CAIRO CABAL

CALIBER
BOOKS

Also from ALAN CAILLOU

CABOT CAIN Series
Assault on Kolchak
Assault on Ming
Assault on Loveless
Assault on Fellawi
Assault on Agathon
Assault on Almata

TOBIN'S WAR Series
Dead Sea Submarine
Terror in Rio
Congo War Cry
Afghan Assault
Swamp War
Death Charge
The Garonsky Missile

MIKE BENASQUE Series
The Plotters
Marseilles
Who'll Buy My Evil
Diamonds Wild

IAN QUAYLE Series
A League of Hawks
The Sword of God

DEKKER'S DEMONS Series
Suicide Run
Blood Run

Rogue's Gambit
Cairo Cabal
Bichu the Jaguar
The Walls of Jolo
The Hot Sun of Africa
The Cheetahs
Joshua's People
Mindanao Pearl
Khartoum
South from Khartoum
Rampage
The World is 6 Feet Square
The Prophetess
House on Curzon Street

The Charge of the Light Brigade
A Journey to Orassia

CAIRO CABAL

Copyright 2025 Eagle One Media, Inc.
Original Copyright 1957 under the title Alien Virus and copyright 1974 Alan Caillou
All Rights Reserved.

No part of this book may be copied or retransmitted without the express written permission of the publisher and copyright holder. Limited use of excerpts may be used for journalistic or review purposes. Any similarities to individuals either living or dead is purely coincidental and unintentional except where fair use laws apply.

For further information visit the Caliber Comics website:
www.calibercomics.com

Cover image by: Dubya2x

King Farouk's Cairo is the background of the violent and ruthless tale of espionage and counterespionage, secret agents, spies and dark conspiracy.

CHAPTER 1

When he awoke, the sweet sickly scent of the brothel was thick in his nostrils. The purple satin quilt had fallen to the floor so that it lay brightly close to the red plush armchair on which his clothes had been carelessly, hurriedly thrown. His jacket was too far tossed over its back so that the pockets were upside down and their contents had fallen out and were strewn untidily over the floor. A nylon stocking lay beside them on the green carpet, a thin ladder in it clearly visible as if put there deliberately to disgust him with its cheapness. He was not disgusted; it was too constant an episode in his life.

He reached for a cigarette and, lighting it, lay back among the white sheets of the rumpled double bed, his hands behind his tousled head, sucking the smoke down deep into his lungs, staring at the mirror on the ceiling. When he was fully awake, he stubbed out the cigarette and padded on bare feet over to the dressing table. He poured some eau-de-Cologne into his palms and rubbed them over his face, smarting at the sharp sting, and grimacing at the scent of it. Then he went to the window and flung open the dark green shutters, letting the hot sun in to strike his face and blind him with its sudden brightness.

He screwed up his eyes and rubbed the back of his neck lazily, wondering what time of the day it was.

Scratching his stomach idly, he stood for a while looking down on the street outside, where the coffee seller sauntered by, clinking his tiny egg-shell cups together in a pleasant morning tintinnabulation, the big brass urn, brightly polished, slung over his ragged shoulder on a broad leather strap, his bright red tarboush with its black tassel stuck far back on his head, the deep dark shadow of its accustomed place clearly showing lower down on his brow, his feet bare, his bony brown ankles protruding gawkily from his baggy white *sharawallis*.

He looked glumly up at the hot blue sky and saw that the heavy haze from the desert was closing in, and wished that he had been awake earlier to breathe in some of the cool morning air before the *khamseen* hit the town. He heard the shrill sharp cry, "*Café...café...ahwe...ahwe ya effendi...*" and watched while a passerby paused, neat and elegant in his brown silk suit, mopping at the sweat on the back of his neck and waiting for the coffee-boy to fill the little cup. He watched the black liquid run from the tall, thin spout, the urn dropped down and pulled up sharply, an expert motion bringing the cup upwards, too—a scimitar of practiced motion. He saw the man wipe the cup with a grubby cloth, and tuck a coin into the folds at his waist.

He bent over and coughed, straining at the depths of his bowels, his hands on his naked hips, retching deeply, and the woman on the bed opened her eyes and stirred, pushing the white sheet off her body, lazily, with one long leg, stretching her arms high above her shoulders, twisting her body to make room for them, squirming deeper into the center, yawning, murmuring lazily: "*Again, I want it again...*" then dropping once more into sullen sleep, twisting her body over on to her stomach, her white rump large with morning-after inelegance, her black hair long and shiny and tousled about her shoulders, and a red-painted toenail at the other extremity of her soft white body semiconsciously scratching at an ankle.

He moved over to the bed, stood looking down on her for a while, then slapped her sharply. She twisted and sat up, suddenly awake again. He grinned at her as she rubbed her flank, watching him through half-closed eyes, pouting her full lips.

"No, that's not nice..."

"Time to go, *cara*. Where's my watch?"

"Who knows?"

She lay back and stretched herself again, contorting her white shoulders, yawning widely. "*Là...sur la commode...je n'sais pas...*"

He walked over to the dresser and took his watch. Strapping it on his thin wrist, he said:

"Nearly eleven o'clock. *Porca miseria!* Did I pay you last night?"

She nodded her head. "Again...once more..."

He said: "*Ce soir, demain,* when the apricots come..." He took a handful of black hair and twisted her head around, then sat on the bed beside her and kissed her lips, his fingers sinking deeply into the white flesh of her shoulder. She lay back and watched him dress, watched him shake himself awkwardly into his trousers, pulling them up over his thin brown legs, slipping his arms into a gaudy shirt with a bright green stripe to it, tucking it in at his narrow waist.

She said: "*Maquereau!*"

He grinned at her and said again: "Tonight...tomorrow...when the apricots come. Who knows?" He stood for a moment looking at her, holding his tie in his hand. He said softly: "You have the greenest eyes I have ever seen. What's your real name?"

"What's yours?"

"Who cares? Carlo? Gianni? Giuseppe? Call me Gianni."

"Italian?"

He nodded, staring at her, watching the white curve of her breast and its soft oscillation as she moved, admiring the small waist and the sudden out-curving of her hips and the smooth white sweep of her thighs. He said: "Do you always live here? Can I always find you here?"

"*Bien sûr.*"

He looked at his watch again. "*Porca miseria!*" he said, "I should have been out of here an hour ago." He began slipping off his clothes again. He said: "Move over."

It was in the café downstairs that he found the paper.

At that late hour of the morning, in that part of the town, the couples were coming in for their *apéritifs*, some beginning their day, some ending it. It amused him to watch them and look for the difference.

The new ones were bright and eager, their clothes neat and newly pressed, the women smart and well made-up, relaxed, bright-eyed, their men elegantly expectant and full of smiling repartee. Then the others, ending their long day; they were tired, with delicate shading under their eyes, the men unshaven, the women with their make-up carelessly, hurriedly put on, their hair not properly set, their faces tired and strained but happy. They showed that eagerness to get to a cold shower and their own beds, to the comfort of their own dressing-tables with the special eyebrow pencil or the favorite razor just in its accustomed place where they left it yesterday, or the new jar of foundation cream on the ledge by the window, carelessly left open; the smell of too much eau-de-Cologne on their bodies, but still cheerful and happy. *Tatty but happy*, he thought, watching them, and tried the phrase in Italian and then in French, smugly smiling at his own linguistic agility.

Sitting at the table on the pavement under the shade of a big blue and white umbrella, he sorted out the papers in his jacket, pulling them out of the pocket in which he had hastily, carelessly thrust them when he picked them up from the green-carpeted floor, turning them over and putting them into their proper places; two letters, a list of groceries, an old receipt, three driving licenses in different names; half-a-dozen assorted visiting cards, an unexpected pound note ill-folded among some scraps torn from a note-book...

And then he saw the list.

He frowned at it for a moment and started to crumple it up. And then the names suddenly caught his perception and he saw that there was something intriguing in them, and he examined it more carefully. It was a typed list of names, no more. He read:

> *Mr. Oswald Pearman*
> *Captain Ahmed Saleh*
> *Ibrahim Shulam*
> *Sergei Reizen*
> *Stefan Bolec*

The name *Captain Ahmed Saleh* had been crossed out, and underneath was written in pencil "*Major Kamel Irani*."

There was nothing more. He frowned at it for a moment, staring at the names, the dark forgotten reserves of his agile mind quickly dropping everything into its proper perspective. The picture of the

CAIRO CABAL

finding, unnoticed till now, was sharply in focus; the notes and scraps of paper, the old and long-folded envelopes that had slipped from his breast pocket, the list lying a little removed from the others, deeper under the gaudy purple bed that was still surely reeking with her warmth; the hastily gathered-up papers stuffed hurriedly into a pocket...

The clock in the deep and shaded recesses of the café struck midday. He drained his coffee and went quickly back to the brothel.

As he turned the corner and made to cross the road, he stopped abruptly and stood staring at the policemen outside the building. A police car drove up and he watched an inspector go quickly into the house. Then, frowning a little, he straightened his jacket and followed him in.

Half-an-hour later, a little pale and still trembling, he went into a 'phone box and called John Trent.

They met at Groppi's.

The sun struck sharply down on the bright canvas awning, casting clear and vivid lighted streaks where it passed through the tiny rents and long thin slits where one piece overlapped the other, striking with hot summer brightness. It groped down towards the people below who sat in the cool secure depths of the shadows, sipping their Pernods, and the cappuccinos and their thick rich Turkish coffee in little white cups that rang like high-pitched bells when they struck them with their spoons to summon the *sofragi*.

It was the late lunch hour and the place was crowded. There were Egyptians in their neat silk suits and tarboushes, Greeks in shabby brown serge, a few leftover Englishmen in their customary khaki drill and brown suede shoes, their khaki stockings almost washed white, and a sprinkling of Italians, French, Armenians, Czechs and Poles, all talking at once in a dozen different languages, gesticulating broadly, idly worrying the flies with their horse-hair switches. Little ragged boot-boys tapped their brushes on their little wooden boxes, persistently calling out "Shoe-shine...shoe-shine," and slipped in and out among the tables with incredible lissomness, grimacing at each other, settling down to the slow and serious work of polishing with a kind of slow, deliberate intentness, rolling up trouser-cuffs, slipping little pieces of red-stained cardboard into the sides of already high-polished shoes. They wielded their brushes with a gentle, rhythmic cadence.

There was gravel underfoot, clean grey gravel hedged in with geraniums, and the walls were hung with morning glory and bougainvillea and honey-suckle, and in one corner a huge magnolia tree was green and white and cool in the shadows where not even the midday sun could reach with its probing fingers. At one end of the courtyard, up a few steps, were the bar and the way out on to the back street. At the other end, the strongly scented pastry shop was sweet with cream puffs and chocolate eclairs and sickly *milles-feuilles*; and the sales-girls, smart and bright in their yellow overalls, were rapidly and efficiently putting pastries and *petits fours* into thin white boxes that snapped briskly into shape. Beyond the shop lay the main entrance and the dusty, crowded, lunch-time street. The sun was beating down on the pavement, and the policeman at the corner was dozing in the shadows of the Bank Building, standing up but almost fast asleep and nobody worrying about it at all.

In a corner of the courtyard, lolling back in his canvas chair and reading the *Egyptian Gazette*, John Trent sat waiting. He was small, and thin, and wiry, and darkly tanned, his lank hair black, his startling pale-blue eyes set deep under heavy eyebrows. He folded his paper and clapped his hands for the *sofragi*.

The waiter hurried to his table, his sharp, professionally watchful eyes alert under his fez, his long white gown with its bright red cummerbund spotless and freshly starched.

Trent stifled a yawn. He said: "More coffee."

The *sofragi* nodded quickly. "*Turki, effendi?*"

"*Saada.*"

The waiter said: "*Haader...*" stringing out the vowel sound, bowing slightly, a well-filled tray balanced on his arm, sweeping away with the quick grace of a ballerina. The sun, moving slowly round, sent a sudden shaft of light on to the deep purple flowers on the wall.

Trent looked up and smiled half-heartedly as Perugino came in. He was wearing a green-striped shirt with a white silk tie; Trent looked at the tie and shuddered. He said affably:

"Sit down and have a drink, Perugino."

Perugino nodded eagerly. He said: "May I join you, Mr. Trent?" It was all part of the ritual. "Perhaps you will allow me...a beer, perhaps?"

Trent nodded. He said good-humoredly: "I've just ordered coffee, but a beer would be fine. What's on your mind? Sit down, for God's sake."

Perugino dragged up another chair. He said hesitantly:

"I don't know, Mr. Trent. Frankly, I don't know." He spoke carelessly precise English. He said: "I have something which I think will interest you, but I don't know what it is."

"Or what it's worth?"

Perugino spread his hands elegantly. "A man must live," he said. "As usual, I shall be happy to rely upon the generosity of my friends. Perhaps it is worth a great deal, perhaps nothing. Frankly, I don't know." He smiled quickly, showing his strong white teeth. "Perhaps I hold a fortune in my hands. I don't know."

Trent waited. The *sofragi* hurried up and slipped a delicate white cup in front of him, then leaned forward to pour the coffee from a tiny brass pot with a long rosewood handle, the thick black liquid pouring softly from under its rich brown froth. Grinning broadly, he said:

"*Saada, effendi,* very bitter." He paused and stood in front of Perugino, waiting expectantly.

"Two beers." The waiter nodded and hurried off.

Perugino took a paper from his pocket and laid it on the table. He glanced round the garden, his eyes lingering on the women in their bright summer frocks. He said apologetically:

"Not the best place, perhaps, to discuss business. But it is a convenient rendezvous. One can always use the other exit...in case of emergency." He grimaced.

Trent picked up the paper and frowned over it. He said softly: "For a man of your accomplishments, no place is better. And it's the coolest spot in Cairo. What is this meant to be?"

Perugino raised his shoulders, spreading his arms in a gesture of helplessness.

"As you see, a list of names...no more. But there is a certain significance, both in the names and the place where I found it."

"Which was...where exactly?"

"A place I don't think you would know of, Mr. Trent. In the Birka. I didn't feel like going home last night— my place is terribly hot, you know—so I stayed out rather late and slept at the house of a young lady...a Turkish girl you may have seen dancing at the Pigalle de L'Orient..."

"A friend? Or a...a casual acquaintance?"

Perugino placed the tips of his fingers together and wondered if it was time for a manicure. He said: "No doubt you do not approve, Mr. Trent, but...shall we say, a casual acquaintance. I had met her once before, I seem to remember. I found this paper quite by accident on the floor of her apartment. I assure you I had no intention of...of stealing it." He added apologetically: "It really is very hot in my little apartment; really."

"And now, this list, what's it supposed to be?"

"It mentions your Mr. Pearman..."

"*My* Mr. Pearman?"

"And Ahmed Saleh. His name, as you see, has been crossed out."

"Uh-huh."

"And the others. You know who the others are?"

Trent nodded casually. "Some of them I know. Who's Stefan Bolec?"

Perugino said carefully: "Am I to understand that we can do business, Mr. Trent?"

"Come off it, Perugino," Trent said amiably. "If there's anything worth buying, you know I'll buy it. What's the connection?"

Perugino reached over and pulled the paper towards him. Taking out a silver pencil, he wrote opposite the names:

Mr. Oswald Pearman...Security, British Trade Delegation (MI5).
Captain Ahmed Saleh...Counter-Espionage. Deceased.
Ibrahim Shulam...Political Police, Intelligence.
Sergei Reizen...Russian MVD.

CAIRO CABAL

Stefan Bolec...Query?

He underlined *Major Kamel Irani,* and passed the sheet back to Trent, "Stefan Bolec, whom you do not know, is the key to this puzzle. You agree with my comments? On the others, I mean?"

Trent said mildly: "Mr. Pearman? What do you mean by Security?"

"Mr. Pearman," Perugino said promptly, "is in charge of the Trade Delegation's security. Officially, there's some Scotland Yard man or other attached to the party, but the only man of any consequence is Mr. Pearman, who belongs to MI5." He glanced surreptitiously over his shoulder. "Am I not right?"

"Right or wrong," Trent said, "these things are supposed to be secret. How do you come to know about them?"

Perugino shrugged his shoulders. "Everybody knows about it."

"Everybody?"

"Well, everybody in...in my line of business." He said firmly: "In my business it is necessary to keep one's ear very close to the ground."

"So I see. Well, what about the others?"

Perugino began to tick them off on his fragile fingers. "The two Egyptians; Ahmed Saleh we all know...Military Intelligence. He was killed last week in a motor-car accident. And his name is crossed off the list."

"Is that significant?"

"In this business, Mr. Trent, everything is significant. But frankly, Saleh was a man of no consequence. But Shulam...there is a sheep of a different color. You know Ibrahim Shulam, Mr. Trent?"

"I know him."

Perugino hesitated. He said: "I mean, Mr. Trent, do you know what his present duties are?"

"Suppose you tell me?"

"He is commonly regarded as the best of the new breed of policemen. And he has recently been ordered to investigate these strange and recurring cases of sabotage that we have read so much about in the papers recently."

"This is Egypt," Trent said briefly. "Sabotage is second nature to these people. Any outburst of nationalism..."

"Quite. But there have been rather a lot of them recently...all of a pattern. A pattern, Mr. Trent. True, in this country these outbursts of nationalism have never been exactly spontaneous, but none the less, a constantly recurring pattern... There are all kinds of dubious, half-formed rumors in the market... Does it not seem strange to you?"

"Not sure that I know just what you mean. Care for another beer?"

Perugino raised an elegant hand. "Allow me," he said. "Allow me..." He clapped his hands and the waiter came scurrying.

He said: "Two more beers." As soon as the *sofragi* had swept away, he went on:

"There was the destruction of the cotton warehouse at Giza recently; then the burning of the Jordan Hotel; then the Turf Club again; then the timber yards at Heliopolis; and several others in the same pattern. Perhaps there is nothing strange about this to you; but I can assure you that the Government have put their best man on it—on what would normally be a routine job for a couple of constables and a sergeant. Why should they choose Shulam for that job? Why? In this business, Mr. Trent, the answers to these puzzling little problems are always interesting."

"Interesting and profitable, is that it?"

"I will tell you why, Mr. Trent." Perugino ignored the remark. "They fear these outbreaks are no less than...than a rehearsal, shall we say. They think they are merely training for something bigger and better. You know that in the new Government, they are all at each others' throats, watching each other...and fearful of their own downfall. And they would very much like to know just what *somebody* is rehearsing *for*. And now we find some person or persons unknown linking your Mr. Pearman's name with both Reizen and this Shulam. Do you not find it interesting?"

"Are you thinking of Shulam's work at the Russian Embassy?"

"Precisely. For nearly two years now, he has been at work on the Russians—liaison officer of some sort. To spy on them, of course. Why should he be taken from this work for which he is admirably suited—did you know that he speaks Russian?—to investigate a few cases of arson? That is the question, Mr. Trent."

CAIRO CABAL

Trent wondered about the devious reasoning of the little Italian's agile mind, puzzling out the little anomalies, fitting them carefully into place, putting a jigsaw together until there should be enough of it to comprise a saleable product... He said:

"And Bolec? What about him?"

Perugino smiled broadly. "Bolec," he said, "is a man you will certainly know nothing about. A displaced Czech, a great oaf of a man, but one with certain endearing qualities. He has a very interesting profession. He organizes the...what shall I call them? The shoe-shine boys, the beggars, the porters at the railway station—all those unfortunates who live on the edges of our civilization; Bolec organizes them." He pointed to a grubby shoe-shine boy who was squatting on the floor by the next table.

"You see this cheerful urchin? He pays his dues to Bolec; if he did not, then a dozen of the other boys would descend on him and beat him to a pulp—because Bolec will tell them to. You want a cheap case of whisky perhaps? Bolec will have it stolen for you off one of the boats in the harbor at Port Said or Suez. You want a woman watched, or a man? Bolec's beggars will faithfully report every move he or she makes. But what has Bolec to do with our Russian expert Shulam? And what have they both to do with Major Kamel Irani? This, I must tell you, came to me as a shock. *Mr.* Kamel Irani has been making inquiries about Bolec for the last two weeks—you understand, a man in his profession must live a secluded life. *Mr.* Kamel Irani is a tourist from Istanbul who has constantly been asking questions about him. At first, when this came to my notice..."

Trent asked, "How?"

Perugino said diffidently: "My sources of information...you understand...it came to me confidentially that he was asking questions a little too much. At first, I thought he had some proposition to make, but then...it went on for too long, Mr. Trent, too long. Too many questions, too many...and now this; *Major* Kamel Irani. It is too much. The man is an impostor. I will find out what he is up to. He seems to spend his nights at the Pigalle; I think I will have to watch him for a while."

"And what, then, is the significance of all this?"

"I do not know." He said lamely: "I thought perhaps the

juxtaposition of the names would mean something to you. Who could class these people in one category? And why? That is the question. What have they in common? If you can answer that, then you will know what is the significance."

Trent said pleasantly, draining his beer and wishing it were stronger: "I don't think there's very much here, Perugino. Where can I find this man Bolec?"

"Ah! Then you are interested? I have brought you something which is of interest to you."

"Well, a little. I don't think it's worth a great deal."

"Ten pounds, maybe? I could very happily make use of ten pounds just now, Mr. Trent, My old mother..."

"Say a couple?" Trent picked up the list and put it in his pocket. "Where can I find this Bolec?"

"Through me, Mr. Trent. I can always bring him to you. Perhaps a little more than two pounds? My mother is very sick and badly needs a doctor. I can't afford to give her the things she wants. Perhaps five pounds would not be too much?"

Trent took out his wallet and passed across five one-pound notes. He said affably: "You haven't got a mother and you know that I know it. I don't see why the British Government should keep your mistresses in too much luxury."

Perugino slipped the money quickly into his pocket. He said: "There's something else you should know."

"I know that. I've been waiting for you to tell me the name of the lady in whose house you found this."

"Not that, though I will tell you that with pleasure. You may have seen an attractive Turkish girl dancing at the Pigalle, the one with the green eyes, like a tiger's. She called herself Princess Higran..."

Trent said sharply: "*Called?*"

"Exactly." Peering eagerly at Trent, Perugino said with relish: "When I saw that this list was not the kind of thing that ought to be left lying around in a brothel, I went back...to ask her where it might have come from. She was dead. Somebody had...someone had disembowelled her." He shuddered slightly.

Trent, staring at him, fancied he detected a delicate fascination

coloring his restrained excitement. He said again, his eyes gleaming:
"Disemboweled, Mr. Trent. Not just killed. Disemboweled. She was a very attractive woman."

CHAPTER 2

The leader was showing them how to improvise a landmine.

He was sitting in a white-washed room, a small hut on the outskirts of Abbassiya, the desert stretching far across to the hills in the distance, hot and dry and dusty.

In the tiny room, four men were grouped around him, watching nervously. One of them, a small man with anxious eyes, was clearly scared stiff; the others, their mouths hanging open in idiot wonder, were fascinated, hypnotized by the drill, watching it in silent awe.

He drew the bow back and forth slowly. Sitting there, grasping between his knees an ancient Turkish shell dug up from the burrowing sand where it had carefully been hidden against just such a time as this, grasping the tarnished brass tightly between his knees, with one bare foot wrapped around its base, his prehensile toes gripping it firmly, he slowly twirled the iron-tipped wooden drill with the bowstring, slowly, gently, with infinite precaution, drilling into the percussion cap.

Only the anxious little man, who had been in the army, shuddered; he looked once or twice towards the door as though wondering if he could run for it, but finally began to count his beads instead, his lips soundlessly framing the hopeful phrases of the Koran.

The leader paused in his work, touching the cap with delicate fingers, feeling the indentation he had made, thinking with his fingertips, then drilling again, two or three more careful twists. The nervous man swallowed hard. The leader did not look at him, but kept his eyes fanatically fixed on his work, willing the great shell not to blow up, twisting once more, feeling the infinitesimal thickness of the copper left at the center of the detonator. He stopped and wiped the sweat off his forehead, then stared at the others.

"*Heik*..." he said. "Like that."

He raised a delicate hand, grimy and lined, but delicate as a dancer's.

"*Heik*...almost through. If you go any farther..." He threw up his hands to Heaven.

"Then take a nail...like this..."

With his long fingers he held it close against the cap, then wedged it ever so gently into the hole he had made. The nervous man squealed. Not looking up, he went on:

"Plant the bomb deep in the road, upright, like this...put a piece of wood over the percussion cap. See that the nail is upright, like this. Then cover it with sand...smooth it over... The first car to go over it..." He raised his slender hand, the fingers outstretched, and made as if to tap the home-made striker. The nervous man closed his eyes and groaned. The others watched, fascinated, nodding their foolish heads eagerly, seeing the lorries of the infidels blown into Hell, but not the miscarriage of their own dangerous handicraft; not seeing the final protest of mistreated shells blowing themselves and their seducers and all about them, high into the hot and stifling air around the fragile mud-and-wattle house, nodding their stupid heads and saying, "*Aiwa...aiwa...kwayis...*"

The leader took out the nail and put the shell down gently, laying it down on the floor in the corner. "Watch it," he said briefly. He pointed to the other five shells standing by the wooden bed. He said: "Get them done by tomorrow. Then take them out to the Dead City. Hide them there, then tell me where you've put them. *Fahim?*"

The others nodded. The leader walked over the nervous man, took him by the cloth about his neck, and shook him, raising him up so that his face was within a few inches of his own, glaring into his eyes, his black fanatic's eyes wide and angry.

He said: "You do the first one."

Then he glared around the room, spat, and walked out.

CHAPTER 3

The pale blue flowers of the jacaranda trees in the driveway lay spread on the ground like a summer carpet, blue and white with tiny tinges of brown, thickly clustered in great round patches; they made a sharp crackling sound as Trent drove his Jaguar over them, individually popping a chorus of protest. He drove slowly into his allotted parking space, and sent into the office. He pushed through the wide swing door, turned down the corridor, and entered the room marked "Communications Section."

Pearman was waiting for him, sitting on the chair by the big empty desk, scribbling some lines into a notebook. He was tall and awkwardly formed, with watchful, expectant eyes as though more ready to receive than to give, as though he had just made a statement and were waiting for you to contradict him. His clothes were made for a colder climate, but he looked incredibly neat and cool, his long thin frame too tightly clad in a dark blue suit that seemed out of place in Cairo, his white collar and cuffs spotless and unmarked by perspiration. Trent, sweating slightly in the afternoon heat, wondered idly how he did it. He said cheerfully:

"Hope I haven't kept you waiting. Your cover's blown wide open. Did you know that?"

Pearman froze in mid-motion. Half-standing, his gaunt, angular form was queerly twisted, a gawky Manet picture, his worried eyes peering sharply over the longest nose in the Foreign Office. "No!" he said. "No! Not really? Are you sure? I mean...you mean the Egyptians?"

CAIRO CABAL

Trent sat on the edge of the desk and took out his tobacco. "Too damn hot for this time of the day. *Khamseen* still blowing. Not only the Egyptians; everybody. Heard in town from one of my boys, fellow named Perugino. Makes a living of sorts selling information to anyone who will buy it. Small stuff. Trade secrets, military intelligence, anything to anybody. He mentioned it almost casually—says everybody knows it. And if he knows it, then everyone else does."

Pearman sat down again, frowning at the creases in his too-tight trousers. Joe said fussily: "But it's disgraceful! I'm supposed to be here under the tightest possible security. How could they possibly find out?"

Trent shrugged his shoulders. "Who knows? Come to that, who cares?" He said affably: "You can't keep these things quiet for very long, you know. Not in Cairo. They're bound to find out sooner or later. But does it matter? There's precious little they can do about it."

"But...but it's quite monstrous! Aren't you supposed to take care of that sort of thing?"

"No, I'm not. As far as I'm concerned, you're just a guy passing through with the delegation and upsetting the careless routine of my everyday existence. I don't really come into the picture until they start taking pot shots at you. I just have to see that you don't get into trouble."

"And you don't call this trouble? Good heavens...do they also know...what I'm doing here?"

"They know that you're tied up in something murky; more than that I can't say." He slid off the desk and went to the window. Hands deep in his pockets, making bubbling noises with his pipe, he stood for a moment staring at the long green lawn with its borders of poinsettias. Over in the shade by the corner, treading delicately on the close-cropped turf, a peahen was strutting, casting jerky eyes about for its mate.

He said slowly:

"I don't know. Perhaps not. I could tell you that if I knew myself what you're supposed to be doing. I know that you have nothing to do with the Trade Delegation; what the hell would a Trade Delegation need with an MI5 man? But more than that, I'm quite in the dark. This confounded secrecy... But I think if your business were known, then Perugino would have mentioned it. He wouldn't be able to resist the temptation; one of my own occasional stooges telling me what goes on in my own department."

"Of course." Pearman was faintly embarrassed. He said carefully, apologetically: "These things are not entirely in my hands, you know. Anyway...now..." He said abruptly: "Colonel Brand's waiting to see us."

Trent turned and raised his black eyebrows. "The Colonel?"

"I called him as soon as I got your message. He said he'd better see us as soon as you came back."

"Then what are we waiting for? Let's go." Trent tapped out his pipe into the waste-paper basket and held the door open. He said: "I've got something for him too. A messy business to tell him about. A girl got herself killed this morning, and there's some sort of connection between the two of you."

"Really? In what way?"

Trent shrugged his shoulders. "One of the things I have to find out." Shepherding Pearman down the long corridor he said: "Your name was on a list found in the girl's room. Who she is, and how she comes into all this, I don't yet know. The list was given to me by the fellow who knew you were tied up with MI5. One of the men whose name was on that list was killed; a motor accident, so they say. That's the sequence of events. The connecting link is the thing I have to worry about."

"*An accident, so they say*. Does that mean...?"

"Well...could be, I suppose. When an Intelligence man gets killed in Cairo... I suppose it could have been an accident. The police think it was. Unfortunately, the police and the new Army don't always see eye-to-eye on a great many things. We'll find out."

They turned the corner of the cool lobby and went through to an office marked "Private." The girl at the desk stopped her typing and looked up and smiled quickly at them. She said: "The Colonel's waiting for you; you're to go straight in." Trent patted her affectionately on the shoulder as he passed. He knocked at the door of the inner office and they went inside.

Colonel Brand stood up and held out his hand. He was in

civilian clothes, a short, stubby barrel of a man with three or four chins and flabby jowls. His eyes were tired and his heavy flaccid features were pale, but he was smiling broadly. The left sleeve of his jacket was pinned up over the stump of his arm. He walked towards them, extending his hand. He said amiably: "Come on in, Pearman, come in and sit down. John. What's all this I hear? Your cover blown open?"

Pearman nodded crossly. "So Trent says. He picked it up in the bazaar."

"John?"

Trent pulled up a chair and offered it to Pearman. "That's right, Sir. Not the bazaar, exactly, but...you know this fellow Perugino? The one who was involved in..."

"I know him. Not a very reliable source."

"I agree. But he gave me this..." fumbling in his pocket. "I had a call from him this morning and went over to Groppi's to meet him." He handed across the list of names.

The Colonel said: "Perugino's notes?"

Trent nodded. "The list was just the typed names, and he added the notes in front of me. It seems that he's pretty well in the picture. I asked him how he knew about Pearman here, and he said it was common knowledge. I can't guess the extent of his knowledge, because I myself don't know what Pearman is really doing here."

"For a very good reason."

Studying the paper, the Colonel said carefully: "Nobody in this organization knows what he is doing here with the exception of myself. I toyed with the idea of letting you in on it for a while, as you're supposed to be looking after him and it might have been an advantage of sorts...but ..." He hesitated, and stared at the list. He said at last: "In a case like this, when information gets out, it's very nice to be able to say to London, 'Nobody in this office even *had* the information.' Also makes it very much easier to trace the leak. Now, you'll have to know. But first of all, tell me more about this scrap of paper. Do the names mean anything to you?"

"I agree with Perugino's comments. I know, of course, that Reizen is mixed up in anything that will embarrass us here... I don't know Bolec or Kamel Irani."

"Uh-huh. Who typed this list out? Do you know that?"

"I wish I did. As it stands, it's one of those things that mean nothing except that we ought to know a good deal more about it."

"And where did Perugino get it?"

"He picked it up in a brothel. From one of the girls..."

"Have you seen her?"

"No, Sir."

"Are you going to?"

"No, Sir. She's dead."

The Colonel opened a drawer and took out a file. He said: "I see. That does make a difference, doesn't it? Not a natural death, I take it?"

"No, Sir. A very unnatural one." Trent felt the distaste again, remembering the excited, sensual gleam in Perugino's eyes. He said: "According to Perugino, she was disemboweled. Literally." He felt the Colonel's eyes on him and looked away. He said: "Are we jumping to conclusions if we assume that she was killed because of this list? It could easily have been something else..."

"Have you checked with the police?"

"No, Sir, not yet."

"Well, don't do so unless you have to." The Colonel dropped the cardboard file on the desk. He said: "I want you to read through this, before you leave the office. But first of all, I'd better tell you something about Pearman. He's nothing to do with MI5." Trent said nothing.

The Colonel stood up and wandered about the spacious room, looking down at his feet.

He went on: "I'm afraid it's a little involved. Officially, as we all know, he's here as head of the Trade Delegation that's so much in the news just now...buying cotton, selling machinery, that sort of thing. That's why he moves about with them and uses their office. Unofficially, as Perugino has found out, he's attached to MI5 and is interested in certain aspects of the trouble over the Israeli border disputes—the attempts by the Arab States to strengthen their alliance, to get into a better bargaining position. It's quite an important problem just now, but we won't go into it. So far, so good. An important man doing an important and hush-hush job; and that's just what we wanted them to find out. Actually...actually, there's quite another problem which Pearman is handling."

He perched himself on the ledge of the window, frowning.

"The Trade Delegation is his cover story. Underneath that, when they start digging, is the Israeli business. That's a cover story, too. Underneath that, too deep to be dug up easily, there's the truth. And the truth is the Trade Delegation again, the thing they have already discarded as a mere cover story. And it's top secret. Now listen."

The Colonel slipped a cigarette case out of his pocket and opened it. He said: "I won't offer you one of these for reasons which you know. Help yourself from the box." He extracted a cigarette and lit it, using his one hand with rapid dexterity. Inhaling the smoke deep into his lungs, he said:

"Egypt has always been governed by someone else. The Romans, the Babylonians, the Mamelukes, the Turks, the British. Now, for the first time in two thousand years they're independent, and we all know what that means. The social trend since the beginning of man's history has always been towards amalgamation—towards alliance and integration. We started out with tribes and clans, then moved through states and countries to continents and finally to...what shall I call it?...to half-worlds. A natural trend, and a desirable one. But we've lost sight of one important fact; while the other half-world is sensibly consolidating itself, we on the contrary have pulled out of...out of too many places and left the tribes and clans to their own devices again. They've even invented a name tor it; self-determination." He growled: "Precious little progress we'd have made if they'd let the American Indian self-determine himself. But nowadays, what we recently controlled by force of arms, and would in time have controlled by more agreeable means, we now try to contain from a distance by a kind of avuncular benevolence. But it won't work. They don't want well-meaning uncles who speak a language of sociology that means nothing to them. They want to stand on their own feet and they'll take whatever props are offered to them—from East or West. And what's good for them is not always what we feel *ought* to be good for them. Today Egypt's a sick country."

There was a pungent scent in the air, not dissipated through the open window, but hanging stationary in the air over the center of the room. Pearman was watching the Colonel curiously; Trent felt, rather than saw, that he glanced quickly across to him and he avoided his eye. The Colonel went on:

"This is what you might call a Western part of the world. The habits, the way of thought...even the clothes and the food and the cars they drive, they're Western rather than Eastern. So are the weapons they use; tanks, aircraft, guns and so forth. Until recently. Now, while the West is busy forging its comic chain of defense all round the world—an interlocking system of uneasy alliances and doubtful friends...while all this is going on, the Russians are busily moving in, several thousand miles on the wrong side of the chain that is laughably meant to contain them. Ha!" The Colonel snorted. "We made the vacuum for them to rush into. First tanks, then aircraft; next it'll be troops. I tell you, the new Egyptian Army will be entirely Russian-equipped if we don't watch out. Their technicians are here already. And what's the next step?"

Pearman said softly: "Arms factories. And in case of war...in case of emergency..."

"Good God," the Colonel said, "while we are busy equipping all the Allies with the same type of weapons, standardization to a remarkable degree... I tell you, right here in our own backyard the Russians will have an outpost more useful to them than Japan is to us..."

Balance of power, Trent was thinking bitterly, *who hits first with the most...* He said politely: "And is there any fear of such an emergency now, Sir?"

The Colonel glared at him. He said sharply: "You know damn well there isn't. And you know, too, that we can't afford to wait until there is one before we do something about it. Pearman is here to sell them an arms deal. British weapons. It's a ticklish job. In the Army, that's what they want. But they realize that popular feeling is against any indication of British influence. It was this feeling that put the present Government in power, and they know that it can just as easily put them out again. Pearman's dealing with the Minister in person; if any news of their talks gets out prematurely, it could easily mean the downfall of the Government and a new one would simply have to abandon the whole deal. Even so...tanks and aircraft from Czechoslovakia...good God, they're using them already. Pearman's here to see that they don't get any more. To see that the arms they use are British."

Trent said bitterly: "And the Israeli problem? Won't they use them against the Israelis! If this new Army of theirs gets any stronger..."

The Colonel said sardonically: "I don't doubt that there's someone in Tel-Aviv at this minute selling them arms, too, but that's no concern of ours. Don't think I like it any more than you do. But you've got to make your mind up on one simple point; either the British Cabinet is trying to prevent a war, or they're trying to start one. Make up your mind on that one point and what you're thinking becomes either patriotic or treasonable, depending upon the choice you make. We've insufficient knowledge to look farther than that. It's a dirty business. Good God, if we had any morals at all, we'd all be hermits. But we're not; we're here to do what the Cabinet tells us to do, and corporals don't win wars by thinking better than their Generals. Now, where were we?"

Pearman said: "Now that Trent knows what I'm doing, could he find out if anybody else knows? Just how far the cover story is gone?"

"No...the top cover's off, but no more. Of that I can assure you, and it would be gratuitous to start asking questions about that all around the Mousky. They've found out what we wanted them to find out. Now they'll leave you alone."

"And it's a good cover," Pearman said. "The Russians are very interested in the Israeli question, so I can legitimately interest myself in them. And should any of my real activities leak out, then they'll assume it's all part of the cover story they exploded, and they'll drop it. Meanwhile, I can get on with my work peacefully."

Trent said: "Not perhaps the best choice of word."

"Don't regard me," Pearman said, "as a kind of international arms broker. I'm not." He said doggedly: "My job is simply to see that the new Egyptian Army uses Allied weapons, not Russian. And that it hires Allied technicians, not Russian. And that if this country has to take foreign troops again, they'll be Allied, not Russian. Satisfied?"

"Fair enough." Trent said carefully: "All the same, I think we shall have to watch Pearman very closely from now on."

"You must." The Colonel stubbed out his cigarette, coughing slightly. He said: "I don't like the look of this list you've found. I don't like it at all; it smells. The necessity of being *ready* increases; we must look to it." He dropped the end of his cigarette into a small white envelope and popped it into his pocket. He caught Pearman eyeing him and said briefly: "My medicine." He sat down at his desk. "Find out who wrote that list," he said, "and find out quickly. Try and leave the police out of it if you can. Any ideas?"

Trent nodded. "It won't be easy, but I'll find out who visited this girl yesterday. It's too much to suppose that it could have been dropped any earlier; surely her room must be cleaned out every day..."

"A brothel, you said. Which one was it?"

"Well, not exactly a brothel. One of those apartment houses where girls can stay and entertain...an apartment in the Birka. A girl who called herself Princess Higran. A dancer at the Pigalle de l'Orient..." He broke off; the Colonel was staring at him.

"Higran?"

"Yes, Sir."

The Colonel dropped his eyes. He said abruptly. "Well, keep me in the picture." He turned and went to the window. As they left the room, he was staring out into the sunlight across the garden, his stubby broad back more than ever like a beer barrel. They saw him take the silver cigarette case from his pocket as they closed the door.

The girl at the desk looked up as they passed. Trent said softly: "He's taken two of them; he's in a bad way today."

She nodded miserably. "I wish there were something we could do."

"There's nothing. Nothing at all. Don't worry too much about it."

"It's no use, is it?" She went on with her typing, blinking her eyes.

When they were in the corridor again, Pearman said: "What in heaven's name was all that about? Do you realize what that was?"

Trent said briefly: "He's a sick man."

"Sick! But heavens above, don't you know what that was he

was smoking? Smelling the place up with marihuana..."

"Here we call it hashish."

"But good heavens! What kind of sickness is that supposed to cure? If anyone found out...in London... openly like that! If London got to hear of it..."

"They know, in London. He's too good a man to lose."

"But drugs! Of all things, drugs! It's...it's quite unbelievable! It's monstrous...a man in his position...it's the most fantastic thing I've ever heard..."

Trent looked at him sourly. He said: "It's common enough out here. Not among the British, perhaps, as a rule, but...I told you, he's a sick man."

"But there's no sickness marihuana will cure."

Trent said savagely: "Oh, shut up! For God's sake, shut up!" He turned at once and said: "I'm sorry. Please forgive me. Call it the heat. Come and have a beer; what do you say?"

Pearman hesitated. "Well..." he said. Then: "Of course. Let's go and have a beer."

Trent grinned quickly and they went out into the hot sunlight and got into the Jaguar and drove off over the blue jacaranda flowers which patched up the driveway and popped under the wheels, and turned out through the old-fashioned iron gates and down the road which led to Sharia Emad-el-Din.

Trent looked at his watch. He said: "Four-fifteen. Like to join me in some investigation? Have you got a little time to waste?"

Pearman nodded. "Nothing to do for the rest of the day. What's on your mind?"

"I want to have another talk with Perugino. He's a useful little bastard to have around."

The sun was hot on their faces as they drove slowly through the dense traffic. A big green open Buick tore past them with a load of freshly-killed meat piled up on the back seat, its white-robed driver furiously banging with the flat of his hand on the side-panel of the door and the jaywalkers not paying any attention to him at all, banging away at his improvised horn, swinging the loose steering-wheel from side-to-side, skidding to a squealing stop behind a bus as one wheel locked when he braked. It swung round slightly and quivered beside the Jaguar with a dismal thudding noise, smoke billowing from the engine, steam hissing angrily up from the radiator, the flies swarming blackly over the red meat in the back. The driver pushed his tarboush back with an impatient gesture and shouted an imprecation at the driver ahead, gesticulating with the outstretched flat of his expressive hand, not being heard and not letting that worry him at all but shouting and cursing and calling on the unheeding passers-by to witness the iniquity of the bus-driver. Then he turned his head and saw the Jaguar idling silently beside him, and his face twisted into a new form, his white teeth gleaming quickly, deep lines of humor suddenly appearing round his eyes, a happy, instant transfiguration. He moved his fingers up and down in a gesture of admiration, pointing at the Jaguar, waving his arms with abandon. He gestured at his own protesting motor which rumbled and boiled and groaned beneath him and threw back his head and roared with laughter, then as suddenly turned again and shouted at the driver ahead, shouting his curses with marvelous eloquence.

Trent said mildly: "Wish I had the command of language these fellows have. Nice to be able to swear like that." Rolling the words round his tongue, savoring the euphonious sound of them, he said: "*In al abu dahya illa sabhat riglak...* Speak Arabic?"

"Not well enough. Just a few words."

Trent translated. "*A curse on the father of the midwife who yanked you out by the leg ...*" He said dreamily: "Imagine the thought behind it; forget the delightful rhythm of the words—just admire the imagination. By the leg, mark you; and not the midwife herself, to hell with her, but her father. I hear you were at the Pigalle the other night?"

"Er...yes. Most difficult to get used to the idea of being followed everywhere I go." He said pompously: "Rather felt like taking in some of the local color, you know. Very good food, I thought. But I had a dose of diarrhea afterwards."

"Remember seeing a girl called Princess Higran?"

"Yes. I thought of her while you were telling the Colonel... A rather good-looking woman, I thought. She had green eyes; not grey-green, but a real deep jade, almost...quite incredible. A terrible thing, terrible..."

CAIRO CABAL

"This fellow Perugino, who gave me the paper, was with her last night, and apparently picked up this paper in her place by accident. When he went back to see her about it, she was dead."

"Quite terrible..." Pearman said hesitantly: "You said she was disemboweled...does that point to an Arab...surely a European wouldn't kill a woman like that...not that way..."

"The first thought that occurred to me, too. And, I'm quite sure, to Perugino. I want to get him to work on it. That is," he added, "if he hasn't already gone to work along those lines. With a man of his type, you don't have to tell him what to do; he's already done it."

"What is he, a sort of...of leg man for you?"

"Good God no! Works for anyone who'll pay him. But in this case he'll be working for himself. He knows we'll buy anything he can dig up. He knows he's on to something important, even if he doesn't know what it is." He added wryly: "Any more than we do. Here we are now. That's the house, where the policeman is."

They pulled to a stop and parked up by the curb a few yards away. Trent said: "Let's go and have a beer and wait for Perugino."

"Is he coming here?"

Trent grinned. "He will. If I know our friend at all, he's in there now, trying to bribe a policeman. When he comes out, he'll see my car and know that I'm waiting to see him. That's the way he reasons these things out. Let's have a beer."

They walked across the road to the tiny bistro on the corner. It was empty, the man behind the bar sitting half asleep at the cash register. They ordered beers and carried them across to the tiny table by the window. Trent said: "I'd better put you in the picture a bit. Did you see the names on that list I gave the Colonel?"

"No, I didn't."

"Well, they wouldn't have meant anything to you. There was an Egyptian MI man, a Russian newspaper correspondent—you know what that means—a policeman from the Political Branch, a Persian we've never heard of, a displaced Czechoslovakian Fagin...and you. Interesting, isn't it? You're in good company. One of them is dead."

Pearman said uneasily: "You mean..."

"Well, possibly. A car accident, I believe. But now, with this girl...I don't know. Maybe I'm over-suspicious. But from now on, be very careful about letting me know your whereabouts at all times. And if you want to go to places like the Pigalle, let me know and I'll go along with you."

"I see. You make it sound very...very sinister."

"It's perfectly innocuous. But if you start the evening there, you might easily finish it in some other, less innocent place."

Pearman said stiffly: "There's no fear of that at all. I don't go in for that sort of thing. I merely went there once to see what the native dancing was like. I'm very interested in seeing how other people live. I think it's a very necessary part of a man's education..."

"Uh-huh. Here's health. Anyway, there's a man on your tail, day and night. And if you feel like going to any of the brothels in the Birka..."

Pearman said frigidly: "Really, Trent, I wish you wouldn't talk like that. It's quite unseemly. I wouldn't dream of visiting such places; the very idea revolts me."

Trent said amiably: "Come off it. This is Cairo."

Pearman sipped his beer uneasily.

CHAPTER 4

The Commandant at the new barracks was having his shoes shined at his desk and drinking a cup of Turkish coffee and reading the early morning edition of the paper when the duty officer reported to him. He perfunctorily acknowledged the Lieutenant's salute and went on reading his paper.

The Lieutenant said hesitantly: "*Ya Pasha*...there is a theft to report, *ya Pasha*."

The Commandant put down his paper wearily. "Again?" he said. "Again? What is it this time? Cigarettes again?"

The Lieutenant stammered. "No, *ya Pasha*...not cigarettes..."

"Well, out with it, don't stand there trembling, don't you see I'm busy? What is it? What is it this time?"

The Lieutenant said: "*Islah, ya Pasha*. Arms No. 4 Store was broken into during the night. Thirty-two rifles and seven cases of ammunition are gone..."

"*Allah!* Thirty-two rifles? Where was the guard? Why did they not hear them? What was the Sergeant of the Guard doing?"

"They heard nothing, Sir. It seems they had a key..."

"A key?"

"Yes, Sir. The padlocks were all unlocked. Nothing was broken."

"By the life of God, where would they get a key?"

"I don't know, Sir."

The Commandant glared at his subordinate. He said: "Inform the military police at once."

"It has been done, Sir."

"I see. I want a full report. Dismiss."

The Lieutenant saluted, turned, and went out.

The Commandant brushed aside the boot-boy with a curt "get out," then left his office and walked across the parade ground to the camp gates, acknowledging the salute of the sentry on guard there. Once outside, he crossed the main road, threading his way through the noisily clanging tramcars, blinking his eyes at the dust as it swirled along in their wake, and went to the public phone box on the corner.

He went inside and dialed a number.

"*Hawaga* Reizen?"

The voice at the other end was guarded. "*Min?*"

"Colonel Saudi. Last night. Thirty-two and seven."

"Correct. It has already been delivered."

"And the money?"

"It will be delivered to your house as arranged..." The Colonel passed the tip of his tongue over dry lips.

"But when, *effendi?* I am a poor man..."

"As arranged. In a few days. There is nothing to worry about. Don't call me here again."

The Commandant heard the sharp click as the receiver was replaced at the other end. He went out of the phone booth, put his swagger cane jauntily under his arm, and stepped briskly back to the barracks.

CHAPTER 5

They had finished their third glass of beer when Perugino walked in. He had found time to change into a neatly pressed grey flannel suit, the knot of his yellow tie too big, and too much blue cuff showing at his thin wrists. As he came in, he looked round the little room; his eyes lingered on the two women seated at the bar, waiting for the evening crowds to come in from their siestas. He came and sat down beside Trent.

"I saw your car here, Mr. Trent." He said: "I wondered if you were perhaps looking for me. Did you know that I was here?"

"I guessed you would be. What have you been looking for?"

Perugino smiled quickly. "I like to anticipate my client's wishes, Mr. Trent. I went to see Higran's friend, a girl named Maria Gamal who lives close by. I used to know her slightly, as a matter of fact. The last time she was here...also a dancer."

"Oh? Anything of interest?"

Perugino was faintly embarrassed. He said: "As a matter of fact, she wouldn't see me. She has an Arab servant...a hulking great fellow who would not let me in to see her. A woman of no great consequence, Mr. Trent. Very little intelligence."

Trent said unkindly: "You mean you couldn't make the grade, is that it? Well, never mind, I'll see her myself. What did you say her name was?"

"Maria Gamal. A dancer at the Pigalle. Quite pretty if you like that type... She comes, I believe, from Beirut, but like all the girls here, she moves about all the time on the great cabaret circuit—to

Damascus, Beirut, Athens, Alexandria, Cairo. When one town gets tired of them, they send them off to the next."

"Maria Gamal? Isn't that the one with the hair?"

"Long red hair. She dyes it. I don't think she'll be of much use, Mr. Trent, but perhaps...a word of some sort, some little thing might offer a clue..."

"All right, I'll look after it. What are you drinking?"

"No, please, allow me." Perugino fumbled graciously in his pocket. "Well...if you insist, a beer please. Very good beer they make here. From onions. I also gained entrance to the girl's apartment..." He waited till the Greek waiter, who had put a freshly-starched white apron round his waist, had brought his drink and gone back to his silent meditations at the cash register. He went on:

"The police are still there, of course, but I thought you would like to find out how that piece of paper got into her possession."

Trent smiled imperceptibly. "And?"

"Are you interested in this line of approach, Mr. Trent? It will take a good deal of effort to find out."

"About ten pounds' worth of effort?"

Perugino said deprecatingly: "That was the figure that occurred to me. Of course, I don't want to...to hold you up for too much. Customer relations are most important to me. But it would need a certain amount of care and persistence..."

"And just what would I get for ten pounds?"

Perugino said promptly : "A note of her movements, a complete note, all during the last two days. That piece of paper must have been dropped there yesterday; any earlier, it would surely have been found."

"Yes, I agree. What do the police say about the woman's death? I take it you have friends in there?"

Perugino shrugged. "It's a nasty case," he said. "A very unpleasant way to kill anyone, especially a woman. Especially a beautiful woman like that. I think the police tend to believe it was a crime of a sexual nature. I heard the phrase 'sexual maniac' used. There is a young Inspector handling the case. I know him slightly and he was able to confide in me to a certain extent."

Trent had a picture of the crowded room, the detectives and the cameras and the medical men and the policemen, and the young Inspector standing fastidiously by, watching his men milling about the place, stumbling over each other, and Perugino moving about on the edge of their conversations, talking interminably, passing a few piastres surreptitiously in the right places, his excited eyes gleaming, calculating.

He said: "Didn't you have trouble accounting for your presence there?"

"I was forced to be a little careful, Mr. Trent." Perugino stared at a woman who came in and joined the others at the bar. "Beautiful," he said, "really beautiful. *Regardez ces tetons*..." He went on abruptly:

"It occurred to me that they might find traces of my presence there last night, and I did not wish to be sent for and questioned like a common criminal. So I went in and told them quite frankly that I had spent the night there. I said I had left at ten o'clock and gone back shortly afterwards to see her again..." He said slyly: "There is nothing unusual in this, after all...after a glass of Marsala or a zabaglione in the cafe downstairs, one often wishes one had not left so soon. I told him that there had been no reply to my knock, so '*Now*' I said, 'I am trying once again.' I affected suitable surprise to find the police in possession of the apartment and I must say that the young Inspector was most sympathetic. He told me of several other places in the same building, one of which, I must confess, I did not previously know of. I think a man is happier, Mr. Trent, if he learns something useful every day. Don't you agree? We chatted for a while and I was able to learn a great deal from him. They are as anxious as we are to find out who visited her yesterday and today, and I think for a small sum of money...for a little ready cash we could persuade my police friend to keep us informed."

"Uh-huh."

Trent said nothing for a moment. Then: "All right, try and find out what her movements were yesterday; who she was with—who came to see her. But the facts must be certain; guesswork won't do, Perugino."

Perugino looked at him reproachfully. He said primly: "Really, Mr. Trent, with me it is a matter of professional pride. I have my future to think of. I have never been guilty, Mr. Trent, of selling you any guesses."

"Uh-huh. How long will it take you to find out where she was yesterday?"

Perugino smiled happily. He said: "It all depends on how long the police take. As soon as they know, I shall know, too. Could I promise my friend a little money? A policeman's pay, as you know, is not very much. Not even an Inspector's."

Trent said crossly: "I think I'd better put you on the payroll, Perugino. Wouldn't you prefer that?"

"No, if you don't mind, Mr. Trent." Perugino hesitated, choosing his words carefully. He said: "Of course, I am flattered that you should think of me for permanent employment, but...well, I'm afraid my background is not...you might not find me suitable."

"In other words, you think you can get more out of me by bringing in bits and pieces?"

Perugino said placidly: "Dribs and drabs. Such a pretty phrase. Really, English is not nearly so dull as we foreigners usually believe. Of course, if you insist..."

"You're a bloody rogue, Perugino," Trent said, "and if I had any sense at all, I'd have nothing whatever to do with you."

"So should I offer my friend a little money? I assure you it would be very useful to have him on our side..."

Trent stood up abruptly. He said: "Bring me something worthwhile and I'll pay you for it. You know that. The rest is up to you."

"One moment, Mr. Trent," Perugino said smugly. "Would you not allow me to buy you a glass of beer? Mr. Pearman too, perhaps?"

Trent stared at him. "All right, Perugino," he said. "Out with it."

"She had a friend, Mr. Trent."

"A *maquereau?*"

Perugino shook his head. Trent fancied he saw a shadow of distaste at his use of the word touch the sharp features, no more than a guilty flicker at the back of his conscience, wiped out for ever the moment it appeared.

"No," he said. "Not a pimp. A friend. She had spent the last few days in his company. Long talks at café tables, in the bars, at the Pigalle..." He said softly: "I think it is this fellow Kamel Irani. The description sounds very much like him."

Trent sat down again. He called the waiter and ordered three beers. He said carefully, worrying the idea at the back of his mind: "This could be very important. How sure are you, Perugino? How certain are you of that?"

Perugino nodded. He said: "I understand your interest, Mr. Trent. If Kamel Irani killed her...from his name, he must be a Persian. He speaks good Arabic, but he is a stranger to Cairo and his accent is more...more Syrian, they say. If he killed her, it means quite definitely that somebody outside the country is interested in this business. It can no longer be a purely domestic affair. Is that not so?"

"Possibly." He said again: "How sure are you?"

"I can very easily find but. I know Kamel Irani by sight, and the concierge has seen him with the girl. If I bring the two of them together...she can tell me if this is the man she has seen with Higran. There is another thing." Perugino was enjoying himself enormously, bringing his cards out and laying them down on the bar counter one by one. "My friend the Inspector told me that this woman was seen in a disreputable café the other day with a sergeant from the Political Police. They were seen by a detective who tried to find out what they were talking about; he was not very successful, but according to the sergeant's report, she was making inquiries about a list of people whose names she carried on a piece of paper."

"Oh? That might be very interesting. Do you know this sergeant?"

"By name only. He has a local reputation for selling information...a most dishonest individual. But I myself have never had any dealings with him. However..."

"You mean he's the competition?"

Perugino sounded hurt. "No, Mr. Trent. I am conscientious about the people with whom I deal. However, the detective talked to him afterwards and was unable to find out any more; apparently he took fright and refused to talk. Now, of course, they will pursue the matter further."

"I see... It seems to me that the first thing to do is to get Kamel Irani identified. Would you take care of that? Though this might turn out to be a domestic affair after all and as such be none of my business.

Perugino said, smiling: "I will not charge you too much. Besides, there are too many indications that this is *not* a domestic affair. The girl was killed by a foreigner, whose name has been connected with people in whom you are interested."

Glancing quickly across at Pearman, he said: "There is already a nasty smell in the air."

"Well, get your concierge and Kamel Irani together. You might take her along to the "Pigalle tonight; he'll probably be there..."

Perugino interrupted him. "Not the Pigalle. It is too...too indiscreet a place. Somewhere a little more secluded would be more fitting; I would not like my wife to hear that I had been taking this lady out... I think she would object, and when my wife objects to something, Mr. Trent, she has a very vigorous way of..."

"Your wife?" Trent was momentarily startled. "Don't tell me you have a wife, Perugino? And is your concierge the kind of woman your wife would be jealous of? You astound me."

"Oh no." Perugino leaned forward earnestly. He said: "That's the point, Mr. Trent. The concierge is old and ugly, like most concierges—who else would want such a job? And if my wife heard that we had been to the Pigalle together..." He shuddered slightly.

"But, God dammit!" Trent protested, "you're out with a different woman every night; doesn't she raise hell about that too?"

"Oh no, Mr. Trent." Perugino shook his head emphatically. "That is different. A young girl...a beautiful woman...my wife knows that I am human, what else?" He spread his hands eloquently. "But she'd be very suspicious if she heard I had been out with a woman with whom I could not possibly go to bed. She wouldn't know what to think, and that would make her suspicious. Surely you can understand that?"

"I can't understand," Trent said resignedly, "how a man like you happened to get married in the first place."

"Ai, ai, ai...that..." Perugino shook his head sadly. "She used to be a lot younger and not bad-looking. Not beautiful, mark you, but not bad-looking at all. It was in the time of my youth when I was obsessed with the form of the feminine breast...nothing else mattered to me; you recall those early fetishes perhaps? Ai, ai, ai, I was very young then...my tastes have now matured quite considerably, but in those days... She was a peasant girl, and like so many of our peasant women, quite well developed at a very early age, and nothing pleased me more than the leisurely contemplation of those globular protrusions...it was quite disastrous. Well, somehow or other she became with child, and her father... There was nothing I could do, Mr. Trent, nothing. At first he just said he'd kill me if I did not marry her; you know the righteous indignation of the lower classes under these circumstances."

He said miserably: "I fought hard, Mr. Trent, I fought hard. At first, he was just going to kill me, and then he found out that I was going on a business trip and so...he concocted some wicked charge against me together with the local *maresciallo* of police, a loutish beast with no finer feelings at all, and I was faced with the choice; either prison—or her. I chose badly. I should have considered more deeply. After all, one can always escape from prison, but marriage...for an Italian, a Catholic, you understand?"

He brightened suddenly. "However," he said, "we have come to quite a reasonable working arrangement; in return for a certain freedom of behavior which she allows me, I no longer beat her. But the concierge to the Pigalle...that, *boutana Madonna*, that would be too much. I will take her to some other place; to his hotel, perhaps. Leave it to me."

Pearman picked up his drink and saw that it was getting flat. He said unexpectedly: "Your good health, Signor Perugino. I see we need no introduction."

Perugino leaped to his feet with a flourish. Trent suspected that he had not been addressed as *signor* for a very long time.

He said, beaming: "A great honor, Mr. Pearman. Of course, I know you by sight, by reputation. A great honor indeed, I assure you."

There was a screen of charm, almost of genuine courtesy, that kept back any sycophancy, that barred the intrusion of any obsequiousness. His pleasure was eager and unfeigned.

Trent sighed. "Oh well, that's that," he said. "Get to work, Perugino. And where can I find this fellow Bolec?"

"I will find him and bring him to you. When would you like to see him?"

Trent looked at his watch. "Tonight? At the Pigalle?"

"In one of the private booths? Perhaps ten o'clock would be a good time?"

"Ten o'clock then. Tell him to ask for me. They know me there."

"Ten o'clock in the Pigalle. Shall I come too?"

Trent smiled gently and shook his head. "No," he said, "not this time. Just Bolec and I. *Arrivederci.*"

As they walked across to the car, Pearman was feeling the effect of the beer. He said, gently reproving, "I really wouldn't have thought that that extraordinary fellow would know my name. There really doesn't seem to be very much security here, does there?"

"Of course he knows your name! So does every beggar on every street corner! It's no good trying to hide such simple things from them. If we call you Smith or Brown, every petty informer in Cairo will be making enquiries about you. Let them know so much, and they won't try to find out very much more. Not to worry; you're in good hands."

"Well...I suppose so. What an extraordinary fellow that was."

They drove off down the crowded street, the hot *khamseen* dropping now, and a fresh cool breeze starting to blow in off the sands in which the city stood like a crowded, conglomerate oasis. They went to the Semiramis Hotel to drop Pearman, and Trent went on to his office where the night-duty officer was just settling down, checking the locks on the office doors, and gathering together the contents of the waste baskets, checking the desk drawers for used carbons and carefully stuffing them into the incinerator bag.

He went to the bathroom on the top floor and took a cold shower, rubbed himself down briskly, then went to his room and sat down at the telephone.

He made some calls, wrote out a report, checked through the daily file, reading all the reports over carefully and initialing them, and at nine o'clock drove round to the Pigalle for dinner.

The Pigalle de l'Orient lies halfway along the more interesting half of Sharia Emad-el-Din, the half to which tourists flock to stare at

CAIRO CABAL

the pictures outside the nightclubs and to stand in their doorways experiencing the throb of the whining music and the sweet aphrodisiac scents that come through them, the scents of strange cigarette smoke mingled with rich cooking and pungent jasmine and faint distant odors, susceptible only to the trained palate, of arak and brandy and cheap champagne; and above all, the persistent whining of the violins and the rhythmic metronome of the drums, and the soft drape of red plush curtain that must not be inspected too closely lest the depredations of the moths destroy the illusion. It lies sandwiched in between a tall red building that might be anything, and a grubby little shop that sells bicycles and newspapers.

The street cars thunder past it all day long, clanking their yellow overcrowded way along, the passengers clinging to their sides, slipping with the agility of custom from side-to-side as the hazard of an approaching vehicle draws near on the other line, or when the conductor moves along with a hopeful clinking of his collection bag. The big green buses thunder past the decrepit taxis and the sad horses that pull the *arrabiyehs* which wind their huge iron wheels relentlessly over the potholes, the coachmen sitting high up in front with their long thin whips, and the tarts in the back on the worn leather benches; and the cafés across the road with the pavement tables (and everybody stumbling over them and cursing as they hurry by in the bright sunlight, for this is a busy street in the daytime), and the coffee-sellers and the boot-boys with their shabby *galabiyas* reaching down to their bare feet cheerfully exchanging insults, and the posters on the walls in Arabic and French, and a music shop on the corner blaring out the latest melody from the film studios at Heliopolis, and the grubby little urchins selling their pornographic postcards to the tourists (and with marvelous sleight of hand contriving to switch packets at the last moment so that the tourists, retiring to the nearest privy to gloat over his purchases, finds that he has bought instead some pictures of the Pyramids); and everywhere bustle and noise and dusty urgency.

But at night time, the scene changes. The beautiful Cairo moon, the loveliest in creation, shines down azurely (you can easily read a newspaper by its light) and everything is quiet and softly luminescent. The businessmen have all gone home, and the stores are closed, and only the cafés that serve the railway station are still open, for everyone in this quarter is in the nightclubs. There are some soldiers standing outside the Crescent Bar, swaying slightly, taking in the night air and counting their money and wondering if there is enough left for another round, looking somehow sadly out of place now that so few of them are left. A prostitute saunters up to them on the dim street and says: "Hullo, dearie, you come home with me?" Just as if she had been trained in London. But this is almost all the English she can speak, and she knows the same words in French and Italian and Greek as well, and the pulsing blood in her smooth animal limbs is Arab and Turkish and Negroid and Berber; the milk in her breasts is Babylonian and Hittite and Phoenician and Tartar. She is young and beautiful and a thousand years old.

In the Pigalle, under the bright white lights of the spots, the tables were only just beginning to fill. The Greek maître was disposing the Sudanese waiters, tall and straight and slim in their spotless white gowns, allocating the tables, checking the service, his small sharp eyes watching the door and the bar and the entrance to the kitchen, and at the same time lingering with professional interest on the navel of the new girl who was dancing on the small round dais, dancing slowly to the soft whine of the music, to the plucked strings of the lute and the thumping of the drums, twisting her torso slowly, holding her arms above her head, snapping her fingers together in a particularly oriental gesture, swaying slightly, moving the round mass of her hips sensuously, feeling and caressing the soft smooth drape of the net that hung between her white thighs, the tiny blue veins showing under the harsh whiteness of the spotlight, her big mascaraed eyes almost demurely cast down to her gold-painted nipples and the sweat glistening on her body and running in a tiny, fascinating rivulet down her chest.

Trent watched her for a moment, standing at the entrance to the red-curtained booth in the corner. He signaled to the maître. The rotund little Greek came hurrying over, smiling pleasantly, rubbing his hands together. He said: "Good evening, Mr. Trent. A long time since we see you here. We have a new show; very good. You like the new girl? Arrived from Beirut today."

Trent nodded. He stood watching her for a moment, marveling

at the litheness of her, wondering at the fleshy contortions of her mobile stomach. He said: "Fellow coming to see me here, Angelos. I'll be in the booth. What's for dinner?"

"We have what you want, Mr. Trent. Some lobster perhaps, or you like a filet mignon? What do you say to a filet mignon with some asparagus tips? We have some very good steak today; I tell the cook to make it very rare..."

"Fine. And have them bring a bottle of arak and two glasses, will you?"

"Certainly. You want arak from Syria, or this local stuff?"

"Syrian."

"Certainly. I send it to you at once. And the steak...very rare, not?"

"Very." Trent pulled the curtain aside and sat down. When the waiter brought the bottle, he poured a glass of the strong liquid, added a touch of water and watched the whiteness come swirling, and gulped it down. When his dinner came, he ate with enjoyment and deliberation, poured himself another drink, then lit his pipe, and sat back to wait for Bolec. He pulled the curtain open a little and watched a couple of girls dance a bolero, swaying sinuously in and out of his line of vision through the gap in the curtain, the lights streaking across the room, the smoke clouding and spiraling up to the ceiling, the pleasant clink of wineglasses and the faintly indistinct sounds of inconsequential conversation coming to him.

It was exactly five minutes past ten when Bolec came in.

The half-open curtain was pulled back sharply, and the shadow of the big untidy man fell across the table. For a moment, he stood looking down on Trent, frowning slightly, his heavy face scowling, his tiny porcine eyes watchful and alert. For a moment he said nothing, standing there framed in the red plush curtain, the music rhythmic behind him, the spots cutting through the smoky air and making a shaft of light behind his enormous shoulders. Then, with a gesture, he swished the curtain shut, and sat down. He put his hands on the table and waited. Trent noticed that a finger of his left hand was missing.

He said: "I look for Mr. Trent. You Mr. Trent, no?"

Trent nodded amiably. "Good of you to come. What will you

drink?"

Bolec shook his great head, his heavy jowls quivering.

"Thank you, no. I drink nothing this place. Maybe they poison me. Whisky here made last week from old army alcohol, one hundred eighty proof. I know. I sell it to them. What you want with me?"

The man looked like a suspicious bullock. Trent offered his cigarette case. Bolec shook his head. "I not smoke, Mr. Trent. When I first come to this country I work for undertaker. Not smoke any more."

"An undertaker?"

"Yes, undertaker. You take dead man smoke too much, when you squeeze his lungs in your fist, like so...nothing but nicotine come out. Now I not smoke any more. What you want with me?"

"Er...quite." Trent tapped out his pipe and lit a cigarette. He said carefully: "Well, as a matter of fact, I don't really know. Wanted to meet you. Thought you might be able to help me."

"You from police?"

"Sort of."

"Military police?"

"Yes. Does that matter? Does that put you on the other side?"

Bolec smiled warily. He said: "No other side, Mr. Trent, all one side. Military police is good, O.K. I ain't got nothing to hide from military police. Sometimes little trouble with Egyptian police, but you got nothing to do with them. Better you be honest with me. You too well known around here. What you want with me?"

"Sure you won't have a drink?"

Bolec picked up the bottle and examined it critically. He sniffed the cork suspiciously and said: "O.K., maybe I have little bit."

"Help yourself."

He picked up the slim white bottle and held it up to the light, then poured himself a tumbler full; Trent watched him curiously. There was something deliberate, plodding, persistent, about all his movements. He drank it quickly, feeling the harsh fire of it in his throat, burning his stomach, then wiped his mouth with the back of his hand. He said: "Is good Syrian. But you want good arak, I get it for you. Better than this, cheap. I get off Greek ships in Port Said. Now, what you want?"

CAIRO CABAL

Trent asked: "What did Perugino tell you?"

Bolec grinned broadly. "Nothing. Perugino pretty good man, he don't tell me nothing. He tell me one Englishman want to see me tonight at Pigalle, name Mr. Trent, better you go. So I go. Now, what you want?"

Trent said abruptly: "Do you know a man called Reizen?"

They were watching each other carefully. Bolec shook his head. "No," he said, "not know that name. What is, German, maybe?"

"A Russian." He saw, or thought he saw, the slightest change of expression flicker on Bolec's broad face, no more than a momentary glimmer, so slight that he mistrusted even his own carefully cultured awareness of it. "Do you know a man called Kamel Irani?"

Bolec hesitated. He said carefully, his sharp little eyes watchful, "Maybe I know him. Why you ask about him?"

Trent said: "I'll tell you, Bolec. No reason at all why I shouldn't tell you. His name was linked with yours on some matter that concerns my office. I'll be quite frank; I don't know what you're up to, and I intend to find out. It's as simple as that."

"You think maybe you scare me, I tell you something, eh?"

"Something like that."

"And what this got to do with that fellow, what you say his name, Reizen? A Russian? I don't know no Russians. Kamel Irani maybe I know; maybe. But I don't know no Russians."

"How long have you been in Egypt, Bolec?"

"Fifteen, sixteen years maybe. Why?"

"About 1940? Where did you come from? Czechoslovakia?"

Bolec said nothing. Trent went on blandly: "My dear Bolec...with a name like that...I can find out from the police pretty easily."

"From Prague."

"If you left Prague in the early days of the war, or thereabouts, you're a refugee. Didn't you like your new rulers? The Germans? Then why didn't you go back when the Russians took over? Or didn't you like them either?"

Bolec stood up. He said angrily: "Mr. Trent, your people never get foreign troops in your country. You not know what this is, this occupation. You British, always you occupy. Never get occupied. If you understand what this means, then you don't talk to me this way. I go now. I got no business with you. I got nothing to talk to you about."

Trent said smoothly, glad that he had cleared up at least one problem:

"Sit down, Bolec. All right, you don't like the Russians. That's what I wanted to know. And I'll tell you this—I believe you; let's leave it at that. Now. Tell me about Kamel Irani."

Still standing, Bolec said: "Better *you* tell *me* about Kamel Irani."

"What do you want to know? Has he been making inquiries about you, is that it? That's what I hear. I hear he's asking a lot of questions about you."

Bolec said slowly, a deep frown on his face: "I think maybe Mr. Irani is policeman. Don't you know?"

"No, I don't know. All I know about him is what Perugino tells me, and that's precious little. I'd like to know a lot more."

Bolec hesitated, made up his mind, and sat down. "Then I tell you. He come to Cairo three weeks ago, live in Lido Hotel, down by the station, not far from here. I hear he start asking where he find me, but you understand, in my business, a man got to be careful little bit..."

"What is your business, Bolec?"

"Merchant," Bolec said promptly. "I buy things, sell them again. Sometimes a little black market... Why I tell you this? Because I think maybe you know who this man is. He ask too many questions about me. I know you not work for police. I know your business, everybody know it. But if this man not policeman, maybe you tell me what he want from me. I got friends in police headquarters. Down there, he don't ask no questions; only in cafés, in bars, in brothels...if Kamel Irani on the level, he ask for me by police. What you think?"

"What is he, a Persian?"

"Irani...is Persian name. But I think Kamel Irani is Turk. One of my friends tell me he hear him talking to one Turkish girl, dancer here. Not talking like foreigner; good Turkish, he say."

Trent said casually: "You know who the girl was?"

Bolec shrugged his massive shoulders. "Some girl," he said.

"Some Turkish girl dance here. Been here long time, you see her, maybe. Princess Higran; pretty girl, too fat little bit. But not bad. She come on floor show tonight; you see her."

Trent nodded, watching him carefully. He was conscious that Bolec was watching him too, puzzling out something. He said slowly: "Maybe our Turkish friend is working with the Russians, Bolec?"

"With Russians? What he do with Russians? They not do nothing here" This Egypt, not Czechoslovakia."

"Uh-huh. I wish I knew. Frankly, I can't even guess what they are up to. I may be chasing a wild goose all over the bloody country, but...I'd still like to know who associates your name with friend Reizen, and why."

"Who is this Reizen, Mr. Trent?"

"A Tass Agency correspondent, which means...well, he has to collect military and economic information, that sort of thing. Small stuff. Nobody of any consequence, but...I'd still like to know."

Bolec said slowly: "Perugino say you pretty good fellow. I want to help you. If I find out something about this fellow Kamel Irani, I let you know. You like that?"

"Well...there's not much you can do. Afraid you can't help me very much. Sorry to have brought you along for nothing." He indicated the bottle. "Have another glass of arak?"

Bolec shook his head, a lock of black hair falling dankly over his wide, low-browed forehead. "No," he said. "No. I go now. I make few inquiries about this man. I like to know what he want, too." He stood up and pulled the curtain aside. A red-headed girl was writhing on the floor of the stage, crouched on her knees, her thighs spread, her long hair hanging down over her white shoulders, her head thrown back so that the long red mass seemed to sweep the floor behind her, her breasts up-pointed and the spotlight bright on the jewels at her waist; she was moving her arms sinuously, her long white fingers carefully poised. Bolec said: "I find anything out, where I get in touch with you?"

"See Perugino. He knows where to find me."

"O.K." The big man hesitated, mentally twisting his cap. He said diffidently: "Maybe I give you my address? Some time, maybe you need me. My house not very...very fancy, you know...but you always welcome there. I live that big building on corner of Bab-el-Louk and Sharia El Gher, just beside Bab-el-Louk market. You know where I mean?"

Trent nodded.

I live on top floor, on roof. Just two-three small rooms I fix up pretty good. Very small, but maybe you come and have food with me one day, eh? I cook pretty fine food, Mr. Trent. You like it."

"All right, Bolec, I'll do that. One day soon. Thank you. Can you cook *kibdha?*"

Bolec threw back his head and laughed heartily, a quivering mountain of good humor. "You like *kibdha?* Sure, I make best *kibdha* in Egypt. I make special for you. You see."

Still laughing, Bolec pushed out through the curtains and snapped them shut behind him. Trent waited two minutes, timing it by his watch. Then he stepped through the curtain and looked around the room carefully. There was a faint smile on his face. He went across to the bar and said hello to the barman. The red-headed girl was just finishing her dance. He said: "What's her name, Charlie?"

"Maria Gamal, Mr. Trent. Pretty hot stuff by the look of her. Can I pour you a drink?"

"I left my bottle of arak in the corner booth."

The barman sent a waiter for it, and as the girl on the stage stood up to take her bow the lights came on all over the house and he caught her eye and smiled at her. A few moments later, she came out of the dressing room and sat on a stool beside him. She put on a bright, quick, smile, and said: "You like my dance?"

"Uh-huh. What are you drinking?"

"Champagne."

He said to the barman gently: "Bring a whisky and soda, Charlie," and when Charlie moved off to get the *Artistes'* bottle, the one that contained only cold tea, and poured some into a glass and added a splash of soda for the look of the thing, he said: "When you've finished, where can we go and talk?"

She leaned forward, pushing her breasts into him. "Anywhere you like. You got a hotel?" He shook his head. "Maybe we go to Lido. It's only fifty piasters, not too much."

"What about your place? Where do you live?"

CAIRO CABAL

"You don't like a hotel? All right, we go to my place. Is not too far. Ten piastres in taxi." She spoke English with a prettily clipped French accent, tossing her head with studied effect as she spoke, feeling the great mass of her hair on her bare shoulders.

He said: "Good. Finish your tea and let's go."

She grimaced and said to the barman: "I come back, Charlie, for three o'clock show."

"Fine, Maria."

He was polishing glasses, watching them slyly, the bald spot on the back of his head reflected in the mirror behind the bar. Trent slid off his stool, laid twenty piastres on the counter, and took her arm. "Goodnight, Charlie."

"'Night, sir."

In the taxi she sat close beside him, and he put his arm round her and kissed her once or twice, and put his hand on her thigh, more out of principle than anything else, and she kissed him and fondled him a little, feeling the tight muscles of his shoulders, and when they got to her room on the third floor of one of the new apartment houses on the edge of the Birka, she started slipping off her clothes. He watched her for a minute, admiring the smooth form of her, wondering if Higran had been as lithe and animal as this girl, worrying about the unknown hazards for her. He said abruptly: "You were a friend of Higran's, weren't you?"

She stopped in mid-movement, her dress held out halfway to the bed, a sudden look of alarm on her face. Suddenly, there was danger in the place, and fear. She glanced towards the door quickly.

Trent said gently: "There's nothing to worry about. I want to find out who killed her."

She held her dress over her body, a slow, defensive, frightened movement, then slid slowly to the bed and sat down, her eyes alert. Trent noticed that she had moved unobtrusively within reach of the bedside telephone. She said: "You from the police? I think you are English, no? No English in the police anymore."

"English, yes. Police, no."

She picked up the telephone quickly, almost expecting a quick movement from him, her wide eyes on him, showing fear. He said nothing, smiling at her. She spoke rapidly into the phone, just two rapid words, in Arabic, "*Send Ahmed,*" and in scarcely a moment he heard the rapidly padding footsteps down the hall and when the door burst open he was leaning back in the armchair, his hands behind his head, a smile on his face. He said to the Arab who came in, speaking quietly, almost affectionately: "No trouble. You can wait outside."

The Arab was fat and flabby, fat with the deceptive fatness of great strength, dressed in the uniform of a houseboy, a professional chucker-out, with all the unexpected lightness of movement of a heavy animal. The girl stared at Trent for a moment, wondering, then said: "What you want? Why you come here?"

"Tell Ahmed to wait outside. You have nothing to fear."

Not taking her eyes off him, she said: "*Stanna barra, Ahmed,*" and the Arab, looking him over carefully, measuring him, went slowly out into the hall and gently closed the door behind him. Trent said again:

"There's nothing to be afraid of. I want to find out who killed her. Don't you?"

She nodded, staring at him wide-eyed, a frightened child with the full breasts of a woman and the dyed red hair of a courtesan. He took out his identity card and tossed it on the bed beside her, noting with a sudden feeling of pity that she caught her breath and trembled sharply as his hand went to his pocket, and realizing the extent of her fright. She picked it up and looked at it, and pondered it for a moment, he wondered if she could read the Latin alphabet, then she handed it back to him silently.

He said gently: "Not frightened anymore?" She shook her head, still sitting motionless.

"That's good. I tell you, I only want to find out who killed her. Now. Tell me about her friends. You knew her well, didn't you?"

Still staring at him, hesitating, she said: "Yes. A long time we know each other. We meet in Damascus, in Beirut...sometimes in Athens. But now, this time, she stays for two seasons in Cairo, and each time I come 'ere, I find 'er at Pigalle still. I think per'aps she likes it 'ere, per'aps she 'as rich friend 'ere."

"That's exactly it. Who was her friend, Maria?"

Maria let out a deep breath as though feeling her danger was past. She stood up and walked to the door and took a housecoat off a hook behind it and slipped it over her shoulders. "I don't know. I don't know. She 'as plenty of friends. Sometimes I think..." She paused.

"What do you think, Maria?"

"Well...sometimes I think she is doing something...something wrong. Always she is whispering with one man. When I go to their table one night, she does not introduce me; always before, she introduce me to all 'er friends, but this one, no. And I think at first she is jealous, because 'e is...a fine man, very big...and then I think '*Why she whisper with 'im always?*' and I think per'aps they are doing something which is not good..."

"Such as?"

She shrugged her shoulders, walking up and down the little room in bare feet. "Now...she is dead." The tears were starting to come to her eyes and she dabbed at them with the hem of her robe. "Tonight, when she does not come in time for the floorshow, Mr. Papadopoulos send a rickshaw boy to fetch 'er, and when this boy comes back...'e tells us all what 'appen. 'Oo did this to 'er, Mr...what you say your name was?"

"John."

"John." She stopped sniveling; and found a handkerchief. "Johnny. Is a pretty name."

Trent winced. He said: "You mean the police had not told Papadopoulos before? Hadn't they been round asking questions about her? They must have known where she worked."

"No...no police come. Mr. Papadopoulos is very angry about it."

"I see." It did not make sense. He said: "The more I hear about this, the more it smells...the police were not round at the Pigalle during the day? Are you sure?"

"Of course. If they come round and ask questions, everybody will know about it. But nobody know."

"What about a man called Reizen? Do you know the name? Have you heard Higran mention him?"

She shook her head. "No, I do not know this name."

"What about Kamel Irani? Did she mention him at all?"

"Kamel Irani? Yes. This is the name of 'er friend, the one I tell you always whispering with 'er. 'E come to the Pigalle tonight."

He said sharply: "Tonight?"

"Yes. 'E was sitting at a table near the bar, stay a little while, then go. I think per'aps 'e was looking for Higran."

"I see. Do you know any of her friends in the police?"

"The police? Girls like us...we 'ave no friends in the police, Johnny. Always they want money us, or..." She made a gesture.

"Was she worried about anything...did she seem preoccupied, upset about anything?"

"No...only...only I think per'aps she...she told me one night, I don't know 'ow to say it, but she ask me if I stay 'ere long, and when I say per'aps I finish season 'ere with 'er at Pigalle, she says no, is better I go away from Cairo soon. I think per'aps she is making some big trouble 'ere..."

"What sort of trouble, Maria? This might be what I want to know."

She sat down on the edge of the bed. "I don't know, Johnny. Only trouble...she said better I go away from Cairo very soon. When I ask 'er why, she shake 'er 'ead and say nothing."

Trent sighed. "We haven't got very far, have we?"

Maria got up and went to the cupboard. She took a slice of mango from a gauze-covered bowl and offered it to him, holding it like a speared fish on the tines of a fork. "You like mango?"

He shook his head and she started eating it noisily, then went to the tiny kitchen and put the coffeepot on the gas ring, piling the powder high on the upturned brass cone. She said: "Why you want to know all this, Johnny? Per'aps Higran is working for you? Yes?"

"No...not for me. I'd just like to know..." He got up and went to the kitchen with her, standing with her by the gas ring while she shook the pot gently and waited for the water to bubble up, standing close beside her and feeling the nearness of her, smelling the rich scent of her, watching the bright spread of her hair. He said: "You haven't been much help, have you? Not scared anymore?"

She shook her head. Holding the piece of mango in her hand, holding it between them, looking up at him, her eyes serious, she said: "You want to make love to me, Johnny?"

He said gently: "Not this time. Later, maybe. You're a nice girl,

Maria. See you at the Pigalle sometimes?"

"I see you there, any time you want..."

"Are you going back there now? Shall I walk you round?"

"No...I eat a little supper first. Then go back."

He stroked her hair for a moment. She said: "You not like to drink some coffee with me? Is nearly ready." The little pot bubbled up and she took it quickly off the fire, held it a moment, then put it back, watching it carefully.

"Not now. I must get some sleep." He put his hand on her hip and stroked it gently for a moment, then turned and went out into the hallway. He paused at the door and smiled at her, and she stood by the kitchen with the coffeepot in her hand, watching him, smiling at him regretfully. He hesitated for a moment, then closed the door softly. As he walked down the stairway, feeling vaguely troubled and already wishing he had stayed, he heard the soft padding of the Arab behind him, and looking back, saw him standing massive and silent at the top of the stairs, bulkily framed against the light of the upstairs landing.

He walked quickly back to the Pigalle in the clear moonlight, picked up his car, and drove home. When he reached his apartment, he took a cold shower, drank a glass of brandy, and when he climbed into bed and pulled the sheet over him, the last thing he heard was the clock on the tower in the *midan* striking half-past three.

He dreamed that he was making love to Maria, and when he rolled off her body, the red cumulation of her hair turned suddenly and frighteningly into blood and Perugino was standing by watching him and gloating and saying, "Disemboweled, Mr. Trent... disemboweled..."

He was glad when daylight came.

When he got to the office in the morning, he noticed with some sorrow that the gardener had swept up the jacaranda flowers and the driveway was clean and neat in the nine-o'clock sunshine. The bright red hibiscus in the corner under the window was startlingly vivid against the dark green backdrop, and the long pointed leaves of the scarlet poinsettias, which the Egyptians call *bint el onsul*, the consul's daughter, were sprinkler-washed and lovely in the crisp morning air.

The flowerbeds were neat and tidy, and the steam from the night's hosing was beginning to rise perceptibly, dark patches of water still showing where the humid mango trees cast their heavy shadows across the driveway; and faintly odorous, a heavy, pungent smell tinged with the scent of frangipani, the still-wet ground was preparing itself for the onslaught of the oppressive sun. The air was heavy with the fresh aroma of watered earth.

The girl at the desk smiled brightly at him when he came in, noting the heavy shadows under his eyes, as she handed him a report. He sat on the edge of her desk while he read it, one leg dangling idly.

> *"In accordance with your instructions I went to the Pigalle last night, at twenty hundred hours. At twenty-fifty-five I saw you come in and take a seat at the corner booth. Ten minutes later I saw (presumably) Stefan Bolec come in and I heard him ask for you. He went straight to your booth on the direction of the head waiter, and was with you for twenty minutes. Several other people came in behind him, but as only the spotlights were on at this time, I could not see them clearly. When he left, he was followed out of the room by a man who had been sitting near the bar, and who, I believe, was one of those who came in behind him. I followed him.*
>
> *Subject was about fifty years old, five feet nine inches, about 230 pounds, with short black hair, a small black moustache, swarthy complexion, and a very thick neck; his most noticeable feature was the powerful build of his shoulders. He looked rather like a prizefighter. I would say that he was Egyptian, or possibly Turkish. As soon as he was outside, he made no attempt to follow Bolec, but merely watched him go off in the direction of the Birka. He then walked to the Lido Hotel, making no effort to hide his movements. I regret to say that I think he knew I was following him, though I took all normal precautions. I would say that he is no beginner in this business, since I believe he spotted me at once; this is only conjecture, and I may be wrong. When he reached the hotel, I heard him ask for the key to room 36. I went to the bar and stayed there for two hours. Then took a room there myself. While registering, I saw that room*

36 is occupied by one Kamel Irani, whose address is given as Istanbul. He booked in on September 12th."

The report was signed, *Henson to Mr. Trent. Confidential.*

Trent went into his office and slid the paper into the drawer of his desk. He sat down to think for a while, and then went in to see the Colonel.

CHAPTER 6

The old, old man was sharpening his knife on a whetstone. The movements of his wizened shoulders were smooth and rhythmical, his whole upper body moving smoothly forward with his hands, pushing gently forward.

From time-to-time he tested the blade on a thick and broken thumbnail, then set the stone straight once more, easing his haunches on the ground and gripping it firmly between his toes as an ape does, sometimes spitting on the stone, then testing the blade once more and examining it critically with his wrinkled, ageless eyes, then honing again more gently, with a soft and cadenced motion.

Sometimes he looked up and watched the passersby, looking up at them from the dusty gutter, twisting his frail old head this way and that, his wicked, mischievous lace grimacing as he muttered to himself.

At last, he took the long curved blade, which had three large holes bored down the center of it (to cause a deadlier wound), its brass and silver handle tarnished with age and bound at a broken point with a piece of galvanized wire, and he drew it slowly and carefully across the wiry white hairs on his forearm, blowing the shaved hair away with a sharp hiss through his broken yellow teeth.

Then he inspected the blade once more, sheathed it, and tucked it out of sight in the ragged cloth band around his waist.

His tiny, screwed-up, beady eyes were old and tired and vicious and impatient.

CHAPTER 7

The Colonel said angrily: "Confound it, it's nearly twenty-four hours since you found that list. I want to know the reason for it, and all about it, and I want to know now. If anything happens to Pearman... Good God, if anything ever happens to his negotiations..."

Trent fidgeted uneasily, mentally squirming. He said: "As a matter of fact, Sir, we haven't done badly at all. I have a direct lead to Kamel Irani and we've associated him definitely with Bolec. Irani was watching him last night at the Pigalle, so we know that he..."

"You know nothing," the Colonel said sharply. "You know no more than you did at this time yesterday. You know that Bolec and Irani are implicated in something that concerns Pearman. But you don't know what it is, and you don't know how. You knew that yesterday and you still don't know what it is. Now. What are you going to do about it?"

Trent said patiently: "Shulam, the Egyptian MI man, we know all about and we can discount. Saleh is dead. Reizen we know is a Tass correspondent, and therefore involved in espionage of a sort. Pearman we know about. That leaves only Bolec and Irani, and those are the two I'm working on. I'm convinced that they don't really know each other...that they're not working together, anyway. I've dreamed up a reasonable excuse and asked the Egyptian police for a report on Bolec, and I should get a copy of his local dossier today. But if we could get a wire off to Istanbul asking about Irani...he came here three weeks ago, presumably on a passport, so it won't be hard to find out..."

"Good God in Heaven!" said the Colonel testily. "How would you like me to ring up Scotland Yard and ask about a man named John Smith of London? In the Middle East, every Tom, Dick and Harry is called Kamel Irani. No. You know where he's staying. Get into his room and search it. Get a look at his passport and all his papers. Get him held up and robbed on the street if necessary, but get a look at all the papers he carries. Nothing will tell you more about a man than the contents of his pockets. What about this other girl, what's her name? Maria Gamal?"

"The only thing of interest from her is that she said Higran was expecting something to happen which made it advisable for Maria to clear out of Cairo..." He said lamely: "It's not very much, I know...she also verified the fact that she was very close to Kamel Irani."

"Getting her friends to clear out of town...that points to one thing, and one thing only..." The Colonel took out one of his cigarettes and lit it, watching the smoke curl up and hang above the desk. "What about Bolec? Where does he fit in?"

"A report should be in today, Sir. Meanwhile, I had a drink with him last night. Seems a decent enough sort of fellow..."

The Colonel snorted. He said: "You're not old enough yet to tell whether a man's a decent fellow after just one drink, and you probably never will be. And don't forget that there are plenty of decent fellows on the other side, too."

"That's exactly the point," Trent said wearily. "We don't know who or what the other side is. All we know is that someone has associated our man Pearman, in black and white, with a couple of undesirable characters. It's precious little to go on. And it may mean nothing at all."

"You think so? Then tell me why the girl was killed."

"It could be coincidence."

"Poppycock! In this business, there's no such thing."

The Colonel stood up abruptly and started pacing the carpet. He was angry and tired and irritable. "Perhaps I should have put you in the picture earlier. Pearman's work on the arms deal is delicate and it's vital. Among the Egyptians, he's working at Cabinet level, and at that level we know who is on our side and who isn't. As far as their security is concerned, there's not too much to worry about, because they know that if news of the talks leaks out prematurely, their heads will roll. They're too fond of their jobs to run the risk of that, and they've been too-long trained in the craft of deceit. It's the lower echelons we must worry about...at that level, nobody must know what he's doing. We know, from the very existence of that list of yours, that somebody has an idea he's not what he's supposed to be. And I'm anxious about the inclusion of Reizen's name; that can also only mean...it's outside interference again, and it's dangerous. I tell you it's deadly dangerous; it smells. You've got to find out quickly who wrote it, where it came from, where it was going, what it's about. Your best leads? Find out first who killed the girl..."

Trent raised his eyebrows. He said mildly: "That's not going to be easy, working from under cover..."

The Colonel repeated coldly: "First, find out who killed the girl, and unless it was a *crime passionelle*, which I doubt, take it from there. Second, find out where she got the list from. Third, find out all about Irani and Bolec. If that doesn't get you somewhere, I'll take over myself."

He stopped his pacing suddenly, standing in front of the picture that hung on the wall beside the big map. It was a photograph of a violin, a black and white photograph of the kind taken to advertise expensive cameras, an enlarged photograph of a violin that lay in three-quarter profile on a bed of silk, the bow lying silent beside it, the highlights striking the soft and beautiful sheen at the graceful curves of the wood. He pinched out his cigarette and said slowly:

"Am I bad-tempered this morning, John? Forgive me...sometimes I feel... Forgive me. Do you need any more men?"

Trent shook his head. "No, not yet. The police are finding out about Bolec for me, and I'll put Perugino on to Irani. He ought to be able to get into his room..."

"No, do that yourself. It's too important. How sure are you of Bolec?"

"Well, not at all, really. Only my own judgment...after a single meeting. He came here from Prague in about 1940. That makes him a refugee from the Germans who did not return when he might have done, when the Russians moved in. Unless he were planted here...is that possible?"

The Colonel shook his head. "We'd have found out about him long before this. It's too much to expect that he could have kept his cover for so long. Try and get him on your side. If he's a Czech, he's almost certainly violently opposed to people like Reizen. Can you get a line, a discreet line, on to the police investigations of the girl's death? That's really the only thing we have to go on."

"Yes, Sir, I have a lead already."

"Good. Assume one thing. Assume that the Russians are behind whatever's going on. If it turns out that we're wrong, then it isn't our problem anyway. If we're right, then we'll be glad we assumed that in the first place. Understand?"

"Yes, Sir." Trent stood up and went to the door. He turned and said: "Did you know there's a violin concert on the BBC tonight?"

"Yes, John, I know. Thank you...one thing more."

The Colonel sat down at his desk. "Get a list of the people who saw that girl during her last twenty-four hours. See the concierge, the waiters at the Pigalle, the taxi-drivers; I want a list of every single soul she spoke to. Understand?"

"Yes, Sir. I'll have it by tomorrow."

"Tomorrow won't do. Set it by tonight."

Trent sighed and went out. He said to the secretary: "What's he upset about?"

"Upset?"

"Like a bear with a sore head." He sat on the desk beside her, looking at the pale grey of her eyes, feeling a closeness to her. He said: "Come out for a drink at lunch time?"

She smiled and shook her head. Slipping some paper into her typewriter, she said: "Too much to do. Lunching off sandwiches in the office." He grinned at her and swung off the desk.

"There's a message for you in your room. Did you see it?"

"No, from whom?"

"Your Perugino. He wants you to call him. I made a note of the number."

"I know it." He picked up the telephone and dialed the number. Perugino's voice sounded strangely high-pitched. He said:

"Mr. Trent? I tried to find you earlier. My friend Bolec told me this morning that he wanted to see you badly. I took the liberty of suggesting that you might go round now. Call him and tell him I'm on my way there, will you? Is he on the phone?"

"Yes, Mr. Trent. His number is not listed, but I will call him for you. Shall I come too? If you wish to see me..."

Covering the mouthpiece with his hand, Trent said: "Persistent little bastard." Into the phone he said: "No. I'll pick you up after lunch. Say...three o'clock outside the Hambra mosque. Is that all right?"

"At three o'clock? Yes, I will be there."

He rang off and went out, fumbling in his pockets for his pipe and tobacco.

Bolec's place on the top of an old apartment house that overlooked the big market at Bab-el-Louk was a tiny affair made up of three small rooms up on the roof that had once been servants' quarters, and had been joined together by interconnecting doors. There was a small hallway, a single living room, and a bedroom, and a kitchen, all the rooms square, and all of identical size. They were furnished haphazardly, with comfortable odds and ends picked up at the auction sales.

When he opened the door, Bolec was standing with a cast-iron frying pan in his hand, hanging down at his side. His great belly spread over the top of his belt, and he was wearing white drill trousers and a singlet. He was clearly excited. His tiny black eyes were shining with excitement and he used his frying pan, a ten-inch affair of some considerable weight, as though it were a fly-whisk, gesticulating with it wildly. Poking it at Trent he said:

"Now I know you are my friend...this time, I find out what they try to do with me, I say to myself, this time my friend Mr. Trent want to know this thing. So I tell Perugino. Is O.K.?" He put his frying pan down with a bang on the table.

Out of deference to Bolec's undress, Trent undid the belt and buttons of his drift jacket and sat down in a leather armchair, spreading his legs out wide and fanning himself with a magazine. He said:

"Go ahead. I'm anxious to know what you have to say."

"First," said Bolec, "first you try some of my wine. This I make myself, is good. Is hot, no?" He wiped the back of his bull neck on a towel and dropped it on the divan, then took a long slim bottle of clear white wine and poured a tumbler full. Raising his glass, he said:

"*Nazdarovye*. You remember this man Reizen, this Russian fellow you tell me about? Now I tell you something about him. Is up to no good, Mr. Trent. I think he want to make trouble for me. I tell you. You like this wine? Is good, no? I make from bananas."

Trent sipped it suspiciously. Bolec drained his glass and poured himself another, setting his huge bulk on a wooden chair, his great, thighs spread wide, the buttons of his trousers bulging. He clapped his hands, and the servant came in, a young Arab girl of sixteen or so, dressed in village black, slim and dark and solemn-eyed. Speaking rapid and fluent Arabic, he said brusquely: "Go to market. Bring eggs." She nodded and left, moving silently on bare feet. He watched her go, letting his eyes linger on her as she closed the door behind her. He said cheerfully: "I keep girl servant, is better than a man. Is pretty, no?" He went on: "First I tell you about my business. You know, sometimes I do jobs not very legal, like black market, very difficult times now, have to make a living, no? You understand? Sometimes the police make me trouble, so I like police very much, you understand, eh? I tell you this because I know you not tell the police about me, yes?" He waited.

Trent said carefully: "Perhaps I should tell you, Bolec, that I'm getting a copy of your dossier from police headquarters. Frankly, I don't expect to find anything in it that conflicts with my own interests. Whatever mischief you're up to with the police—that's none of my business. Do we understand each other?"

Bolec nodded eagerly. He said: "O.K. Is good. Now, I tell you. Somebody come to me last week, ten twelve days ago, ask me to do little job. I tell you, I got plenty...plenty friends. You know, all shoeshine boys on street. They all work for me. They pay me little bit money every month, I fix with waiters, barmen, hotel porters, people like that, not to make them trouble. So they go into bars, hotels, cafes, places like that, make plenty business. Any boy not pay me, I tell waiters, barmen, you keep this boy out of your place, then boy got no work except on streets. So I tell other boys, maybe you fix this boy up little bit, taking your work, so then..." Bolec spread his huge arms eloquently. "They make trouble for this boy, then next time he pay me his dues. Is like union, Mr. Trent," he said righteously. "Poor boys got no union, so I fix. You understand? Sometimes, friends want little job done, like follow somebody, find out where she live, find out about somebody's wife; so my boys find out for me, I make a little bit money, not much, enough to pay rent."

Trent said affably: "All this will no doubt be in your dossier, and a lot more. As I told you before, it's none of my business."

Bolec said uncomfortably: "Maybe you let me see that dossier when you get it, Mr. Trent. Maybe they write plenty lies about me. I put them right for you, no?"

"No."

Bolec was glum, all the troubles of the world on his shoulders. Brightening, he said: "I can tell you about your friend Reizen, then maybe you show me, yes?"

"It's a confidential document, Bolec. It will help me to check on the truth of what you have to say." Bolec nodded miserably. "But," he protested, "I don't tell you no lies. I tell only truth. Police, different matter. To my friends I tell only truth, I got nothing to hide from my friends. But few days ago one fellow come to see me, make a proposition. One Egyptian fellow name Shakri, no good. He say, I tell my boys drop nails all over roads, make lot of trouble for motorcars, you understand? He pay me one hundred pounds. I say, 'Where you get one hundred pounds, you good-for-nothing Egyptian?' This Shakri is poor man, got no money. He say, 'Never mind, I pay you, I give you twenty pounds now, eighty after.' I say, 'When after?' and he say, 'When I tell you start throwing nails.'"

He hesitated, letting the significance become apparent. He said: "You see this thing before, Mr. Trent. When taxi-drivers go on strike, boys drop nails all over roads, make plenty trouble for private cars, buses. Sometimes we do this outside places fix punctures, good for their business. But this fellow Shakri, he want one hundred boys on this job. Now, this is too much! I put ten, twelve boys do is work, make already plenty trouble, plenty. But one hundred boys...sure, I got one hundred boys working for me, I got more than that, but this is very big trouble, Mr. Trent, too big. Another thing. He tell me he want some boys working outside police garages, at Kasr-el-Nil and Abbassiya, all big police garages. I say, O.K. I put twenty boys on this job, one hundred too much, make too much trouble. He say no. We argue little bit, have little drink, and this fellow Shakri get drunk. I find out he supposed to pay me two hundred pounds, and I think this very big job. I don't want nothing with it, is too big. But I agree. I say O.K. I take fifty pounds off him..."

Trent raised an eyebrow. "Fifty?"

Bolec grinned happily. "Fifty. I tell you this Shakri get plenty drunk, I take fifty pounds off him. Next day, I see him again, I say better you tell me who put you on this job, maybe we get more money for both of us, because this is very big trouble coming up. Nails on road outside police garage very dangerous work, maybe some of my boys get caught, then what? We talk little bit, but Shakri don't say nothing. Sometimes he's a smart fellow." Bolec shrugged his shoulders, "O.K. I got to make a living, I tell him I do it. But I'm a pretty smart fellow too. I find out this Shakri got girlfriend, Arab girl, very dirty. But Shakri talk to her too much, he tell her everything. So I talk to her, give her little bit money, tell her to find out what Shakri up to. Last night, after I leave Pigalle, I go to see her. I find out who tell Shakri to do this thing. Is your friend Reizen."

Trent sat up stiff and straight in his chair. "Reizen! Are you sure? Are you sure about this?" He said sharply: "Don't feed me rumors, Bolec. I want to be sure about this."

Bolec said placidly: "Is sure, Mr. Trent. This fellow Shakri talk plenty to his girl. You don't believe me, I bring her to you, you talk to her yourself. Maybe beat her little bit, find out she tell truth."

Trent stood up and stretched his legs. There was a frown on his face. He said: "Tell me one thing, Bolec. This nonsense about strewing nails on the road to stop the traffic...it's been done before, of course, often. I know, it can be a damn nuisance. But how big a scale is this compared with...for example, the Black Saturday riots, when they burned down Shepheards? How many boys were out on that caper?"

Bolec said solemnly, laying his fat hand on his chest, "Believe me, that time I don't know nothing about it. The British are my friends; that time, I don't know nothing about it at all. I have to hide,

CAIRO CABAL

like all other Europeans, plenty trouble for me, too. But that time, you remember, all cars off the road by midday. Maybe ten, fifteen people cause all that trouble, but not my boys, somebody else. Is easy. Each man buy five, ten pounds two-inch nails; then he walk down street, keep on dropping them, nobody see, cause plenty trouble. That time, Black Saturday you call it, no cars on street after first two three hours. No police cars, no nothing. All get punctures, police sweep up nails, boys drop more. Is easy."

"So this is a pretty big effort. It's the same thing all over again. Where were your boys to work? Only at the police garages?"

"No, I write down list. He say, corner of Fuadel-Awal and Emad-el-Din; in Midan Ismailia; places like that, all busy places in Cairo. You see, pretty soon no police cars on road, no other cars either. But I not work for Russians, Mr. Trent. I think this maybe pretty big trouble, I don't want nothing to do with it. Maybe I even give Shakri back his fifty pounds. What you think? Is big trouble, big riots coming again?"

"That's what it looks like. But I don't know...it's like groping in a haystack..." He paced up and down the small room for a while, his dark face frowning, the deep lines showing round the corners of his mouth.

He picked up the tall wine bottle. "May I?"

"Of course. Is good wine, help yourself. Maybe I cook you some lunch?"

Trent shook his head. "Have an appointment. Thanks all the same."

"I make pretty good *shikshuka*, Mr. Trent. You like *shikshuka?*" Bolec stood up and went to the cupboard. He said: "You try my *shikshuka*, you feel pretty good afterwards."

Taking out some eggs and ripe tomatoes, he said:

"What I do about this fifty pounds? Maybe I give it back to Shakri?"

"No, don't do that." Noticing the pleasure in Bolec's eyes, he asked: "When were you supposed to start work on this project?"

Bolec went to the tiny kitchen and turned on the gas on top of the stove. "Don't know," he called. "This fellow Shakri tell me, 'Have your boys ready, I tell you when to go ahead.' But I not work for the

Russians." He came back to the doorway and stood hugely framed in it. "I do this thing for anybody else, but not for them. Make trouble for police, I don't care. Police make plenty trouble for me, too, sometimes. But what they want here, these Russians?" He said savagely, "They make me plenty trouble in Prague, what they trying to do in Cairo? You tell me that."

Trent sipped his wine slowly. "I wish I knew," he said. "I wish to hell I knew. Anyway, don't let me influence you one way or the other. What about Shakri's girlfriend? Will he find out you've been talking to her?"

Bolec came to the door again and leaned against the jamb. "I don't think so," he said slowly. "How can he find this out?"

"You gave her money?"

"Little bit, twenty piastres."

"If Shakri finds she has money...presumably he doesn't give her any? What sort of relationship is it? Could she pick money up elsewhere?"

"Oh, that..." Bolec went back to the kitchen. "I tell her, 'You let Shakri see you got money, he think you got another lover. Maybe he kill you.' No, I don't think so. Anyway, Shakri no trouble. Is good-for-nothing Egyptian."

"And let me know next time your little bastards start strewing the roads with nails. I want to keep my Jaguar off the streets."

"I do that." Bolec was grinning happily, slicing tomatoes with a rapid sliding motion, using a long butcher's knife, drawing the keen blade sharply, obliquely across the taut red skins, dropping the slices into the pan, smelling the rich scent of the frying butter which filled the tiny apartment, watching the red slices sizzle and bubble, gloating in the pungent aroma of them. Carrying his glass, Trent went into the kitchen and watched. He said:

"You'll lose another finger if you don't watch out."

Bolec shook his head, grinning. "Not with my knife, Mr. Trent, not with my knife." He held up his left hand. "I tell you how I cut this finger off? I tell you." Gesticulating happily with the bright blade, he said:

"Cutting wood, in Czechoslovakia. We live on farm when I was a boy, not very big, small place, you know. One day, I cut wood for the stove, and my axe...too sharp, like razor. My mother call for me from window and I look up and bang! Axe come down on my hand, chop one finger off, right off. Well, my father fix for me, put on disinfectant, bind up with bandage, then I go back to finish chopping wood. So I see my finger lying on...how you call it? Chopping-block? I see my finger there, and I think to myself, 'O.K. Stefan, what you going to do with that finger?' I think maybe I send it to my girlfriend, but I ain't got a girlfriend, not steady, just a young boy still. So I think a little bit, then take finger and sneak into kitchen and put it in goulash on the stove. Pretty soon, dinner ready, and I begin to wonder who get my finger. First time round, nobody get, so I ask for more and go help self at stove, fish around in casserole, find finger, cover him with sauce so my mother not see, then eat him. Taste pretty good. Soon, my father see bones on plate and say to my mother, 'What sort of meat you put in goulash, wife? Look like rabbit bones; rabbit got no place in goulash.' So I tell them. 'That's my finger, taste pretty good.' My mother faint right away, and my father take his belt and beat hell out of me. But no good wasting fresh meat, Mr. Trent. What you think?"

Trent shuddered slightly. "Quite," he said, "no good at all."

Bolec tossed some eggs into the pan. He said, "Pretty soon ready. Why you not stay and eat with me? Not take long."

Trent looked at his watch. "Well, if you'll show me you still have most of your fingers left before we start eating..."

Bolec took a spatula and turned the mixture. He shook some chilies into a grinder and ground them over the pan. His great belly was quivering with merriment, his beady little eyes twinkling. He said: "I feel pretty good today. Make new friend, feel pretty good."

The Arab girl came in silently and took some brown eggs slowly, one by one, out of a piece of rag, laying them gently in a white bowl in the cupboard, her long thin fingers moving delicately, a ballet movement of even so prosaic an act. Bolec said in Arabic:

"Fix table. My friend eat with me."

She put some plates and forks on the table, with two wine glasses and the tall bottle, then stood back and waited silently.

They sat down to eat.

CHAPTER 8

Reizen was the General, and the Captains stood around him.

He sat at his desk in the hot and stuffy room, none of the night coldness penetrating through the heavy sailcloth of the drawn curtains, the smoke from a dozen cigarettes thinly climbing and lingering, and the chink of tiny porcelain coffee-cups interpolating its high falsetto to the deep low voices around the room. He sat at his desk with his maps and his papers and his pencils and his notes all spread out in front of him; he was the boss, the general, and the men around him took their orders from him.

He was thin and slight, with a long beaked face that obtruded nasally over the table; his long sharp nose was no longer an embarrassment to him, but in his youth it probably was, when schoolboys would giggle and jeer, and the girls would turn away from him in disgust; it was thin and long and beaked and seemed to be always there, so that when you went to see Reizen, you saw his nose delicately feeling the air like a proud beak of a toucan, and then you saw the man appended to it, following it, so to speak, and blindly going where it led him. On its thin bridge were perched a pair of aimless glasses. His forehead was wide, receding, his hair straight and limp; it was always falling over his forehead. His eyes, which were blue, were shrewd, inquiring, cold; but you somehow had the feeling that Reizen was a fraud. He had the ingredients in him of an intellectual eagle; but he was no more than a belligerent sparrow.

He spread his long, bony fingers out on the map in front of him and spoke to the men sitting about the table.

CAIRO CABAL

"First," he said, his voice low, quiet, solemn, "first comes Pearman. Rashid, you know what you have to do. Until Pearman is dead, nothing happens. Then we start here..." jabbing his fingers on the map "...then here, then here, then here. As soon as Pearman is dead, Abdul Rahman will give the signals. First he will go in his taxi and tell the students at the University to be ready to start their demonstrations. Then he will go to the corner of Fuad-el-Awal and Suleiman Pasha where you, Shufik, will be waiting outside Russo's Bar. As soon as Rashid gives you the signal, get your men together and start work. Next, Rashid, go to Midan Opera; Saleh will be waiting outside the Badia. As soon as you get the signal, Saleh, walk across to the Continental Hotel and throw your grenades into the lounge. Rashid, you then drive over to Abbassiya and tell Yussuf Destur; he will start his procession. Then, over to Gezira and do the same with Gamal Suleiman. Now, at this point, I will call the others to start work. They know what to do. Within six hours, there will not be one Britisher alive on the streets, nor one British building standing."

There was a gleam in his eyes. It was not the destruction of all he had been carefully taught to hate that pleased him so much as the thought that they had successfully accomplished such a lot that was beyond the usual scope of his activities. Behind the pleasure shining out of his eyes was barely a conscious rehearsal of his lines: *"Yes, Comrade Minister, this has been done, and that has been done, and the other has been done, yes, Comrade Minister thank you, Comrade Minister, thank you...I have always tried to do my best, my very best, perhaps if Moscow were to hear about it?"* And then he said to himself, *"Or shall I take it for granted, a good man doing a good job, quietly, no thought of profit, perhaps they will be more impressed..."*

He glanced from one to the other of them, his eyes peering over his glasses, moving rapidly from face to face. They sat there nodding at him, smoking their cigarettes, drinking their coffee, their features cast in a dozen different molds; there were the weak and the strong, the composed and the tightened, the suave and the uncouth; they were tall and short, sallow and florid, old and young.

One thing they had in common: hatred.

It shone from their eyes and vomited from their mouths. It hung like the smoke in the air and was their common denominator.

Somebody (the wisp of smoke drifting and losing its intensity) said:

"What about the money?"

Reizen nodded. He said: "You will have plenty of notice. One day before we start work, I will call you all here again. There will be plenty of money. The money is coming. You will be paid, and told when to start work; it will be twenty-four hours later. The money will be here."

"By God! if my men do not get their money, they will not work."

"There will be money. Plenty of money. More money than you have ever seen before. The money."

The meeting broke up.

CHAPTER 9

Perugino was waiting for him in the shadows by the great grey-walled mosque, close beside the huge oak doors, bleached to a stone greyness and embossed with age-green bronze studs. The doors were open, and inside, in the cavernous cool depths, white-arched, rush-carpeted, the three-o'clock prayers were being said, and the faint mumbles came clearly out into the hot street, a crescendo of sound trembling over the bowed backs of the kneeling white-robed figures neatly lined up on the mats, rumbling into the dust and the heat and the blinding brightness outside.

They drove slowly round the *midan* in the Jaguar. The air was hot and dry and crisp, the sun striding down with all its force, a last desperate burst of heat before it started to lose its intensity, the tall white buildings glazing white in the heat, casting their huge masses of sharply-etched blue shadow like cool oases on the hot tarmac. Two Arabs were standing in the middle of the road, arguing volubly, one of them taking off his tarboush and looking up to see if the sun had started to go down, wiping the sweat from his forehead, paying no attention at all to the heavy traffic.

The Jaguar slid unheeded past them and braked to a sudden stop as a child ran swiftly across the road, clutching a great bundle of newspapers against his thin, undernourished side, his brown face happily gleaming with strong white teeth, his black eyes sparkling, his bare feet soundless on the road.

Perugino said carefully: "There is something I do not like about it, Mr. Trent. It is not that the police have found out nothing; they are not *trying* to find out anything. A crime like this...a *crime passionelle*...on the surface at least. I think they wish to let it go at that and do no more about it. Their investigation seems to me to be merely a token affair, as if they wished to announce their good intentions to the world. But behind the scenes, there is very little activity. I was able to procure from them a list of the people whom she saw during her last day of life, Mr. Trent."

"The last twenty-four hours is all we want... How complete is it?"

"It is complete. My friend the Inspector gave me a copy of his report..."

"Oh? And what excuse did you give for wanting it?"

"Two pounds, is that all right? He is too wise a man to ask any stupid questions...for a man of his mentality, a little money is enough." He pulled a slip of paper from his pocket and handed it to Trent. "Some names, some descriptions. I have added my own comments where necessary. As you will see, the Turkish fellow referred to is without a doubt Kamel Irani, and the girl with the red hair must be Maria Gamal. I found out where Irani lives, also. The Lido Hotel; you know where that is?"

Trent nodded. "What about the concierge?"

"Tonight, Mr. Trent, I have arranged to take her to the little café opposite his hotel, and we can wait there until we see him." He shuddered delicately. "I only hope my wife does not get to hear about this. I assure you, I would not do this for everybody."

"Tonight?" Trent said thoughtfully: "Then you can do something else for me. I want to get into his room and have a look at it. We'll wait downstairs in the café, and when he goes out, I'll go in. You keep watch and sound the horn for me as soon as you see him coming back. All right?"

Perugino said eagerly: "Perhaps it would be better if *I* were to go in and search his room. It's very hard to get into someone else's room at a place like the Lido...perhaps I could do this more easily?"

Smiling faintly, Trent shook his head. He said: "You sit in the café and watch. If and when he comes back to the hotel, sound the horn of my car. Can we assume that he will be going out some time in the evening?"

CAIRO CABAL

"I think so. As far as my information goes, he has his dinner every night in the hotel at about seven-thirty, and then goes out for the evening, almost always to the Pigalle. But what shall you do if he goes as far as the corner and then decides to come back? He might be a very dangerous man to play with."

"That's why I want a warning from you in time." Trent was keeping an eye on the road and trying to read Perugino's notes at the same time. He said: "I want to give this a good going over, Peiugino; you'd better get out here and I'll get back to the office. Meet me tonight at that café...what's the name of it, opposite the hotel?"

"The Embassy, I have to be there with my new girlfriend at seven o'clock. I do not expect him to appear for more than an hour, but I thought we had better make sure of it."

"Good. Then I'll see you there at about eight. If he has left by that time, you'll have to let me know. Otherwise, as soon as he goes out, I go in. And as soon as you see him returning, blow the horn on my car. Got it?"

Perugino nodded. They pulled into the side of the road and stopped. Perugino slipped quickly out and stood by the curb straightening the drape of his checked jacket, pulling his bright blue tie into position against a crimson silk shirt. Trent grinned at him and slipped the car into gear. Perugino said: "When you see this woman tonight, you will understand what I mean. About my wife."

"Don't recognize me when I come in. I'll sit by myself."

"Of course, of course."

He took his foot off the clutch and the big car slid silently away. He turned back once and caught a glimpse of Perugino looking at his reflection in a plate-glass window, patting the side of his hair and setting his clothes more neatly. Then the long shiny body of the car merged in with the afternoon traffic.

He drove back to the office.

Half of the red neon sign outside the Embassy Café was broken, and only the first few letters glowed brightly against the dim grey walls opposite the oasis of light that was the Lido Hotel. There were four or five tables on the pavement, some of them occupied by tourists waiting for the evening train to Kantara and Port Said.

Trent went through the stuffy room to the lavatory at the back, then came out and sat outside in the cool air. He saw that Perugino was there, inside, close to the window, the woman with him, sipping Bolinachi whiskey.

He brushed the crumbs off the shabby white table, ordered a glass of arak, and waited.

There is something special about the stillness of a summer's evening in Cairo. The great bustling square of Bab-el-Hadid, outside the old-fashioned, squat and ugly railway station, the newly-resurrected statue of Rameses towering mightily above it, was just across the way. The taxis and gharries were rolling up incessantly, the hawkers making a last desperate and noisy bid for the remaining piasters of the travelers, touting their carpets and their scarabs and their ornamental, silver-bound bull-whips (made, they tell you, from the stretched and elongated penis of a bull), and their copper trays and their zircon rings and all the exotic paraphernalia of *il gran' tourismo*, dropping their prices down low to scrape the near-empty pockets of the tourists before they went happily off to meet other hawkers in Port Said, or Suez, or Ismalia, encircling them, pleading, urging, persisting, cursing...

The tramcars were still clanging their noisy way along, now brightly lit and cheerful; the early tarts were just coming out of their lairs, freshly-groomed, disinfected and sweetly perfumed, prettily painted, smiling expectantly, showing their strong white teeth under their full red lips; the *tamarhindi* man was dropping great pieces of dirty ice into the huge glass jar slung over his shoulder, shaking up the clear brown liquid, small pieces of golden date-skin swirling lightly with every movement of the sweet and pungent juice. The coffee-sellers were still meandering about, clinking their cups; the infant vendors were yelling across the great square, darting in and out among the cars and the carriages; a team of water-buffalo was hauling a broken-down cart loaded with green and shiny melons, its big iron wheels rattling noisily over the potholes.

Yet here, in the small quiet side-street, the noise of the close-by bustle was muted, no more than a distant intrusion at which a man might idly glance and then turn back his head, back to the consolation of his wine glass and his thoughts.

This was the way they would march, he thought, *down from the big square to the wide streets and the* midans, *chanting their slogans, carrying their leaders on their shoulders, holding aloft their placards. And the experts would watch and know just when to set the fire. And there would be shots fired in the dark alleyways, and a man would be kicked to death and the crowds would gather to watch the fun and then to take part in the burning and the looting and the destruction and the killing. And bombs would be thrown and men would lie bleeding on the streets after they had passed... There was an alien virus at work.*

Across the narrow road, the big brown entrance hall of the Lido was well-lit, but empty. Through the open glass doorway, with its hanging bead curtain to keep out the flies, Trent could clearly see the Greek clerk at his desk, a fat balding man with a tired look; he was idly picking his teeth with the blade of a pocket-knife.

Down these streets they would come, marching and singing and waving their flags, carrying sticks and knives, and staves, an old Crusader sword, a 1914 rifle, a stolen Bren gun...and flaming torches...

He leaned forward suddenly, and glanced quickly through the window at Perugino. A heavy, swarthy man with the bull neck of a prize-fighter was coming down the stairs, moving stolidly down the wide stairway of the brightly-lit hotel across the narrow street, his hands deep in his pockets, moving lightly on his feet, holding himself well, uprightly balanced. Inside the small café, beyond the window, Perugino looked across at Trent and slowly nodded. He turned to the woman beside him and spoke to her, and watching, Trent saw him look up and nod again. then turn away. He saw the wrinkled suspicious eyes of the concierge, distrustful and alert, flicker briefly in his direction, and then Perugino engaged her in conversation. He watched while Kamel Irani got into a taxi and drove away in the direction of the Birka. Then he folded his paper, dropped it on the table, and sauntered across the road.

He walked through the wide foyer of the Lido, nodding at the clerk, and went into the bar. He waited five minutes exactly, drinking a single glass of arak, then tossed ten piasters on the counter and walked slowly up the stairs. The clerk watched him idly speculating on which room he was going to. There was Veronica in 42...or Toinette in 31...or Samia in 39...he tried to fit the right girl in, wondering about it, then realized that it was none of his business, thought with considerable distaste about his wife for a moment, and then went back to picking his teeth.

At the top of the stairs, Trent went straight to room 36. Glancing around him quickly, he took his toolkit out and slipped the thin steel slats into the keyhole of the lock. In two minutes of careful manipulation, the wards sprung into place and the lock slipped back. He went inside, closed the door behind him, and slipped a chair under the handle. Then he went to the window and looked out. The night was clear and fresh and crisp. Below him there was a drop of fifteen feet or so to the darkness of the alleyway at the side of the building.

He drew the curtains carefully, and switched on the light.

It was an ordinary third-class hotel room. There was a big brass bedstead covered with a white counterpane; a mahogany washstand bearing a toilet kit and a brightly flowered jar full of water standing in a washbasin; two glasses and a flask neatly covered with a white napkin; a chamber-pot discreetly tucked under the bed; a heavy dressing table with a fly-blown mirror above it; a small chair and a table with a portable typewriter on it, and some paper; a wardrobe; a dilapidated sofa in the corner; and an enamel bidet half-hidden by an Indian screen. The room was wide and high and on the walls were two pictures, the "Bath of Psyche" and a nude from a highly-colored calendar. On the dressing table there was a bottle half-full of Haig whisky and a vacuum flask full of ice. A suitcase lay on the sofa. It was unlocked.

He poured himself a drink and looked carefully round the room, not moving; then he pulled the mirror and the pictures away from the wall and looked behind them, prizing off the thin board backing. He opened the suitcase and tipped the contents on to the bed; three shirts, some ties, two pairs of shoes, some woolen socks, some underwear, a bottle of lighter-fluid, a silver cigarette case. Trent flipped it open; there was no inscription inside. There was a silk cravat, and the label on it, like those on the ties, bore an Istanbul address. There was a long and heavy pocket-knife, a switch-bladed weapon of some weight. He flicked it open and scowled at it, feeling the long sharp edge of it with his thumb. He closed it and dropped it into his pocket. There was nothing else. The wardrobe contained three suits, empty-pocketed, made by an Istanbul tailor; he examined the labels on them carefully. Then he went to the typewriter and inserting a sheet of paper in it, slowly pecked out the words: *The quick brown fox jumps over the lazy dog* and then in capitals, THE QUICK BROWN FOX JUMPS OVER THE LAZY DOG.

He folded the paper carefully and placed it in his pocketbook. Then he finished off his whisky and began a precise and careful search of the room.

It was a long and painfully slow process. At the end of an hour-and-a-half, he had brought into the light only one thing of interest; inside the vacuum bottle, closely wrapped around the glass container, were eight hundred American dollars, in hundred-dollar bills. He wondered about the latest rate of exchange, congratulated himself on his good fortune, and slipped them into his hip pocket. There was nothing else. No papers, no documents; nothing.

Badly wanting to smoke, knowing that he could not, he poured himself another drink, and made his preparations.

He filled the water-flask from the big porcelain jar and stuffed a sock in the neck for a stopper, then set it on the floor by the door. Then he switched off the light, unscrewed the bulb from the light socket and laid it on the bed, opened the curtains, closed the window, took the chair from under the door handle, and sat down to wait. He waited an interminable time.

He could hear the ticking of the clock on the dressing table, and when it stopped suddenly he felt a tightening of his muscles and knew that he was nervous. He sipped his drink and waited, feeling the heat mounting up in the closed room, feeling the dampness of his armpits, hearing the beating of his heart. *This*, he told himself, *this is the difficult time...when he comes, strike hard, you will not get another chance, if he dies, then that's too bad but you can't run any risks*, and he thought of Perugino saying again *Disemboweled, Mr. Trent*, and he steeled himself as he waited... There was the sound of the car horn below, the resonance of it repeated loudly twice, and he stood up quickly and picked up the water-flask from the floor and held it by its neck, feeling the moisture on the palm of his hand and changing hands quickly while he wiped his right hand dry against the leg of his trousers, saying to himself, *Hit hard, his head will be like a bullet.* He moved the chair a little farther back and pressed himself into the wall and waited. His heart was pounding.

It seemed an endless wait. He could feel the beat of his pulse and there was a tightening at his throat, a dryness in his mouth, and he felt the perspiration trickling coldly down his back and thought for a horrified moment that he was going to sneeze. And then he heard the key in the lock and the door opened.

For one brief minute there was a long shadow thrown on the floor across the room, the light from the corridor streaming in around it and momentarily lighting up the bed. He heard the soft click as the light switch went down ineffectively, and then he stepped quickly forward and bough the heavy flask down on the intruder's head, putting his weight into the blow, hearing the whistling sound and the sharp full stop of it, knowing that the big man was too big to argue with and better too hard than too light, bringing it down with all the strength in his body, raising himself on his toes to do it, forcing the blow home and following through. He heard the flask shatter and felt the water splash all over him, and then he heard the body fall to the ground and knew from the way it fell that it would not get up for a little while.

He shut the door, drew the curtains, fumbled for the light bulb and cursed himself for not finding it at once, then found it and screwed it home, blinking in the sudden brilliance, then turned to the man on the floor. He was still breathing, lying flat on his back.

He knelt down over him, removed the pistol from his belt, took his pocket-book, his passport, the miscellaneous letters and bric-à-brac, stuffed them hurriedly into his breast pocket, quickly wiped the mater off his shoulders, and left.

He was whistling brightly as he walked down the stairway. He nodded at the clerk at the desk, stepped out into the cool of the street, got into his car, and drove off.

He looked at the luminous dial of his watch, straining his eyes to read it; it was half-past twelve. He tapped the comforting bulge of the papers in his pocket, thought of the eight hundred dollars and smiled to himself. He felt smugly pleased with his night's work.

He turned the car in the direction of Garden City.

When he arrived at the office, it was twenty minutes to one. He let himself in with his key and went up to the duty officer's room. He said cheerfully: "Hullo, Morgan. Got some work for you. Turkish. Who's on call?"

Morgan consulted a sheet of foolscap that hung on the wall above his desk, running the point of his pencil down the list of names.

"Turkish? Better get Connie. She's not going to like it, dearie. Probably sitting out on the verandah in the moonlight with one of her boyfriends, getting all worked up..."

"Get her." Trent was busy sorting out the papers from his pocket. There was a Turkish passport, made out to Major Kamel Irani, whose occupation was given as "Military" and dated nine years previously. He said aloud: "1947? I suppose everybody in Turkey was still in the Army?"

"'47? Yes, I imagine so. Why?"

"Oh, nothing."

There was a notebook with several pages torn out, but two of them covered with small neat handwriting; a bill from an Istanbul tailor; a Turkish and an Egyptian driving license; a small account book, twenty-seven Egyptian pound notes and ten pounds in English money; a short list of Cairo addresses and some miscellaneous scribblings, and a recently folded sheet of typing; all in Turkish. He spread them out on the desk and said: "Get Connie to translate every damn thing. This..." holding up the typescript, "this is the most important and I want it done first."

Morgan was at the telephone. He said:

"Connie? John has just come in, dearie. He wants you to come and do some work for him. No, now... No, it won't wait till morning... No, dearie, I'm just passing on the message... He's gone out again, dearie, so I can't really, can I? I'd do it myself, but I don't speak the bloody language... What? Well, give him a bottle of brandy and put him to bed...he'll wait for you...Well, really!"

He put the phone down and said:

"She'll be round in ten minutes breathing fire, so if you've anywhere else to go, I suggest you get weaving."

Trent grinned at him. "I'm off to bed," he said. "I have an idea things are going to start moving now. It all depends on Connie. No..." He looked at his watch. "One o'clock in the morning. Too damn early to go to bed. I'm going out for a drink and I'll be back later on to see what Connie's got for me. I think it'll be worth it. Tell her I'll be in round about three or four."

"Too early to go to bed, the man says. Why don't they ever make you night D.O.? I'd give my soul for a pair of nice clean sheets just now..." He sighed wearily. "All right, I'll tell her you'll be in. Better bring her an apple."

Trent went out again into the cold of the night, filling his lungs with the still moist air, feeling the rich aphrodisiac scent of the frangipani, thinking about Maria, feeling the emptiness and the solitude.

He got into his car and drove round to the Pigalle.

He sat at the bar and ordered a brandy and soda. Charlie was preoccupied and unhappy. He said: "Nasty bit of trouble with one of the girls here, Mr. Trent. You hear about it? Princess Higran?"

"Yes, I heard. A bad business."

"The police were round here this evening asking a lot of foolish questions."

"Oh? A bit late in the day, isn't it? I should have thought they'd have been here yesterday."

"You'd think so, wouldn't you? One of these bright new boys they have in the police nowadays—none of your old-fashioned sergeants with their big white moustaches. Those were the days all right. Fellow by the name of Shulam. Shulam *effendi*, if you please."

"Shulam? You mean Ibrahim Shulam?"

"Yes, that's right. Smooth-talking sort of fellow. You know him?"

"I had an idea he was in the political branch?"

"Well, I suppose it could be, she was Turkish, you know. They probably have to make a report to the Turkish Consul about it. Something like that, I imagine."

"Uh-huh. Dark doings, Charlie, when they get a political police inspector to do an ordinary detective constable's job."

"Well, that's the new Egypt for you. Never can tell what they're going to do next. Not like the good old days."

"Why do you stay here, Charlie? Not many of us left here nowadays."

"Well, I don't know, really... Eighth Army during the war, and then, well, when it was all over I married a little girl I knew... She wouldn't be happy in England, it's too cold there. Too cold for me, too. I like it here...oh, there's always the odd spot of bother, but it's something to be the only English barman in town. Not like the good old days, though. And he pays me good money, Papadopoulos. Not a bad old stick, really. Oh, it's a good enough life... Another brandy, Mr. Trent?"

"Have one yourself, Charlie. What would you do in the case of another blow-up like the last one?"

Charlie looked startled. "You mean like that Black Saturday? I don't think that's very likely, is it? That was the Wafd in power then...it's a different thing now...almost Military Law... You're not expecting anything like that again, are you?"

Trent sighed unhappily. "Don't know, Charlie. Let me in on any bazaar gossip you pick up, would you?"

"Yes, of course I will...but I don't think that's likely to happen again, do you? Needs a deal of organization, that sort of thing. And the Army's in control now, you know. Don't yeah think so?"

"Yes, Charlie. Perhaps you're right."

He saw Maria at a table with two other girls, sitting out the time between the two shows, sipping a glass of cold tea. He caught her eye and she smiled at him, asking a question. He smiled at her slowly and she came over and sat beside him, putting her hand on his. She said: "Why you look so sad tonight, Johnny? Are you not 'appy tonight?"

"Just one of those moods. Let's have some brandy, Charlie, will you? Forget about the bottle of tea."

Charlie grimaced at him and poured the drinks. Trent turned and looked at the girl closely. Her long hair was soft and shone well, her skin white and unblemished. He looked at the smooth flesh of her throat and remembered her standing staring at him last night, her careless motion arrested in mid-movement, staring at him with the frightened eyes of a child, remembering the smell of the coffee and the shiny flesh of the mango she had held poised delicately on a fork, and he felt...he did not know how he felt; he knew only that there was a mood on him, a solitude, an oppression, a fear of something he did not fully understand, an impatience, a feeling of impotence...

He took her arm roughly. Almost rudely, he said: "Come on, let's see what you're like in bed. Your place."

She nodded happily, and he took her round to her apartment and sat on the edge of the bed to watch her undress. The dyed red hair hung down over her white, white shoulders, and he reached out and stroked her breast and found it full and firm and warm to his touch. He ran his tongue over a tiny pink nipple, the nipple of a child on a woman's breast, and she sucked in her breath and held him tightly.

He said harshly: "No, no...I don't even want to wait." He pulled her down and savagely drove himself into her, thinking: *There are times when this is the only kind of relief there is.*

When he arrived at the office afterwards, it was past four o'clock and there was the faintest, almost imaginary, glimmer of light in the east across the open desert, a faintly perceptible forewarning of the day coming up off the hills and the sands beyond Sinai.

Connie had finished her work, and had gone on home again. There was a small sheaf of papers waiting for him, typed out and clipped together. He glanced through them, then sat down to read the translation of Irani's notes. At last he said to the duty officer: "This is it. A good day's work well done."

He tapped the paper with the back of his hand. He said: "Our troubles are over. Or come to think of it, they're really only just beginning. But this is just what we needed. Only question is, where do we go from here?"

He answered his own question. "I'm off to bed. Leave a note for the old man, will you? Tell him I must see him in the morning."

He slid off the desk, yawned, stretched his limbs, and went out. When he got home, he took a shower, lay down on top of the bed and slept till daylight.

Wednesday morning.

CAIRO CABAL

Sitting at his desk by the window, staring out into the wide green expanse of the garden, he let his thoughts wander with the view, on beyond the dark green of the hedges with the tiny orange flowers faintly obtruding, and the bright red flash of hibiscus, and the pale green-blue of a little round petal whose name he did not know, on and beyond to the tall brown mast of the *felucca* that was sailing past on the brown river, its brown sail dark above the pastel brown of the wind-swept desert sand, even the sky now showing that faintly yellow-brown obnubilation of a distant sandstorm.

And then the peahen strutted into his line of vision and brought his thoughts sharply back to the garden and the cool green grass under the window and back to his desk and he yawned. He picked up the papers he had been reading, and went in to see the Colonel.

Colonel Brand was waiting for him. He said brusquely:

"Before anything else, congratulations. A nice piece of work, John. Connie was telling me about it. Let me see it."

Happily, feeling refreshed and rested and pleased, all the oppression and tie loneliness and the brooding gone from him, feeling clean and cool and freshly scrubbed, Trent sat on the chair by the desk and handed across the papers. His eyes were bright. He took out his pipe and lit it, happily waiting.

It was the top paper that interested the Colonel. It was the translation, and fastened to it with a staple was the original, a single folded sheet of paper. It read:

OCO/325 Turkish. Classification: Grade IV only.
Translator—Constance Mayers. Confidential.

Text.
"The Essence of the plan centers round the assassination of the British Official Pearman. The assassin is a man called Omar bin Said Abdullah, a man of no particular consequence, except that he has performed similar jobs in the past for the Wafd and for the Muslim Brotherhood. Pearman's movements are well known, and he is under constant surveillance, At the proper time, the man Omar will be stationed in Garden City close to the entrance to the Trade Delegation offices, and as the car turns out

of the driveway he will open fire with a machine-gun at close range; it is expected that all the occupants of the car will be killed instantly, and careful arrangements have been made for the escape of Omar since he is required for further duties of a like nature. Should anything go wrong with this plan, the alternate attack will be delivered in Pearman's own quarters. He is living in the Semiramis Hotel under fairly tight security. A bomb, however, has already been planted in his room and will be detonated if and when necessary. It is expected that should the attack on the car fail, he will not be moved out from this hotel, as the security precautions there are considered adequate, and they are, in fact, admirable. The bomb, however, has nevertheless been successfully placed into position and is ready for detonation.

With further reference to the presumed leak in the organization, certain details have been discovered by the Egyptian Counter-Espionage unit under Captain Ahmed Saleh. Captain Saleh was liquidated on the Cairo-Ismailia road three days ago, his death having been made to appear as accident, and the local police are convinced that it was nothing more.

More and more evidence of the enmity between the Army and the Police Force continually comes to hand. There is considerable disaffection among the police and the force is ripe for the maximum of mischief. In the Army, several high-ranking officers are known to be violently opposed to the present regime and one or two of them are already actively working towards the plan's fulfilment.

More to follow."
End of text.

The Colonel flipped the page and studied the original, then thumbed through the rest of the notes.

"No signature," he said. "No signature, no address, no date...nothing. Who wrote this?"

"It was written on Kamel Irani's typewriter. And there's another thing. The original list the girl had and which started all this furor, was also written on his machine. I took a sample of its type while I was in his room; it's the same machine. No doubt about that at all."

CAIRO CABAL

The Colonel tapped angrily on the table with his fingers. His pale blue eyes were angry. He said:

"Who the devil is the report *for?* That's the question. And what in God's name is meant by 'the plan'? If the assassination of a senior Foreign Office official is merely part of it, how big, in God's name, is it?"

"There's one thing, Sir," Trent said thoughtfully. "That phrase, 'the maximum of mischief.' Doesn't that sound as though the man who wrote this was on the other side? I mean, opposed to the idea? It's hardly the kind of phrase a man would use who was applying the mischief."

"Well, it's a point. But I don't think much of it. The mischief is always applied deliberately; there's never any pretense that it's anything else. No...I don't agree with you. Are you going to move Pearman? Out of the Semiramis?"

Trent hesitated. He said reluctantly: "Not unless you say so, Sir. I think he ought to stay there."

"You know the risk you're taking?"

"Yes, Sir."

"Does he know about this?"

"No, Sir."

"Don't you think he ought to?"

Trent stood up and stuck his hands into his pockets. Frowning at floor, he said: "I don't think he should. He'll give himself away at once, if, as this report says, he's being watched. If he doesn't know anything at all about it..."

"And supposing '*the proper time,*'" the Colonel looked at his watch, "supposing the proper time is half-an-hour from now? What then?"

"I don't think it is."

Trent said thoughtfully: "We'll have some sort of warning... well, naturally, as soon as Kamel Irani woke up and found his report gone...all this will be changed. But the bomb is only the secondary plan—it will only be put into execution if the first one fails. All we can do is sit tight, tighten up on security all round..."

"Did it occur to you that now this report has been taken it might precipitate things? Blow the place up at once?"

"Yes, Sir."

"What are you doing about that?"

"The hotel room is being searched now, at this moment. Henson's doing it, but discreetly."

"And where's Pearman?"

"On his way here, Sir. He said you wanted to see him."

"I see."

The Colonel lifted the receiver of the telephone. He said: "When Mr. Pearman comes, send him straight in." He replaced the receiver.

He began to pace the floor, stopping to stare at the photograph on the wall. He could feel the strange yet familiar stirring in his fingertips, and rubbing them against the side of his trousers, he said somberly:

"Remember your first love affair, John? The first time you ever touched a woman? It's a moment you can never recapture. The second time...the second time you know what to expect. And if there is no second time...if that sensation is gone forever..." He examined his one hand carefully, passing his thumb over the tip of his fingers, stroking them. He said: "It's becoming psychotic."

"Yes...I know... There's an article I put on one side for you to look at, about the violin makers of Cremona..."

"Ah, Cremona... Stradivari, Guarneri, Amati, they all worked there. I'd like to read it. Do you think Kamel Irani typed that first list out?"

"You're thinking of his own name on it? It's a point that worried me too. A man doesn't write his own name like that. He either writes 'self' or his initials... Could be wrong, of course."

"If he didn't, then who did?"

"Well, there's nobody here who can tell us if the same hand typed them. We know it was the same machine that typed both Perugino's little list and this report. More than that, we can't say. The Egyptian police could make a better analysis, but under the circumstances...I'd say both were typed by somebody who wasn't exactly expert. To the lay eye there seems to be an irregularity of touch, but I'm no expert, I'm afraid..."

"Get photostats and send them to London in the bag. I don't

think it's too important, but..."

The intercom buzzed. The Colonel leaned forward and threw the switch. "Yes?"

Trent heard the soft voice of the girl in the outer office.

"Mr. Pearman's on his way in."

"Good." The Colonial went on: "It's worth a try. Send them the originals and we'll keep photostats. Ask them to cable a reply right away. Ah, Pearman," he said as the door opened, "Come on in, come in and sit down."

Pearman nodded quickly at Trent. He said fussily: "I spotted your man following me today. Surely I shouldn't have been able to do that?"

Trent smiled at him. "An Englishman?" Pearman shook his head. "No, an Egyptian."

Trent said gently: "That's the opposition. They're watching you, too. You won't see my man. He's too good at his job and too fond of it."

"The opposition?"

The Colonel interrupted. He said abruptly: "Pearman, you're sitting on a bomb. They've planted a bomb in your hotel room."

Pearman's angular face dropped, his mouth hanging open, looking a little foolish. He closed it suddenly. "A bomb?"

"Somewhere in your hotel room. I'm sorry it got there. Trent didn't want to tell you. He wants it to lie there till we find out more about who put it there. What do you think?"

Pearman swallowed. "Well, really...really, I mean... You mean just leave it there? A time bomb?" He looked at Trent in horror.

"No, not a time bomb; it's supposed to be detonated at a given time."

"Which is when?"

The Colonel said apologetically: "That, I'm afraid, we don't yet know. There's a man there now, searching for it. If and when he finds it, it will be rendered harmless. What do you say?"

"And if he doesn't find it? Do you want me to go on sleeping there? Tonight, for example?"

The Colonel looked at him curiously. "You mean you'd be willing to? I'm flattered by your faith in us. But it won't be necessary.

John, where can he sleep tonight? Without making it appear that he can't go home? Any ideas?"

"Plenty." Trent said cheerfully, "I could take him on a round of the local nightlife. Stay up till dawn. We could soon find somewhere to sleep if he got tired..."

"I don't doubt you could," the Colonel said. "However...what are your clans for the rest of the day?"

"I have a conference with the Minister at two this afternoon which will last until about six or seven, I expect. After that, I have nothing to do until tomorrow morning at ten, when I have to see His Excellency."

"Good, then it's just tonight we have to worry about. They may have found it by then. If not... There's a party at the Third Secretary's house tonight. I'll get him to invite you both and you can stay the night there if necessary."

He said to Trent: "He's not to go back to the hotel until it's found, is that clear? If it's not found by tomorrow, then he'll have to move out, and be damned to it!"

"He'll find it by tonight," Trent said emphatically. "It's not midday yet, and he's been at it for two hours already. After all, how many places are there in a hotel bedroom where you can hide a bomb big enough to do any damage? It will probably be under one of the floor boards; the only difficulty is that Henson's had to get into the room without being seen...Bradley will be helping him later on..."

"Have you got enough men on the job, John? Watching Pearman?"

"Yes, Sir. There's a man on his tail all the time and I get reports into the office from every shift."

"But surely," Pearman said, "surely they don't think they can stop these negotiations merely by killing me... Don't they realize that I would be replaced at once? That someone else would come out and take over? I suppose it would certainly make things very difficult for us, but they surely ought know..."

"It's not only that."

The Colonel blew his nose vigorously. "One thing will start the ball rolling, and then nobody will be able to stop it. You weren't here in January '52, or you'd know what I mean."

CAIRO CABAL

"Oh, yes. There was quite a commotion in the Foreign Office. 'Black Saturday', the papers called it."

"Black Saturday. It's a good term. In twelve hours of mob control, they made Cairo look like a bombed-out city. It started simply enough. On the Friday a nun was shot in Ismailia, and the British troops tried to round up the people who did it. The local police opened fire on them, the troops answered, and by evening twenty people were dead. The next day, in Cairo, they went to work. It took the city by surprise. At first, everybody just stood by and watched the experts get to work. There were squads drilled in their specific duties; some to break into British buildings—the banks, the B.O.A.C. offices, the British Council, the British Institute, the Turf Club; some to follow them in and start throwing the furnishings on to the pavement; then as they moved on to the next objective, the third details took over with incendiary powders and started the fires. There were squads standing by to keep off any interference. More than a hundred and fifty fires were set in the morning. Anti-British feeling was running high, and nobody stopped them; the police stood by and watched. Then came the next step. They wanted the fervor of a *jihad*, a holy war; so they started on the nightclubs, the cinemas, the bars—anything that could whip up the rigid Muslim element. Then finally they started to appease the have-nots; they went for the jewelers, the department stores, the car dealers. By this time, the Metro Cinema was ablaze, the Chrysler offices were in flames, and the mob started taking over from the experts. By midday, there were twenty thousand people on the streets burning and looting and killing for the sake of it. Eleven Englishmen killed on the streets. In the *pension* opposite the National Hotel—Trent was there with two of the girls from the office—they dragged out eight European women and beat them to death on the main street of the city, then dragged their bodies along..." He paused, staring out of the window.

Trent said somberly: "I saw it. We were up on the roof of the hotel, and there was absolutely nothing I could do. They dragged the bodies along, and wherever they stopped and moved on, there was a patch of red on the pavement. They set fire to a Greek and burned him alive. The mob stormed the National, where we were, and while they were firing the furniture on the big verandah, the manager did something that saved all our lives. An Egyptian Army officer went out on a small balcony above them, waved a copy of the Koran at them, and swore there were no Europeans in the hotel...God knows how much it cost him; I never found out, because he was dead when it was all over. This I can tell you, they were well organized, and ruthlessly led. By the time the mob was in control, and the slogan-shouters had taken over, the organizers had faded away. Their work was done."

The Colonel said: "That's exactly the point. They arrested eight hundred people after Farouk dismissed the Government, but not one of them was a man of any consequence. The people who organized all this are still at large. They had equipment and efficiency, and an organization far, far beyond the scope of the ordinary Egyptian riot mentality. As I say, the Government fell as a direct and immediate result, and whatever chances were left for Britain in the Middle East...they faded from view."

"Yes, I know. London was very concerned it," Pearman said. "I remember that Ibn Saud of Arabia proposed a Middle East Pact; Britain, France, Turkey, and the Arab States, armed with British weapons. When the Egyptians turned it down, Russia moved in with a counter-proposal; she offered to supply Egypt with thirty per cent of her imports, and you know what that means."

"It's a day I won't forget. It's one thing to read about it in the papers...I saw it." Trent said somberly. "Mob rule is the most fearsome thing there is. In twelve hours...that's all it was before the Army took over, and even then...there were trigger-happy soldiers posted at fifty-yard intervals on the streets. Shoot first, ask afterwards. And now, it looks as though they're trying again."

"Exactly. Everything points to it." The Colonel said: "We haven't much time, John. An attack on Pearman... Take him to Saul's tonight, and find that confounded bomb."

"Yes, Sir. It shouldn't take Henson more than the rest of the day to find it. He has to work very carefully, or he'll give the game away. I don't want Kamel Irani to know that we are the people who stole his report. If he sees no activity at the hotel, he may assume that it was just a sneak thief. Is that possible?"

"Yes, it's possible. Did you get his money?"

"Everything in his pockets."

"Good. Then he might put it down to ordinary robbery. I'd better get on the phone to Saul and ask him to invite you up tonight."

"What's the occasion?"

"Saul is getting married. Didn't you know?"

"Oh, that? Poor Saul!"

The Colonel said: "Poor Jeanette! However, it's none of our business. But he won't like having to invite you, John, so try and stay away from Jeanette. She presumably knows what she wants."

"Quite. And, as you say, poor Jeanette!"

Pearman said crossly: "Am I to be involved in all sorts of family squabbles just because you can't keep thugs from putting bombs under my bed?"

Trent laughed. "Not to worry," he said. "You'll be delighted with our genial host, and he'll be impressed by your importance. There'll be lots of drinks, plenty of pretty women, and if you get bored, I promise I'll take you to your old haunt, the Pigalle, and we can go on to one of the brothels in the Birka. You'll enjoy it immensely..."

Pearman was furious. The Colonel said smoothly: "What about the girl Higran? Any further news?"

"Nothing very much. I have a list of the people she saw during the last twenty-four hours. Some names, some descriptions. Mostly Kamel Irani. Nothing else of any interest."

The Colonel looked hard at Trent. "I see." He said bitterly: "I want that man caught, John. Whoever it was. You understand, I want him caught." He said viciously: "I want to see him hanged for it. She was...well, see that the police discreetly get any information you have as soon as you've finished with it. Keep Kamel Irani's passport; it will hold him in the country for a while."

"We could cable Istanbul about him now; his passport information would give them a line on him?"

"And suppose he's reported the theft to the Turkish Consul-General?"

"Ah yes, of course, that wouldn't do, would it?"

Pearman said anxiously: "Have you any idea how long this...this bomb has been there? I mean, who planted the confounded thing, and how? It's not pleasant to reflect that any damned fanatic can sneak into my bedroom with a bomb under his arm every time I sit down in the bathroom for five minutes."

Trent raised his hands expressively: "I'm sorry," he said. "Your guess is as good as mine. One of the servants, probably, though they're all supposed to be screened...we can't be too careful, or they'll realize you're bigger fish than you're supposed to be. It's hard to find the right compromise, but if we had a battalion of Household Guards standing around you wherever you moved..."

This was the crux of the matter, he thought. Guard your base metal too closely, and it's obvious to everyone that the metal is not so base after all. In this sly, deceitful, crafty capital...you can buy or sell a man's life for what? What is the basic unit? A loaf of bread? Then for ten loaves of bread you can buy a woman's body; for twenty a man's life; for fifty, his reputation. Your secret is a secret as long as it is a thought, no more; give it birth, bring it out of the womb into the light of day, and at once you will find it in every barmaid's bosom, on the lips of every *maquereau*, in the pocket of every sly hawker, a thing to trade and barter with; where every eye that scrutinizes you is calculating, where every deed, every thought, every action is coldly and dispassionately summed-up and priced in pounds or piastres, where the beggar on the street corner carries a hundred pounds in his pocket, where the smartly dressed vagrant nibbling at an ivory toothpick and watching the women go by has the names and addresses of your last three mistresses usefully tucked away at the back of his scheming mind...then how do you guard your precious metal—in secrecy?

He said: "Don't worry. We fall down in one place, we pick up in another... My watch has stopped; what time is it?"

"Twenty past ten."

He got up to leave. He said: "If you'll excuse me, Sir, I'd like to go over Pearman's security arrangements with Henson's man." Turning to Pearman, he said: "There's a lot to be done this afternoon... Pick you up after your conference? At about seven?"

"All right. I'll come round here, shall I?"

"No, I'll pick you up at the conference room. Phone me here when you're ready for me. If you want a clean shirt or anything, we'll go on to Cicurel's and get one, then you can change at my place. Or here if you like. I think the hotel will be clear long before the day is finished. Henson's a good man."

Pearman nodded unhappily. He said: "I wish I'd known all this was going to happen. I really ought never to have left London."

"How's the conference going?"

Pearman brightened at once. He said earnestly: "In the whole of the North African area, we're on the edge of a new defense alliance...Morocco, Tunisia, Libya, Algeria...this new nationalism can help the peace of the world, or it can kill off its last hopes...we're on the brink. It's going well, the Minister's on our side, and what Egypt does, the others will too. If we can guide them, if we can keep them on the side of the West, there'll be no trouble in the Middle East. But if we let the Russians get a foothold here, they'll stir up so much trouble... They'll help the Arabs annihilate the Israelis, they'll clamp down on oil supplies to the West, they'll have nothing but mischief to do. The Arabs are gullible people, and we cannot let the Russians dictate the direction of their ambitions. It's a very, very delicate matter. And now...all this."

The Colonel said carefully: "Actually, I don't think you need worry too much as long as you're careful. In this business we all get shot at once in a while. Quite a lot of us survive, you know. If anything breaks out...we should get some warning at least. And you're in good hands. Do you have a revolver?"

Pearman was horrified. "Good heavens! No," he said. "Good heavens! I wouldn't know how to use it."

Trent said: "Well, your escort does, take my word for it. If you'll excuse me, Sir? There's a great deal I have to do."

The Colonel said: "Yes, of course."

As he went out of the room, he heard the Colonel say to Pearman: "Come and have lunch with me, will you?"

He went back to his office and sat down to work.

CHAPTER 10

The shrunken Arab, standing nervously with his hands behind his back, his eyes east down like a naughty child's, was plainly perturbed. As he listened, he sometimes brought his hands out from their respectful confinement to gesticulate, to start to speak, then broke off hurriedly and put them again behind him, nodding his head earnestly, saying, "Yes Pasha, no Pasha, certainly Pasha..." chastising himself, deprecating his own stupidity, conscious at the back of his unhappy mind that this could be trouble for him, serious trouble; conscious that this was something more deadly than the usual run of little annoyances and trifling dangers that were germane to his profession. He was conscious of his shabby suit, aware of its wrinkles and its disrepute, and aware above all of that it was *frangi*, European, its brown pin stripes cut to a form that was foreign. He knew that he should have worn a *gallabiyah* and thereby asserted the pride of his race, and affirmed his independence: *I am an Egyptian, don't talk to me like that, you foreigners don't belong here, if we Egyptians cared to turn you out, I am an Egyptian, the greatest race on earth, a believer, a Muslim, I will not be talked to like this by a cursed infidel, a curse on the religion of your father, may your father's cursed house fall down, you illegitimate son of a donkey and a hundred and seventy whores, don't talk to me like this;* and he nodded his head earnestly and said, "Yes, master...of course, master... I know, master..." And then he thought, *"All right...all right...your turn will come..."* and he hastily concealed the venom that he knew must be showing in his black Egyptian eyes and suffered his castigation in silence, only his concealed fingers nervously twitching behind his back.

Reizen said: "I told you... I told you a hundred times...clearly: *He must not know, he must not know*. You think I learn your filthy language to amuse myself? I learn it to speak to idiots like you, to explain myself to ignorant pimps. This," he said, pointing to his genitals, "this is more use than the brain your father gave you. I said, *He must not know*. Bolec is a Czech, an enemy, a man who..." He broke off disgustedly. "You stupid bastard; what would you know of Czechs and Russians and Poles and English? To you they're the same, aren't they? *Frangi*...foreigners...strange men with better brains who tell you what to do...is that it? Your father was a camel, a syphilitic camel. And he conceived you in a brothel."

Shakri said lamely, "Yes, *effendi*, of course..."

"How did he find out?"

"I don't know, *effendi*. Only he said, 'If I go to this man Reizen, maybe I can get more money for both of us.' "

Reizen's anger crept along his spine. He was trembling. He stood up and brought the black tail of his By-whisk sharply and viciously down on a big blue-bottle fly that had settled momentarily on the wall by the lamp. It squelched abominably and he flicked the mess off the wall and wiped the tip of his finger fastidiously on the side of his jacket, then turned and looked disgustedly at the Arab. He said:

"You know what this means, don't you?"

Shakri nodded miserably. He said: "I...I am afraid, *ya Pasha*."

"Afraid? You weren't afraid with the girl."

"But this...this is different. Bolec is a strong man...if...if anything goes wrong, he will kill me."

Reizen smiled coldly, a twisted artificial smile that showed his broken teeth and wrinkled the coarse flesh round his thin lips. Taking off his aimless spectacles, wiping them carefully on his handkerchief, peering at the Arab myopically, he said: "Well? Is that supposed to be my concern? People like you, Shakri...the *mousky* is full of pimps and gutter-rats like you. I can replace you with someone who will work better and cost less. Well?"

Shakri nodded again, nervously, knowing there was no way out, knowing that in the business he had chosen, the money was sometimes—but only sometimes—hard to come by; that it was easy money all the time, trick after trick and twist upon wicked twist, and then suddenly, out of the limbo which was the controlling force, out of the unknown, little understood, often imagined machinery where the easy money came from, suddenly there came the harshness and the fear and the sudden alarm; and with them came the realization...*only forward now, I cannot withdraw...*

The knowledge was there, trembling at the back of his mind, and Bolec, a giant swollen by his imaginings, loomed large and silent and frightful above him, and he said: "*Yes, ya Pasha...yes*" and wondered if he would live to come to his boss and say, "Bolec is dead."

Reizen said: "Understand this, idiot. You are fighting for your country, no? That is what I do—I fight for mine. You don't know why this is so, but take my word for it. If Bolec knows he is working for me, he will cause trouble. I know these Czechs. To you, it's just another *frangi* and that's why you are an idiot. To me it means something more, and that's why I'm a better man than you are. That's why I can tell you to do these things and all you can do is stand there saying *Yes, ya Pasha, no, ya Pasha*." Pointing vigorously at his chest he said: "I'm the Pasha, understand? You're the idiot who can only do as he is told; don't try and understand these things—accept my word and do as I say. Now get out of here."

Shakri, his fingers twitching, nodded eagerly. He said again: "*Na'am, ya Pasha...*"

"Wait."

"*Effendi?*"

"You know what you have to do?"

"*Aiwah, ya Pasha.* I kill Bolec."

Reizen put his glasses carefully back on his nose, blinked his weak blue eyes and said: "When?"

"Tonight."

"Come and let me know tomorrow morning."

Shakri hesitated. "A little money, *ya Pasha?*"

"Tomorrow morning. Now get out of here." As the Arab turned to go, he shouted after him viciously: "Your sister is a whore."

CHAPTER 11

It was difficult to see across the living room in Saul Stack's riverside apartment. The lights on the walls were shaded with finely-filigreed brass shades that cast intriguing shadows, and some of them had been put out, and although the long windows were open to let the night air drift in from the Nile, the smoke was dense and hung about thickly.

Trent stood scowling about the room and thinking more than ever that it looked like something out of the *Arabian Nights*. Somebody was half-lying on a divan near the gramophone playing through Saul's collection of Arabic records, pretending that he could understand the words and backgrounding the babble with the whine of the music. There was a lot of noise, everybody talking at once, a group in one dimly-lit corner singing a popular bawdy song about the anatomy of King Farouk, another group loudly talking politics, and everybody getting a little drunk but happy. There were too many people crowded into the place, and some of the couples had sought the space and privacy of the bedrooms. One of the girls was tentatively pecking at the piano and exchanging frowns with the man at the gramophone. And standing somewhat aloof from it all, over by the clean air of the verandah, holding a glass of whisky, Pearman was a lost sheep in his neat business suit and new Cicurel silk shirt.

Trent wandered over to him, stepping delicately over a girl who was lying on the floor with her head on a cushion. He said: "Well? Tired of it all?"

Pearman shook his head. "As a matter of fact, I'm rather

enjoying myself. It isn't very often, you know, that I get a chance to go in for this sort of thing...this, this..."

"This barbarous dissonance of Bacchus and his revelers?"

Pearman laughed. "I attend a good many cocktail parties at home, of course, but this...well, it is a little different, isn't it?"

"It's Saul's idea of interior decorating: *vin du pays*, he likes to call it. Always reminds me of a rather expensive bordello. Very chic in a London mews...but a little nauseating when it's only a couple of miles from the bazaar where you buy all these things. He's making a collection to charm the neighbors with in Kensington High Street. But as long as you're enjoying yourself... Have another whisky?"

Pearman drained his glass. "Yes, I think I will. I must say it was a delightful idea to do this. I'd almost forgotten the indignity of not being able to go home for fear of an assassin."

Trent said: "You're a queer bird, Pearman. You ought to be rather scared, you know. The technique of terror is a wicked thing to fight; it's too...too dispassionately purposeful. And competent. We're on the edge of something very horrible. You ought to be scared out of your wits."

"I know. Perhaps I am rather frightened. I'm a diplomat, you know, and this sort of thing...somehow...does it sound silly if I say 'so far from home'? There's a great deal of comfort to be found in the familiar things; the television set in the corner, the clock on the mantelshelf, even the carpet on the floor would be enough. Ever think about that? Put down a carpet and you're home, wherever you happen to be. It's the comfort of familiar property. But here, it's too far away from the things I know, and so I'm frightened. I'm not ashamed of it. I think it's natural. Who's the girl over there, the one with the shoulders?"

"Sharona Wallace. Pretty little thing, I suppose. Want to meet her?"

"We were introduced...I didn't catch her name. What does she do here?"

"Oh, some secretarial job at the Embassy."

"I imagine you know everybody here?"

"Uh-huh. Let me get you that drink. Strong?"

"Not too strong, please."

CAIRO CABAL

"Let's fight our way to the bar."

Pearman said, following him: "You know, I'm rather surprised to see so many British left in Cairo. One rather imagined they had all gone home."

Trent poured a Scotch and soda and took some ice from the silver bowl. The bottles were still neatly arranged in rows at the back of the long white-covered table, the servants standing solemnly by and replacing the empties from time to time. The cook came in smiling and put some fresh canapés in little plates on the buffet.

"Most of them have. Just the Embassy and one or two leftovers from the business world—cotton, oil, that sort of thing. A pretty bloody life nowadays. *Les indigènes* tend to spit at us in the streets from time-to-time; you may have noticed."

Pearman grimaced. "I've noticed."

The Wallace girl saw Trent eyeing her and came over brightly, glass in hand. She was young and fresh and lovely, with a juvenile, sexless air about her in spite of the fact that she had pulled her fashionably expensive dress down over her shoulders, showing her white bust; it was beautiful and quite lawless. Standing above her, twisting his glass idly, he saw that her brassiere seemed to fit closely over her breasts, not supporting or confining them, but rather following their curves as though painted on, clinging to her flesh even between them, and he wondered briefly how she did it; he wanted to put his hand on her to prove to himself that he was unmoved by her. She flashed a quick, smile at him, the bright-eyed kind of smile an actress puts on when anyone in the room might turn out to be a producer, a friendly smile, showing her friendliness, a terribly trusting smile that made him scowl. He thought she considered him avuncular, and wondered if that were perhaps the trouble. He said to himself: "What the hell!" patted her arm, and turned away. He heard her say something bright to Pearman, and he wandered over to the green ferns by the corner of the verandah.

Jeanette was there, sitting curled up on the divan like a cat.

Jeanette, he thought, now there's a cat of a different color. She wore her long dark hair in an unusual style; it was coarse and gracelessly arranged, and there was too much of it. Her features, though perhaps too long, were in themselves attractive; her extraordinary eyes were black and slightly slanted, and her eyebrows were heavy and unplucked. He recalled that at first, when he had met her, he had been a little bored with her. Not with her talk but with her looks. And then, meeting her by chance again and again, he began to discern an animal sexuality about her and wondered how he had not seen it before.

He had watched her one day standing on the diving board at Gezira, dressed in a white bathing costume that was cut low and had no supporting straps to it, and he had suddenly realized that she was waiting there, delaying her dive until everybody should be looking at her and wondering what would happen to the unsupported costume as she hit the water; Gezira in those days was a rather stuffy and respectable club, and as he looked round, he saw that all the men were waiting expectantly, leaving their pink gins and their Pilsners and watching her. Then when she was sure that she had everyone's attention, she dived, and he had strolled over to the edge of the pool in the hot sun, holding out his hand to her, laughing and saying: "Now do that again just for me."

Then, a few days later, they had gone together to the big open-air cinema on Sharia Ibrahim Pasha, and had sat under one of the mango trees at a wicker table while one of the *sofragis* brought them cold beer, for the night was hot and stifling; and then they danced at Doll's and watched the floorshow and she had said: "You know, we mustn't be seen together too much."

"And why not, for God's sake?" he had asked.

"Didn't you know? I'm engaged to Saul Stack."

"That moron? No I didn't know about it. Hell!"

She had smiled slowly. "If you want to make love to me," she had said deliberately, "then we'll have to be a little more discreet."

He had stood up abruptly. "Then let's get the hell out of here and go round to my place."

"Finish your drink, at least."

They went round to the corner apartment which the office rented for him on Sharia Malika Farida, carefully chosen because it had a separate exit on another street, and they made love, and slept close together naked under the virginal sheets and made love again, and in the morning she made some Turkish coffee in the brass *jezveh*, walking about the apartment with a towel below her splendid breasts, round her waist, and all the worries and headaches and loneliness had gone away from him, and then, when he had come out of the shower, she too had unexpectedly gone and left him puzzling about her and deciding not to think too much about it and wondering if that, after all, was just what she wanted.

Looking at her now, sitting on the divan with her feet tucked under her, looking strangely at home among the perforated brass shades and the dim lights and the Persian carpets and the camel-saddle stools and the Syrian leather cushions, detached from all the others, sitting patiently and watching and saying nothing and sipping a green drink out of a tall-stemmed glass, he said: "Still not too late to change your mind."

She said: "Why should I? Do you want to marry me?"

"God forbid!"

"You see? Besides, someone really has to take poor Saul in hand." She gestured across the room. Poor Saul was declaiming to the room at large, being very bright and witty, and nobody paying any attention to him. He looked back at her and wished she were wearing something more colorful than the grey taffeta dress she had on, and he said:

"Why the hell don't you dress more cheerfully?"

"Don't you like this? It cost an awful lot of money."

"I like to see you in bright colors. Reds and greens and yellows."

"Don't be proprietary, John. Are you enjoying yourself? Don't you find it dull?"

"Dull as hell. Come and sit on the balcony with me."

"Then get me another drink."

"One of those ghastly things?"

"Of course."

He fetched her a whisky-and-soda instead and led her to a chaise-longue that was half-hidden by some ferns on the open verandah, and when she sat down he squatted on the ground beside her. He touched her ankle and said: "Really, the nicest ankles in Cairo. I hate women with thick legs."

She leaned forward and brushed her knee with her hand, pulling her legs underneath her the better to examine them. She said: "Do you think so? Are you qualified to judge?"

"Of course I am. At my age, you pay a great deal of attention to these things."

"Not to waste the remaining years of virility? Husbanding what's left for only the very best?"

She looked at him as though he were supposed to make a clever answer, and looking across at Sharona Wallace, who was still chatting gaily with Pearman, he suddenly realized what was wrong with her; she was not *expectant*. Jeannette was a sort of sexual chess player; she would advance a pawn, and wait for him to move, but not Sharona. Sharona probably played table tennis and was healthy and completely undesirable. Jeannette would not give a damn whether she won or lost as long as she enjoyed the stimulation of the game.

He said aloud: "I wonder if I could still mate you?" knowing that out of the context of his thoughts the remark would be misunderstood and not worrying about it anyway.

She laughed and said: "I expect so."

He got up and sat on the edge of the chair beside her, very close, stroking her thick black hair. He said: "Wouldn't it intrigue you to misbehave yourself on this particular occasion? Let's sneak out."

"And who will look after poor Saul?"

"To hell with poor Saul! I'll accept a refusal on moral grounds, but not for the sake of Saul's bloody convenience."

She laughed and shook her head. "Not tonight."

"The wedding's tomorrow."

She smiled at him. Her black oblique eyes were gleaming and there was a redder touch in her white cheeks. She said nothing, smiling and watching him, waiting for him to go on, her claws retracted.

He said: "Only a moron like Saul would have a party when he's supposed to be whooping it up the boys. What time's the dreadful event?"

"Two o'clock." She looked at her watch and grimaced. "Not much more than twelve hours from now."

"He won't be sober." Saul, looking dull and gross with a beer-stain on his suit, was telling some rambling story about an elephant, leaning heavily on somebody's shoulder.

He brushed his face against her, kissing her lightly, leaning close into her. He slipped an arm round her and felt the outline of her breast; she pulled the cushion up on to her lap, a casual movement, just enough to hide his hand. She said: "That's nice." For a few minutes he said nothing. Then Saul came over and said thickly:

"They love that story of mine, they love it."

She asked brightly: "Which story, darling?"

"The one about the elephant." He said to Trent. "Y'see a chap ran into another chap on the street and said to him, 'You know, Barnum and Bailey's Circus is in town, don't tell anybody!' And he looks over his shoulder like this to make sure no one's listening and he says: 'I can get you an elephant for fifty pounds and this other chap says, 'But I don't want an elephant...'"

Trent said brusquely: "I've heard it." He was about to say, "And everybody else tells it better," but he thought *Poor Saul*, and said instead: "I told it to Maynard, he told it to George, George told it to Hastings, you heard it from him. Circuit closed. Come and join the discussion. Jeannette and I are arguing about the Polynesian monoliths."

Saul said unsteadily: "No...no I've got to get some more gin organized. Can't think...can't think where all the gin goes. Last time I looked there were four bottles left..." He walked away unsteadily, seesawing across the room.

Jeanette said again: "Poor Saul. I think I'd better put him to bed."

Trent said, watching Saul hold up an empty bottle to the light, squinting at it in the dimness and putting it down disgustedly: "That's how little bastards come into the world."

She shook her head. "Not tonight, they don't. Are you jealous?"

"Uh-huh."

"Then why did you come? As a matter of fact Saul said he hadn't invited you."

"I wanted to see you. And to show friend Pearman what Cairo nightlife's like. Can't keep him out of the Pigalle."

"Your charge. I hoped you'd turn up."

"For one last look?"

She faced him squarely. "Not a last look. Give me a little time, John, that's all."

He felt his hand tighten on her. He said lightly: "You're an immoral hussy. I'll give you a couple of weeks."

"We're going home for a month."

"Home? To England? Whoever had a honeymoon in England? The man has no soul. Go to Italy instead."

"We'll be back in about six weeks' time."

"I'll still be here. And waiting for you."

"I'll be waiting too, for a real man between my legs." She raised her glass: "To poor Saul."

"Up his ass."

One of the junior secretaries came up to them. He said, beaming at Jeanette: "Looking everywhere for you, John. Message for you. Somebody on the phone."

"Ah, good. In the hall?"

"By the front door."

He said to Jeannette: "Don't go away."

He went into the hall and picked up the phone. "John Trent speaking."

The Cockney voice at the other end was jubilant. "Bradley here, Sir. You might like to know...Mr. Pearman's car is on the way round for him now, Sir."

"Good...good. Is Henson there?"

"No, Sir, he's at your place. He went round a few minutes ago to check up."

"Good... Thank you, Bradley."

He put down the receiver and went to find Pearman. He said casually: "Getting tired? Want to get back to the hotel?"

Pearman took a deep breath. He said with studied calm: "Yes, shall we? Unless you like to stay on, of course?"

"Well, a heavy day tomorrow... Let's make our farewells."

They pushed their way through the crowd to where Saul was telling another story. Trent said affably: "Don't want to break things up...nice party..."

Saul broke off and squinted at them. He said hazily: "Huh? Oh, yes...so glad you could come...don't forget to say goodbye to

Jeanette."

Trent said to himself: "You bastard!" and went across to Jeannette. He took her hand. "Nothing much I can say, really, is there?"

"Are you going?"

He nodded. "Work to do." He looked up and saw that Saul was watching him, still holding Pearman's hand. He said abruptly: "See you in six weeks' time." She nodded gravely. "Don't think too harshly of me, John. Either for this...or for that."

"Well, you know your own mind. You can always come and weep on my shoulder. Have a good trip."

He pressed her hand quickly and shepherded Pearman out into the hall and down the broad stairway, filling his lungs with the fresh air that came up to them from below. Their feet rang noisily on the marble steps of the building.

In the hallway at the bottom, close by the big teak doorway, half-open now with the moonlight streaming in, watching the street outside, a figure was part of the shadow. He heard Pearman breathe in sharply.

The figure moved back into the shadow. Trent said quietly: "Henson?"

The shadow moved forward again. "Yes, Sir. Good evening, Sir. All clear now."

"Good. Is the car coming?"

"Be here in a few minutes, Sir."

"Good. Where was it? Cigarette?"

"Thank you, Sir. Under the floorboards, enough gelignite to blow the top of the building off."

"I see. What about the detonator?"

"Electrical. There's a wire leading from it to one of the rooms downstairs. Don't know which one, Sir. We couldn't trace it without giving the game away, and as you didn't want anyone to know we were looking for it..."

"Did you cut the wire?"

"No, Sir. Just removed the detonator. I left Bradley to put the floorboard back into position and 'phone you when he was all through. Bit of a job, Sir. We thought that's where it ought to be, so we looked for a board that had been interfered with, and finally found one that had had the nails removed and replaced with screws. I told Bradley to run some wax over the place again; I don't think anybody will see it's been touched. Can't think how they could have got in to put it there..."

"One of the servants, probably."

"Must have taken a bit of time, Sir..."

"But it's safe now?"

"Safe as houses. Sorry we had to keep you out so long, Mr. Pearman..."

Pearman said: "It's a great relief. It's not a nice feeling...I'm beginning to watch for moving shadows. When you stepped out of the doorway just now..."

"Don't worry about it," Trent said cheerfully. "Half the damn department's out looking after you. Practically everything else has been dropped."

"It's nice to know you have enough men..."

Trent grimaced. "We haven't. Henson and Bradley and one other man to keep an eye on you day and night...and also to look after this kind of thing. Remember that when you get back to London, if you ever hear them trying to cut down on our estimates. They shrink our budget every year, on principle."

The street was silent outside. Far in the distance they heard a solitary motor-cycle burst into a roar as it shot across the *midan*, then there was silence again as it turned the corner and rumbled out of earshot. There was no wind, and the air was still and humid.

A lonely car was parked across the way, down on the springs at the back. Henson saw Trent staring at it, and said quietly: "I checked it, Sir. Nobody there." Trent nodded.

Pearman shuddered. Then the big black Humber purred up to the curb and they quickly crossed over to it. The driver said cheerfully:

"Sorry to keep you out so long, Sir. But it's all clear now."

Trent asked: "Nobody see you working?"

"No, Sir. Not us, Sir. Me and Henson... We could have found it in five minutes if we'd been able to make a bit of noise."

They stepped into the back of the car. Henson slipped in beside the driver, and they moved off in the silence and the shadows and the cool moistness of the night.

CHAPTER 12

One hundred miles away in Port Said, in the upper story of a warehouse where the floorboards were bare and the rats were scuttling in and out among the tins of ghee and the sacks of maize, and where the air was heavy with a pungent, lingering smell of rancid butter and coffee and corn and spilled tea-leaves, heavily scenting the motionless air, with the dock noises coming up from below through the broken windows, the jagged spikes of glass sharply pointing in to themselves and half-obscuring the light with the dust and dirt and grime on them, a ring of men sat on the floor, cross-legged, thoughtful, paying careful attention. Among them, but on the edge of the circle, the ringleader sat on a bale of cotton.

He was a stranger; that much was obvious. His neat grey suit was fastidiously well-pressed, his shirt was silk, and his brown shoes were clean and shiny; his nails were manicured. But above all, he wore, instead of the tarboush of his class, a red-checked cloth about his head, bound with a double band of black goats'-hair rope—the *hattar* and *agal* from the distant north across the wide expanse of the Sinai Desert. Its color showed that he came from Hebron, a *Khalili* from the ancient grey hills that flank the Dead Sea.

The others were in rags, brown rags, grey rags, khaki rags, their heads bare or bound with grubby cloth; one of them had painted the flesh of his eye-sockets with bright blue dye, and the *kohl*-pot and brush were tucked into a soiled cummerbund about his waist. One of them wore old brown shoes with no laces or socks and had removed one of them and was busily picking at his thick toenails with the blade

CAIRO CABAL

of a knife.

One was incredibly old, white-bearded, broken-toothed, his ancient face lined with craft and wile and cunning. Another was young and virile, and wore shorts without a shirt, a broad leather belt round his slim waist, a strap around his right wrist, and he sat with his broad flat hands on his thighs, his elbows turned outward, a string round his neck hanging with a pendant in the center of his broad brown chest.

The Hebronite was speaking slowly, softly, carefully enunciating the rich mellifluous sounds of his northern dialect, scorning the use of the hard *g* and guttural *k* of the Egyptians, rolling the words softly in his delicate mouth, feeling the softness of them on his tongue, asserting his superiority over them. He said:

"Nothing can go wrong. As soon as the mine is delivered to you, you will throw what to do. There must be no mistake...no delay. Now listen. Listen carefully. The boat will be left in its usual place, down by the water. You understand, Salim? From this time onwards, always leave your boat in the same place. The truck will come during the night, when it is dark, about four o'clock in the morning. There will be a small boat on it, and if a policeman sees you, you are to say that you have been told to off-load the boat; no more. The driver of the truck will keep watch for you, and you Salim, with Saidi, Yussuf, Abdullah and Gamal, all five of you, you will unload the mine. It is big, and heavy." He spread his arms and indicated the size to them. "There will be some boards on the lorry. Roll the mine gently on to the sand, and push it to the edge of the water. Push it carefully, into the water. It will not explode. It is quite safe..."

The young boy interrupted him. He said respectfully: "but...*ya Sheikh*...how do you know it will not explode? I have seen mines. There is dynamite in them. If it goes off..."

The Hebronite said patiently: "It will not explode. There is a time mechanism...you understand what that is? It is like a clock. At a certain time it will explode; not sooner. You can hit it, drop it, jump on it; it will not go off before the time set on the clock. I want you to handle it carefully because you must not make any noise. At four o'clock in the morning, there will be fishermen about, so if the police hear you, they will not worry. But I do not want too much noise, you understand? Now. When the mine is in the water, hitch it to your boat, Gamal, with four meters of rope; the rope will already be fastened to the mine, and all you have to do is tie the other end of the rope to your boat. Then push the boat and the mine out as far as you can into the water. Row it out a little bit if you like—just so that the mine is well under water. It will not be too heavy in the water—it is weighted just enough to sink slowly, but while it is tied to the boat it cannot sink, is it not so? So it will stay just under the surface, four meters down. You understand?"

He waited, and watched their nodding heads. He went on:

"Now is the time to unload the small boat, the one on the truck, remember? Now you can make as much noise as you like. Unload the small boat and put it in the water, and the truck will drive off. Remember, you have been told to unload the small boat, and that is what you are doing there, nothing else. Nothing else."

He wiped his hands together with a small clapping noise, and held his pale soft palms up towards them. He said again: "Nothing else. If the police ask you what you are doing there, you are unloading a small boat. After the truck has gone, you can all go about your ordinary work. Gamal and Saidi—you will have your wares ready, and load your boat in the normal way; baskets, scarabs, *keffiyehs*, fruit, all the stuff you usually take out to the ships in the harbor. Now. Now you must pay close attention. Row out the boat with the mine floating under it at the same time that you usually do, and go first to some of the tourist ships, sell what you can, behave as you generally do, try to forget that the mine is hanging under your boat. Then at midday, row up to the *Shepley* and get close in beside it. At midday, remember? Gamal, start your selling, in the normal way, but you, Saidi, take your knife and cut the mine loose. You understand this? As soon as you touch the side of the big ship, the *Shepley*, cut the mine loose. Then stay there for an hour, no less than an hour remember, and your work is done. Get back to shore and get out of the area. Is that understood? You will all be paid by the driver of the truck when your work is done; he will be waiting for you on shore. Saidi and Gamal will come here after the mine has been laid, and there will be more money for them, because they have the most...the most difficult task. Now. Does anybody want to ask a question? There must be no mistake, remember. Well?"

The young boy said: "From the decks of the ships, they will see the mine in the water."

"No. Under four meters of water, they will see nothing."

"And if they see him cut the rope?"

"They must not see him. Saidi, you understand that?"

Saudi said disdainfully to the youngster: "I know what I have to do, child. No one will see me." To the ringleader he said: "It will take long to sink? The mine?"

"Not long. But it does not matter. It will not go off until the night time."

"And the ship... the *Shepley*...it will stay there all the day and the night?"

The *Khalili* smiled. "You are a good man, Saidi. It will stay there. There will be a strike among the stevedores."

There was a rumble of admiration among the men. One of them said: "What about the money? The driver will pay it?"

"The driver will pay it." He took out a roll of money and let them see it. Peeling off a handful of pound notes, he handed two to each of them, calling their names as he did so: "Saidi...Gamal...Yussuf...Salim...Abdullah... After, there will be more. Plenty more. Now go with God."

He watched them as they went down the rickety ladder into the building below and out through the big wide doors into the hot bright sunlight, the heat haze rising off the dusty tarmac at the dockside and shimmering across the blue water, making the huge grey statue of de Lesseps at the water's edge seem to tremble in the hot air.

He took out a clean white handkerchief and carefully flicked the dust off the seat of his trousers.

CHAPTER 13

He slept late in the morning, and lay in bed ruminating for a while after he woke up, watching the brightness on the underside of the slats of the green shutters and knowing that it was hot outside and reveling in the cool of the dark room. He took a shower and some coffee and dressed unhurriedly in the clean khaki shorts and bush-jacket that the unobtrusive silent Sudanese servant had laid out for him. When he arrived at his office, it was already past ten o'clock and the girls were making their morning tea.

Joan, the Colonel's secretary, was waiting for him. She had a piece of paper in one hand, a cracker in the other. Nibbling, she said: "Perugino just called. I phoned your flat and you'd just gone. Here's the number. He says it's urgent."

He ignored the piece of paper and went to the 'phone. "Don't bother," he said, "I know it already."

"Not this one. I tried to trace it for you, but no one seems to know where it is. It's an unlisted number."

"Oh? Let's see." He took the slip from her. Dialing the number he heard Perugino's excited voice.

"Mr. Trent. You know who this is? Our friend has something for you, Mr. Trent. I think you would like to see him at once. You know where I mean? Where his place is?"

"I know. What's happened? Why are you speaking for him? Is he there?"

There was a pause at the other end of the line. Then: "I think you'd better come around, Mr. Trent. If you can spare the time..."

"I'll be there in five minutes." Trent put the phone down and stood staring at Joan for a moment. He said slowly: "Give me the key to the cupboard, dear, will you?"

She looked up in alarm. "Trouble?"

"No," he said slowly, "I don't think so... But we'd better be careful. Does the Colonel know we found that bomb last night?"

"Yes, of course. The reports have been in for an hour or more."

"Pleased?"

"Jubilant. He wants to know if you can still manage this round-the-clock watch with the men you have."

"We will, somehow." He took the key and unlocked the steel cupboard that lay against the wall, and took out a Browning pistol, a clip, and eight shells. He loaded the clip slowly, a frown on his face, and slipped it into the gun, then stuck it tightly in his belt and closed his jacket over it. He picked Joan's teacup off the desk and gulped a drink.

"As soon as I get there, I'll give you a call—in about five minutes. If I don't...if I don't, give me a ring, and if it doesn't sound absolutely all right, then tell the Colonel at once. All right? Your tea's cold."

Not smiling, she nodded gravely.

He went out, climbed into the Jaguar and drove quickly round to the Bab-el-Louk apartment and parked at the curb outside. He noted briefly that an Arab was standing on the pavement opposite the house, carefully not looking at him. He scowled and went quickly up the stairs, taking the worn white stones two at a time. At the top, he paused, took out his Browning and checked it, slipping a round into the breech and thumbing the safety-catch carefully on, then put it into his side pocket. He knocked on the door.

It was opened immediately by Perugino. He whispered quickly: "Come in, Mr. Trent, come in." Trent pushed past him and went into the little living room.

Bolec was lying on the couch, a bloody white bandage round his forearm, his shirt ripped open and a wide plaster patch on his broad, harry chest. The Arab girl was on her hands and knees beside him, cleaning the wooden-plank floor with a rag and a bucket of water. The water she rung out was red.

Bolec looked up at him and grinned happily. He said cheerfully: "That little bugger Shakri...a knife this big, Mr. Trent." He raised his arms and spread them largely.

Trent said: "For God's sake, what happened?" He went quickly to the couch and bent down to examine the wound, pulling away the plaster gently.

"Shakri...he come to see me. We talk little bit, I pour little drink, then he stick his bloody knife into me. But I move quickly, Mr. Trent. Plenty fat, but I move quick. I twist to one side, like this..." He turned his shoulder and grimaced at the pain of it.

Perugino broke in excitedly: "I found him on the floor, Mr. Trent. He's lost a lot of blood from that wound in his arm, but that, I think, is not too serious. The other one...the chest... I think he deflected the blow. Otherwise he must surely have perished. Otherwise, he would not be so happy now. I do not think he has the brains to realize that this is a very dangerous business..."

Bolec said happily: "That little son of a whore... I hit him, I hit him hard. My left hand still pretty good. I knock him off his feet, and he get up and run quick, like lizard, out of doors. Then I fall down a little bit, get up and go to kitchen to get soap..."

"Soap?"

"Soap," Perugino said scornfully. "I wanted to put iodine on it but he says no. He has blocked the orifice with soap. Really..."

"Best thing," Bolec said calmly. "Best thing, soap. Then I fall down little bit..."

"By the grace of God," Perugino said volubly, his excitement rising, "by the grace of God I arrived at the opportune moment. He was lying on the floor in a dreadful pool of his own blood. The Arab girl was out, of course, and when I found the door open..."

Gesticulating with his delicate hands, using them like an Indian dancer, he said: "What annoys me more than anything else...I saw this man. I saw him walk away from the building as I came in. I know him. Shakri. A good-for-nothing from Alexandria, a *scelerato* of the first order. He had the impertinence to ignore me when I greeted him..."

Trent was still on his knees. He replaced the plaster and said: "The good Lord's on your side, Bolec. That should have killed you.

I'll get you a doctor..."

"No doctor. I not like doctors, no good, charge too much money..."

"Don't worry about that. The office will pay his fee..."

"Ah, then is good. Office pay, I have doctor, is best thing, maybe pretty bad after all." He hesitated and said uncertainly: "Maybe...maybe this doctor take a look at...how you call it?" Gesticulating uncertainly at his backside, he said: "I got hemorrhoids. Maybe he take a look at that, too? Give me plenty trouble..."

Trent threw back his head and laughed out loud. "We'll get you in working order again. But tell me what it's all about... What happened between you and Shakri?"

Bolec said: "Maybe I have little rakia first? You find bottle in cupboard there..."

"No rakia," Perugino said firmly. "Alcohol is most harmful to a man in your condition."

Trent went to the cupboard and found the bottle. He said: "No amount of alcohol will hurt this lump of mutton. On the contrary, it'll probably do him a lot of good." He poured a long glass and gently lifted Bolec's head. Then he glanced at the phone and said: "Perugino, you take care of this. I'll get a doctor." The telephone rang as he went towards it. He glanced at his watch and grinned. Lifting the receiver he said: "Joan? Right on time."

"Are you all right, John?" Her voice was worried.

"Fine. But I want a doctor sent up here right away. Couple of knife wounds to be taken care of. Among other things...wait, I'll give you the address. Tell him to come to the corner of Bab-el-Louk and Sharia-el-Gher. Perugino will be on the corner looking for him. He can't mistake Perugino; he's wearing, for God's sake, a bright green shirt and a yellow tie. He looks like a fragrant calla-lily. Make it urgent, will you?"

"Hold on, John, I'll get him on the other phone."

He heard the muted sound as she laid the receiver on her desk at the other end, and faintly he heard her talking into the other phone. He took out a cigarette and lit it. He said: "Pour me a glass of that stuff, Perugino, will you?"

Bolec nodded vigorously. "Is new bottle," he called. "I make myself. Very good stuff this time, more two months old. Last time not so good, I drink him too soon, but this, very good stuff."

Trent said: "You keep quiet and relax." He took the glass that Perugino brought him and sipped it gingerly, grimacing at its harshness. Bolec called: "Is good? You like?"

"Is good." Into the phone, he said "Joan?"

"Doctor Loblaw. He'll be there at once. Anything else?"

"Nothing else."

"Who is it? What happened?"

"Bolec. Tell you when I get back. And Joan..."

"Yes?"

"In case I don't get back in time...you know Jeannette's getting married today?"

"Yes, I know that."

"Send her a telegram for me, will you? In case I'm not back in time. I think it's at two o'clock."

He measured her hesitation. She said: "Yes, John. I'll send one."

"Thank you, dear. If the old man wants me, I'll be in this evening some time. I hope." He rang off.

Turning to Bolec, he said: "Now, what's it all about? You feel strong enough to tell me?"

Bolec waved a deprecating arm. He said: "Plenty strong. I tell you everything." He took an awkward swig at his glass, the harsh liquid spilling over his unshaven chin. He said:

"This fellow Shakri come to see me. O.K. Before two three days, I tell him, you go see your boss, maybe we get more money from him. Same like I tell you before. So O.K. I think maybe he come tell me about this. So I say, 'What you want, Shakri, you no-good-son of a whore?' and he say 'Bolec, I got to talk to you. Better you send Farida away.' So I tell Farida, 'You go to market, buy pepper'..."

Trent said: "Does she understand English?"

"English? She not even speak Arabic good. Is peasant girl, *fellaha*. You not worry, she not understand us. Besides, is good girl. She know my friends." He stretched out a heavy hand and laid it on her head. She looked up quickly at him, smiling her quick Semitic smile, her fine dark eyes briefly sparkling in her smooth brown face, then got up and went to the kitchen. Through the narrow open door, open to catch the breezes swirling across the hot rooftop, Trent could watch her as she sat in her long black dress on the wooden kitchen chair, her hands folded in her lap, her bare feet twisted round the rungs, showing their pink soles, her long toes almost prehensile. She sat quite still and relaxed, patient, her eyes cast down. He turned away from her. Bolec went on:

"I say to this *levobocek*: 'What you want, my friend? You see your boss about this thing?' Shakri tell me he speak to him, then ask for little drink. O.K. Like I say, Shakri get drunk pretty easy, so I give him drink from that bottle you got there. Why you not drink? Help yourself. Is good rakia, no?"

Trent poured himself a drink and passed the bottle to Perugino. "And then?"

"And then," Bolec went on, "you know what this little bastard do? He throw the rakia in my face, quick like the tongue of a *gekko* when he catch flies, and I go to cover up with my hands, because my rakia pretty hot stuff, burn like fire in eyes. Then I think quick, 'What he trying to do, this little bastard?' and I hold out my hands, like this, and turn away from him, like so...not cover my eyes, look instead to see what this little bastard going to do to me. Then I see this knife come up, fast, like so, and I twist and get knife in arm, instead of in belly, only in chest little bit. So I twist back and hit him hard, on side of head, and I say, 'Bolec, better you hit this little bastard pretty hard, else you going to be a dead Czech pretty soon'. So I hit him hard. Shakri fall down, then get up quick and run away..."

"Did you get his knife?"

Bolec shook his head. "You know these Arabs. You cut off his head, he still hold on to knife, not let go. Then I go to kitchen and fix up little bit with soap, then fall down on floor, and Perugino come. I say, 'Get me a drink of rakia, Perugino,' but he say, 'No drink. Better you call Mr. Trent.' Then you come. Is all."

Trent noticed the perspiration dripping on to the grubby cushion under his head. He said gently: "All right. Leave it at that. The doctor will be here in a few minutes. Get down to the corner, Perugino, and show him up; he'll be looking for your shirt."

"Yes, Mr. Trent." Straightening his tie, glancing at himself in the cracked mirror, looking a little chastened, Perugino hurried out.

He stopped at the door. "This fellow Shakri, he might still be hanging about... What would you like me to do?"

"You won't see him. He'll be halfway to Alexandria by now. Unless..." He crossed to the window and threw open the jalousie. Gesturing down to the street with his head, he said: "That's not him, I take it?"

Perugino crossed quickly to the window and stared down into the street below them. The Arab was still standing on the corner, a dead cigarette hanging from the corner of his mouth. He said excitedly, "No. I have not seen that man before. You think he is watching the house?"

"Uh-huh. Just let him stand there."

Perugino looked up at him in alarm. "You don't think..."

"No, I don't."

He took a pound note from his wallet and handed it to him. He said: "Send the concierge for a bottle of good whisky; Johnnie Walker."

Turning to Bolec he said: "Present for you. Comfortable?"

Perugino took the money and scurried out of the room. Bolec said: "Feel O.K. Is nothing." He was feeling the loss of blood. His left hand was gently caressing the wound in his chest. He said weakly:

"What do you think? You think this man Reizen tell Shakri to kill me?"

"Yes. I think so. Any reason for Shakri to do this for himself?"

"Nothing. Nothing at all. Nothing."

"Then I'm afraid that's what it is. Shakri must have found out from his Arab girl that you'd been talking to her. After that...if he told Reizen what you'd found out from her...we'll have to get you out of here, find somewhere else for you to stay for a while..."

Breathing heavily, Bolec shook his head. "No," he said firmly, "No. I not leave this house."

"I'll find you a place to stay...perhaps you could put up at my apartment for a few days..."

"No."

A shadow of pain crossed his face. He said: "This my house, Mr. Trent. Long time ago, they chase me out of my country. They take my father away, and I not see him anymore. My mother, she get killed, an old woman, nearly seventy years old. She have pretty hard time all her life, we don't have too much money, pretty hard time, then she get killed when Russian soldiers come..." His voice was quivering. "Old woman. Then I ran away from country, come to Egypt. Now, this my home, they not chase me anymore. This time, I fight. I fight little bit before, but no good, too many of them. Now, I fight good. They not chase me from this house. This Egypt. Not Prague any more, I stay here. In my home."

Trent stared at him, seeing the lines about his eyes. "All right," he said. "All right. I'll get you a bodyguard...someone to hang about the place and keep his eyes open..."

Bolec shook his head again. "No bodyguard," he said. "Next time, they not catch me sleeping. This thing, I take care of myself... You not worry. This thing, I take care of myself. Maybe I bring some of my boys here. I got pretty good friends. Do like I tell them. Next time..." He grimaced and felt his ribs. He said anxiously: "Only tell me one thing. Now, you trust me, no?"

"Yes. Of course."

"Then tell me why? Why this man Reizen want to kill me? What I do to him? I never know this man... Why he want to kill me?"

Trent said heavily: "I know the answer to that, Bolec, but I can't tell you much. Only this; you're caught up in some nasty business, and you found out something about it. Not much, but enough. It's something nobody must know about. It's like a plant that grows in the darkness, one ray of light is enough to kill it, and they don't want it killed. You started to bring some light to it, so you had to go."

"But Reizen? You tell me is newspaper man. What he got to do with all this? What sort of trouble they want to make now?"

Walking up and down the tiny room, his buttons undone, the sweat itching at the back of his neck, Trent said:

"I'll tell you this much. You had to immobilize the cars on the road, on a given day. That's the smallest part of it. You were supposed to think it was for some local trouble...a strike...a minor riot, some such thing. But it's all part of something considerably more important. We know more or less what it might be...but we don't know half enough. The only man who does know...is Reizen." He said savagely: "I've a damn good mind to get hold of Reizen and beat the truth out of him... There's a plan. Reizen, Kamel Irani, Shulam..." He stopped his pacing and said: "What do you know about Shulam?"

"Ibrahim Shulam? Is a policeman."

"I know that. Ever have anything to do with him?" Bolec shook his head. "Long time ago, was a sergeant. Then he make a little trouble for me, not much. But is nice fellow. Give him little bit money...no more trouble."

Trent said quickly: "What sort of trouble?"

"Oh, nothing...is little trouble about whisky. Somebody steal some whisky from army stores and he think I got it. So I give him two three cases...no more trouble."

"I see. Nothing since then?"

"Now, I hear he is a big man. Some political job. Security, my friends say. But long time, not see him anywhere. Maybe he work in headquarters some place."

"I think I'll go and have a talk with him."

He sat down on the window ledge, staring into the bright street below, not saying anything, smoking silently, watching the street morosely.

He saw the doctor arrive and pull up beside Perugino, and a moment later he came up the stairs, a thin sparse man with a shock of black hair and thick spectacles, with Perugino following him, dancing attendance on him, carrying his bag up the stairway, enjoying the excitement. The doctor grunted a greeting and went to work at once, his thin white fingers moving quickly, gently, while Trent stood by and watched him. He said:

"How bad is it?"

The doctor shrugged. "A good job he's got so much fat on him. Probably saved his life. It's not too serious, as it is. A day or two...he'll be sore for a while, of course. And he won't like the cleaning out we'll have to do. A knife? A daggar?"

Trent nodded "An Arab's knife."

The doctor grimaced. "Then it won't be too clean." He patted Bolec's great stomach. "A good job you have an appetite, my friend. Those spare tires have saved your life. We'll have to put you in the hospital for a few hours."

Perugino said maliciously: "Don't forget to have the doctor cut out your piles, Bolec. He might cut out your *coglione* at the same time."

Bolec protested good-naturedly. "All right," he said. "You wait you get this thing, you not laugh about it then..."

"It is strange, is it not?" Perugino mused. "Let us agree that the backside is the only intrinsically humorous object which is shared by both the nobility and the bourgeoisie. Bourgeois behinds have a different popular name, is it not so? But all the same, whatever you call them..."

Trent said: "A rose by any other name...?"

"Whatever you call it, it is subject to the same indignities and the same discomforts..."

"This my backside you talking about!" Bolec shouted. "Is enough..."

"If I were a wealthy man," Perugino went on, "it would cause me a great deal of unhappiness to know that from at least one aspect I was no better than the common beggar, but as it is, I can find a certain comfort in it..."

Leaning against the door, watching them with amusement, Trent was conscious of a warm feeling of affection for the preposterous Czech. He said:

"Leave him alone, Perugino. He's a better man than you are."

Touching his fingertips delicately, holding the stage, Perugino groped for the last word. "Of course," he said gently. "And more sensitive, fundamentally."

The doctor dropped his bandage to the floor, threw back his head, and roared with laughter.

Bolec was grinning happily, immensely pleased with the day's events and with his new friends. The doctor said, taking off his spectacles and wiping them: "I think...I think if you'd get me an ambulance..."

"I walk," Bolec said happily. "I don't need no ambulance."

"You'll bloody well do as you're told."

Trent went to the telephone and called Joan at the office and asked her to send an ambulance round, and they laughed and joked until it came, and then he helped the doctor lift Bolec, still protesting, on to the stretcher which the bearers brought up, and they covered him with a clean white sheet against which his linen was an irresponsible grey. As they carried him out, Trent saw his hand stretch out and slip the bottle of rakia from the table and under the sheet, and he grinned and thought that it could have been a lot worse, and that it would be worse when they started to clean the filth and the germs and the dirt from a rusting, ill-kept knife-blade out of the depths of his wound, and he felt suddenly sobered and unhappy. He watched them maneuver the stretcher out through the narrow doorway, lifting it high above the tight iron balustrade. He went back into the room and into the kitchen and saw that the Arab girl was still there, not moving, minding her affairs, her eyes still cast down, sitting patient and immobile on the wooden chair.

He went to her and laid a ten-shilling note in her lap and said: "For food." And she looked up at him briefly, her eyes big and black and sad, the whites of them bright and clear in her child's Madonna face, then nodded her head and looked at the floor again, feeling him beside her and not moving, not touching the money till he had gone away.

He left Perugino there, and went down the white stone stairs, seeing that all the doors were open on the way down, and men in undershirts and women in housecoats and curlers were standing under their lintels, watching silently, leaning against the door-jambs, their arms folded, watching in silence, all the drab unknowns next door who are never seen except when something like this happens and they can wait till everyone has gone and then burst out into excited expostulations and imaginings, the women standing in wide-eyed groups, the men handing each other cigarettes and finding the excuse for a party.

As he reached the street, he saw that the ambulance was just driving away. He waved a hand to the doctor who was just pulling away from the curb. The Arab across the street was gone. A policeman, his rifle slung across his back, was watching them idly.

He got into his car and drove round to see Shulam.

CHAPTER 14

Down in the alley between the two high buildings, there was no sun. The surface was cobbled, and pitted, and broken by neglect. It was close by the busy intersection that cut across the *midan*, but the cats strolled here in peace, stopping only for hair-bristling snarls at the mangy dogs that slunk nervously past them, looking apprehensively over their' shoulders, then darting hurriedly for cover.

A banana skin, rotting in the dank heat, lay in a pool of urine close to a whitewashed wall.

The truck lumbered slowly, tightly between the oppressing walls, awkwardly heaving itself along as though wheezing with antiquity, its cabin doors fastened on with wire, and oil dripping over the engine and foully smelling in blue smoke. The driver was thin and nervous and undernourished, his sallow face pale, his black eyes deep in their sockets. His tarboush was pushed to the back of his head and he was sweating.

As he came to the corner by the main road, he stopped and watched the traffic for a moment. Then the truck swung round the corner and joined it.

Behind him, on the corner of the alleyway, a youth in soiled khaki trousers and a cheap brown jacket, his chest bare to the breeze, his hair long and unkempt, his laceless, lusterless shoes loose on his feet, quickly flicked away a cigarette and picked up the brown packet that lay where the truck had momentarily waited. Looking quickly over his shoulder, he tore away the wrapping and dropped it on the pavement. The box was marked with an arrow and stamped W.D.

Opening it carefully, he pulled out one of the detonators, examined it carefully, replaced it with the others, closed the box, stuffed it into his pocket and walked off.

When he entered the main street, he was singing quietly to himself.

"Baladiya, baidah, ehna bidn'arouh illah'l baladiya..."

He looked back over his shoulder once, a quick sly movement, his lank hair flipping to the back of his head, called a greeting to the policeman on point duty, *"Ahlan wa sahlan, ya habibi..."* crossed the street quickly between two nonchalantly careening cars, and disappeared into the mass.

One hundred and forty-four detonators.

CHAPTER 15

Ibrahim Shulam was one of the new breed of policemen.

He was young, and intelligent, and smooth-mannered, and treacherous. His education at the American University in Beirut and at the Al Hazzar in Cairo had been sound and comprehensive; it had also served to drill him in the techniques of Chauvinism. He hated the foreigners and he aped their ways. He wore English suits and he detested the English. He spoke easy and fluent French, and could not abide the Frenchmen. His education came from an American foundation, and he abominated the Americans.

He had nothing but contempt for the infidel; and in their manners, their speech, their clothes, their housing, their food and their ways he copied them.

His hair was cut short, and shone brilliantly black and was kinked and well oiled, and he affected a thin moustache, cropped short to show the world that he had passed from the childish days when the strength of a man was judged by the luxuriance of the hair on his face. His black eyes were lively, dashing and quick-moving in the manner that, among the gutter-Arabs whom the swank hotels collected and washed and polished up and dressed as desert sheikhs and paid to stalk in natural dignity about their gardens, had so long brought romantic flutters to the maternal maidenly hearts of spinster schoolteachers from the great American Babbitry. He was desperately handsome.

Intellectually, he was a snob. He sometimes regretted that it was no longer fashionable to speak French all the time, and so he cultivated a soft Syrian accent to prove that he was cosmopolitan, a new cosmopolitan of the great Arab world whose boundaries were Damascus and Beirut and Algiers and Mecca and where the mature and ancient cultures had died and been buried in sand and where the new braggadocio had dug up the weapons but not the enlightenment. He was a man with a future, fashionably dressed, slim and athletic, well-to-do and suave, and he believed that most of his problems could be solved on the polo-field at Gezira where, until quite recently, Egyptians had not been very welcome. He groomed himself carefully, and used a lot of perfume.

When Trent came into his office on the ground floor of the big new police building, Shulam got to his feet and held out a languid hand, smiling in the friendliest possible manner, his white teeth quickly gleaming.

"How do you do, Mr. Trent? Forgive me that I keep you waiting unduly."

"Shulam *effendi*... Not at all, a mere half-hour..."

"So sorry. Do sit down, please. Will you have coffee?" Without waiting for a reply he clapped his hands and a servant came in, looked at them quickly, nodded, and disappeared. With a gesture, Shulam dismissed the boy who was squatting at the foot of the desk polishing his shoes. He spoke Arabic, then realizing the perfection with which Trent spoke it, he quickly switched to English. It was always a problem, he thought; the new laws demand the consistent use of Arabic in government matters, and yet...if you talk to a European in Arabic...there was the indefinable sensation of a menial contact, a servant-to-master connotation that still lingered on... He said suavely: "I think we have met before, have we not? I may be wrong..."

"Yes, we did once. At an Army Officers' Club, I think."

"Ah yes, of course. I was still a student then. Political philosophy. And what can I do to help you, Mr. Trent? It is not often that we have the pleasure of a visit from our late masters."

Trent said carefully: "I'll be frank with you, Shulam. I don't really..."

"Shulam *effendi*."

"Of course, forgive me. I'll be frank, Shulam *effendi*; I don't really know whether you can—or will—do anything for me. But tell me this; you know our Oswald Pearman, of course? At the Trade Delegation?"

Shulam smiled broadly, flashing his quick white smile. He said:

"The time has gone, Mr. Trent, when it was not considered necessary for us Egyptians to know what the British were doing in our country. Now, your political activities are well known to us. Mr. Pearman has nothing whatever to do with the Trade Delegation; that is merely his cover story. Mr. Pearman is here to discuss the Israeli dispute with our Minister of External Affairs. I might add that since both the Americans and the British, with their usual perfidy, are supporting the Jews, he is not meeting with a great deal of success. The Minister has been most careful in keeping this a secret, even from us; but you must know that nothing eludes my department for very long. Nothing."

"I see." Trent raised a deprecatory hand. "Of course, all this secrecy is necessary, as you will agree, also from your own Government's point of view. Otherwise, your Minister would not have been so very co-operative with us. What do you know of a man called Kamel Irani?"

"Why do you wish to know, Mr. Trent?"

"Well..." Trent took out his cigarette case and offered it as the boy brought the coffee. Shulam shook his hand. "We Muslims do not smoke, Mr. Trent."

He sighed and put the cigarette case back in his pocket, replacing the cigarette he had half-extracted. Noticing the ashtray on the table, he said patiently: "A man called Kamel Irani has been making inquiries about Pearman; the kind of inquiries that frequently lead to trouble. I could learn nothing down in the *mousky*; we have no other sources of information nowadays, and it occurred to me that if anybody should know about him, you would."

"That's a very gratifying thought. I'm glad that word of my efficiency has reached your ears. It seems a pity, does it not, that we are no longer under your orders? There might have been quite a future for me."

Under his suavity there was an alertness, a questioning, almost a fear. Trent, watching him carefully, said dryly: "I do not doubt for your future, Shulam *effendi*. Who is Kamel Irani?"

"Perhaps you would tell me why my confidential files should be at your disposal?"

Trent said angrily: "For God's sake come off it, Shulam. You know as well as I do that I'm on your side. When you kicked us out of Egypt, only a few of us stayed behind. I was one of them. Why, for God's sake? Why do you think I stayed here?"

"Because a perfidious British Government paid you sufficiently to make you want to stay and spy on us."

"You are a long way behind with your political philosophy. We are still, believe it or not, allies of a sort. I stayed here of my own free will on a perfectly innocuous security job..."

"Communications officer."

"What the hell should I call myself? As I was saying, I stayed here to do an ordinary job simply because I like it here. This is my home, like it or not. I've lived here for more than fifteen years. I like the climate. I like the way of life. And, believe it or not, I even like the people. So stop playing cat-and-mouse and let's be friends. My department works under license from your Government..."

"Under tolerance, Mr. Trent."

"Under license. And I've nothing to hide from you and you know it." He took out a cigarette and lit it, and placed the match carefully in the center of the ashtray. He said: "We're both in the same business, Shulam. So what about some co-operation?"

He waited a long time for a reply.

At last, sipping his coffee drinking it quietly in the European manner instead of sucking it noisily through his lips, Arab-fashion, Shulam said slowly:

"Are you prepared to trade information, Mr. Trent? A *quid pro quo?*"

"Certainly. Your sources are better than mine, but if I can help you, I will. Of course I will."

"You have never done so before."

"You've never asked me. What's on your mind?"

"What do you know about Sergei Reizen?"

"Reizen! Well, that's a happy thought. Reizen. Reizen is a Tass Agency correspondent here, and a minor M.V.D. man. He uses the diplomatic bag at the Embassy to get his dispatches out, and he circulates Communist propaganda among the *fellaheen*."

"So much, of course, I already know."

"Then why do you allow it?"

Shulam said dryly: "Why also do we allow the British to try and convert us? Do not expect us to ask the Russians to leave us alone while you yourselves are still trying to change our way of life. All the flies around the Egyptian honeypot should be killed off, Mr. Trent, or none of them. Do not expect us to pick them out one from the other and say 'This one can buzz around us but not that one.' But the new Egypt is a tolerant country. We allow things we do not approve of, in order to show our tolerance to a skeptical world."

"And do you think Communism is consistent with the preaching of Islam?"

"No, Mr. Trent, no more so than Christianity is. Also, with us it is not a phobia. Do you know what Reizen is doing now?"

Trent said hesitantly: "Well...it's outside my sphere, rather. But there are rumors that he's stirring up some kind of trouble in town. It's only market gossip, of course, but he seems to have some grandiose plan up his sleeve. Don't know very much about it, really."

"What sort of rumors, Mr. Trent? Who, among your informants in the *mousky* could even mention Reizen's name to you?"

"Oh..." Trent waved a vague hand. Knowing he was on dangerous ground, he said: "I heard his name somewhere...nothing definite, you understand..."

His eyes narrow slits of gleaming blackness, Shulam said: "Reizen was mentioned to you by name, and yet you do not know who mentioned him...? Is that what I am expected to believe?"

"Not by name. There was some...some worry about the newspaper people interesting themselves in local politics, somebody mentioned the Tass Agency..."

"Who, Mr. Trent?"

"I don't know. Frankly, it was one of those things that go in one ear and out of the other...just an idea. Please don't attach any importance to it." He was squirming a little. He said boldly: "Knowing the propensity of the Russians for stirring up trouble in disaffected parts of the world...I thought it would be wise to find out something about Reizen myself."

"And did you, Mr. Trent?"

"As a matter of fact, he was the subject next on my list. I was going to ask you about him."

"I see." The danger was past. Trent took his coffee and sipped it silently. Shulam said casually: "Do you know anything about a woman called Higran Hanem?" Not looking up, Trent felt that Shulam's sharp eyes were watching him carefully. He put down his coffee cup and frowned. "Higran Hanem? No, I don't think I do. Higran...the name seems to strike a chord; don't think I know of her offhand. Who is she?"

"A dancer."

"Ah yes...I know now, there's a Higran at the Pigalle, is that the one? Calls herself Princess Higran?"

"That is the one, Mr. Trent. The one who was killed."

"Ah yes, I remember. I read of it in the paper. Should I know her?"

"No, perhaps not. Another business altogether. It just occurred to me that you might have come across her. I know that you frequent the Pigalle. I myself cannot go to such a place very often, of course."

"Off course... Anything to do with Reizen?"

Shulam made his point again carefully. "Nothing, Mr. Trent. Another business altogether."

"I see. And on Kamel Irani? Can you help me there?"

The puzzlement was back in Shulam's cruel eyes. "Kamel Irani? I'm afraid not. I know nothing of this man. If you were to tell me what you have heard about him, perhaps I could find something out for you?"

"That would be most kind of you. All I know is that he has been making inquiries about Pearman. Apart from that...I know nothing. I don't even know where he comes from or where he lives."

"Irani...the name, of course, is Iranian. But when a man is called by such an identifying name, it usually means that he lives somewhere else. A man named El Misri, for example, would never be a resident of Egypt, or the identification would mean nothing. He would be Syrian, or a Jordanian or some such, but originating from Misr, from Egypt. Similarly, a man called Homsi would never live in Damascus, nor would a resident of Palestine ever be called El Falastini. He might be a Syrian perhaps?"

"I don't know..."

"And about Reizen?"

"I don't seem to be able to help you, do I?"

"And yet we both seek information about him. You said you were going to ask me about him too, did you not?"

"Er...yes, I was."

"And why, Mr. Trent? Has he also been making inquiries about your Oswald Pearman?"

"No, it's not that at all. The rumors I mentioned...the talk in the *mousky*..."

"About the interference of the press in domestic politics?"

"Er...yes."

"And you don't regard that as a purely domestic affair yourself?"

Trent said to himself, "You cunning bastard." Aloud, he said apologetically: "Well, these things sometimes lead to international complications, don't you agree? I thought it would be as well if I were to ask you about it. After all, you have a great deal more scope in these things than we do..."

"And what do you suggest we should do about it?"

"Why don't you arrest him?"

"Arrest him?" Shulam smiled a cold thin smile. "On what charges?"

"Oh...charges! You know the way they work. They raise merry hell with the cretins and then move into the vacuum. It's a dangerous business when they start interesting themselves in your domestic affairs. Catch it in the bud and you'll be a lot better off."

"We are quite accustomed to handling the problems raised by the interference of foreign powers in our affairs. We have had a lot of practice at it."

Trent shrugged it off. "You could at least search his office and his home. You might find the results very illuminating."

Shulam stood up and went to the door. He said coldly: "Mr. Trent, if you had told me as soon as you arrived that the object of your visit was to ask me to search Reizen's premises for you, perhaps I would have been more cooperative. But I fear you cannot trick me into following your wishes in this manner..."

Trent was astounded. "My wishes? But...but...what the hell are you talking about?"

"This is not a *quid pro quo*. Your protestations of affection for us are painfully false. Under the circumstances..."

"Oh, for God's sake, get off your high horse. I came here to find out about Kamel Irani..."

"Ostensibly."

"And got instead a lecture on the uses of...of community nomenclature..."

"Good day, Mr. Trent." Shulam stood holding the door open. Trent said resignedly: "What about Irani?"

"Shall I call for my sergeant and have him throw you out?"

Trent got up and went to the door. "Don't make the mistake, Shulam *effendi*," he said, "of not knowing who your friends are..."

"Good-day, Mr. Trent."

"Oh, the hell with you! Good-day." He stamped out of the office, glared at the sentry, got into his car, and drove quickly round to see the Colonel.

Colonel Brand handed him a sheaf of papers.

"I don't see why I should have to do all this," he grumbled.

"Look through this lot and you'll see what's taking shape. Bazaar-gossip, most of it, but one or two items of interest. There's a report that an attempt will be made to blow up the *Shepley* to Port Said."

"Oh? Is she there now?"

"Not yet. She's due tomorrow and she's supposed to offload and turn around at once. But there's talk of a strike among the dockworkers and she may be there for several days. But we obviously haven't a great deal of time to play with. The authorities have been alerted already, so you needn't worry about that."

"What's her cargo, Sir?"

The Colonel looked up at him. "Aircraft parts," he said. "Aircraft parts for the Egyptian Air Force."

Trent whistled. Leafing through the reports, perched on the sill of the big window, he said: "No indication how...?"

"A fire is the most likely method, I imagine. It's the easiest, though, and for that reason, they might try something else. How would you sink a ship if you had to? In harbor?"

Trent said promptly: "Swim out and put a couple of magnetic bombs under it. They're not too hard to come by if you really want a couple."

"In port, with help near at hand, it wouldn't be enough...well, they'll have a look at it in Port Said when she gets in. And the police in Suez raided a warehouse and found nearly three tons of high explosives and seven boxes of detonators. Another thing that's important, very important. On the Suez road last night, a carload of Egyptians were fired on by three men. The car went off the road and miraculously, nobody was hurt. But when the three men found the passengers were all Egyptians, they apologized, warned them to say nothing about it, and went off. You know what that means, don't you?"

"A rehearsal?"

"Precisely. Some overzealous group of saboteurs trying to get their hand in. There's trouble afoot, John, and I don't like the looks of it. What about Pearman?"

Trent walked across to the desk and put down the papers. "Well, Sir," he said. "He's bearing up under the strain. Henson and Bramley turned up the bomb in his room, underneath the floorboards. Enough to blow the building to pieces, apparently. We couldn't find out where the lead wires went without alerting the whole building, so we simply took out the detonators. Bolec was knifed in the chest..."

The Colonel said sharply: "Kamel Irani?"

"No, Sir. An Egyptian named Shakri. Comes from Alexandria. A man of no importance, actually, but the fact of the matter is that they tried to kill Bolec because he found out about Reizen. Reizen's the man behind all this..."

"Behind what, John? How much of the picture have we?"

"Well, we know that there are preparations afoot for large-scale rioting. We know that when it breaks out, the Government is almost certain to fall and with it, our hopes of..."

"But it's the time factor."

The Colonel got up from his desk and stood with his feet widely planted, rooted in the center of the big room, the tall grey-painted walls dwarfing his stubby figure. "The time factor. We know what's going to happen...at least, we've got a pretty shrewd idea of it. But Reizen is not the man behind it all. I tell you, John, it's not Reizen, Reizen is small fry. An informant, an organizer, but not an executive. It will be somebody else. It's too big for Reizen to handle alone."

"You mean an Egyptian?"

"Possibly. But you remember that, after the Black Saturday riots, we found out there had been two newly-arrived Russians in Cairo? From the Oriental Section of the Foreign Ministry in Moscow. This time...well, it might be an Egyptian, I suppose. But I doubt it."

Trent said, worried: "It's rather like sitting on a powder keg. We know what's in it, but we don't know when it's going up. We need a miracle..."

Colonel Brand turned to his desk, bending over it and banging on it several times with his clenched fist, an angry, nervous, rhythmical gesture, his back turned to Trent. He said to the wall, angrily; "Then make your miracle! I don't care how you do it, but find out when. *When*...that's the problem. What about the money?"

"The money?"

"It's going to take the devil of a lot of money. Agitators to pay, palms to be greased... How much was Bolec to be paid for his part?"

"Two hundred pounds, Sir."

"That's nothing. This sort of thing takes hundreds of thousands. And we can be fairly sure that it will be brought in specially. Where will they get it from?"

"It's bound to arrive from Moscow in the diplomatic bag. A pity we can't intercept it. We did that once, remember?"

"Yes...if we knew when. But I don't think so. This is the one kind of thing the Russian Embassy can't afford to be mixed in. It's too dangerous for them. I think it will be brought in specially."

"Is there any way of getting at Reizen? Pressure of some sort? A bribe perhaps?"

The Colonel snorted. "Not a hope. A bribe? First of all, London would raise hell if it didn't work out properly. And I don't think they'd approve if we picked him up and applied pressure of some sort..."

"We might save a lot of lives by doing just that..."

"No, John." The Colonel said sharply: "There was an organization during the war for that sort of thing, but this is peacetime, and we're supposed to be playing a peacetime game. I know how you feel about it, and that's how I feel too. But we have a responsibility... If we start behaving like animals, then we can't expect the others to do any better." He raised his hand.

"I know what you're going to say. But this is not my argument, it's London's. So forget about it. I know it isn't easy. We're here under protest, and we're liable to be turned out at a moment's notice. But we've got to do something, so let's get on with it."

Trent repeated worriedly, muttering to himself: "I still say we need a bloody miracle." He got up to leave. He said: "I'll look through these, Sir, and see what I can find out."

The Colonel did not answer him. He was taking a cigarette from his case, and staring at the picture on the wall. Trent went out quietly.

In the outer office, the clock on the desk struck two. He watched it for a moment and said to Joan, forcing himself to be casual: "Did you send that telegram for me?"

"Yes, John." She kept her eyes off him. He laid a hand on her head, feeling the softness of her hair. He said, "When are they leaving for their honeymoon?"

"Tonight. They're sailing from Port Said tomorrow morning. The *Olympic* I believe it is. Shall I wire some flowers to the ship?"

He smiled down at her. "Yes. Please do."

He went to the door. "If anybody wants me, I'll be in my office for the rest of the day. When the reports come in will you let me see them first? In case I have to go out?"

"All right." She looked up and smiled at him. "Have you had lunch?"

He shook his head. "Not hungry. And no time to eat."

"I'll make you some tea."

"Good. I'll be in the office."

He went out and closed the door. He stood for a moment by the door-end of the corridor, watching the bright sunlight on the lawn, thinking what a beautifully kept garden it was, feeling his affinity for the heat and the color and richness of it and thinking about Jeannette and Saul.

He turned abruptly away and went back into his office. For a few moments, the cool room was dark after the harsh hot brilliance outside, and when it grew slowly lighter, he spread his reports on the desk and sat down to read them. He filled his pipe from a stone tobacco jar; in the soft soapstone of the bottom, underneath, a craftsman had carved on instructions: "J. ALIQUANDO FIDELIS. J."

He recovered his good humor, lit his pipe, and with a sigh got on with his work.

CHAPTER 16

The building opposite the Trade Delegation offices was a tall stone house that had been the Cairo home of an Alexandrian Pasha. It lay back from the road a trifle, and the front garden was still cool and green and friendly. There was an ornamental fountain in the center, rather rococo, now dried up, its bronze pipes green with age and disuse, and the marble circle around it, brought from Italy in the lush old days of the Khedive, was chipped and dulled with neglect.

The house itself was built of white stone and red brick, alternating in garish strata of color up the baroque façade, and the green jalousies over the windows, long since closed and firmly nailed home, were now faded to a nondescript grey, small streaks of red appearing where the damp of the mornings had rusted the nails.

Inside, it was dark and gloomy, and the dampness of the whitewash on the walls gave off a faint pervading stench that hung in the air and did not go away even when the intruder opened one of the windows at the back, pushing the shutter aside to make it appear that it had fallen off.

He spent an hour fitting a padlock and hasp to the door of one of the upstairs rooms in the front, then dragged up a heavy table from the kitchen and set it in front of the window.

When nightfall came, he levered off two or three of the horizontal slats of the once-green shutters, close to the bottom, near-level with the table top, and in the early morning he set his Bren gun up on it so that the barrel pointed straight across the dried-up fountain and the unkept garden, across the black tarmac of the road, straight at the big iron gates of the building opposite.

He clipped a magazine on to the gun, peered carefully down the sights, went out of the room and locked the door carefully behind him. He brushed the dust off his clothes, and went out to buy some cigarettes.

CHAPTER 17

At five o'clock in the evening they released Bolec from the hospital. The wound on his arm was covered with a clean white bandage, and the deep gash in his chest had been sterilized and covered with an adhesive plaster.

Still clutching his half-empty bottle of rakia, he walked steadily in the white sunlight, blinking his eyes against it as he stared ahead of him, feeling the heat go out of it as the evening coolness prepared to move in from the desert, planting his great bulk heavily on his broad flat feet, his tiny porcine eyes alert and watchful.

At the entrance to the apartment building, he paused and looked around him, feeling the vengeful urge come over him, then went in and plodded up the long stone stairway in the cool white hall, pulling himself up by the black iron railing. He threw open the door to his flat, went in and slammed it shut behind him. For a moment he leaned against the doorway, panting heavily.

The Arab girl came running from the kitchen and stood watching him, half expectant, saying nothing. He took her to his bed, and made slow and heavy love to her, saying nothing, then rolling to one side and lying panting for a moment.

Then he got up and went to the cupboard and took a glass and poured himself a long drink of the rakia, and took a pistol from its hiding place under the prised-up sill of the window and laid it on the table beside his drink, and sat heavily in the damask-covered armchair and stared at the floor for a moment.

He said to the girl: "Get Ibrahim Shamar and Youssef bin

Mohamed, and Abdul Ramia. Tell them, come here now."

Then he took his drink, sipped it, watched her go out, stared at the faded family portrait on the wall, and waited.

When you cut your slow way through the thick papyrus of the Nile swamps, the dank steam rising out of the black water and the mosquitoes forming a vicious cloud about your head, and your long bush knife getting blunter with every stroke and your patience vying with your strength in reaching the point of utter exhaustion at which you can go no farther, then you suddenly come across the broad open expanse of wide water that is the immense broad river, stretching as far as your eye can see under the clear blue sky (and you know that it stretches farther still, out into the far distance of infinity, all clear and clean) and you know that suddenly, unexpectedly, all the frustration and difficulty and hopelessness is behind you and there is the smooth continuation stretching wide and clear ahead of you, all instantaneously, kaleidoscopically, suddenly dropped into place.

So with the affairs of policemen, and agents, and spies and counter-spies.

It was towards ten o'clock that night that Trent received the message. He sat at his desk, tired, and hungry, and surrounded with tobacco ash and cigarette stubs and papers and hastily scribbled notes. The sweat was pouring down his face and he knew that he had drunk too much cold coffee and wondered if he was getting a fever. Then Perugino came on the telephone.

He said: "Mr. Trent? I tried your house first...there is a little matter which you might like to know about."

Trent said: "Oh God! Not more bodies?"

"Yes. On the telephone, I cannot explain. But I am sure you would want to know what has happened. Perhaps you could come round here? To our friend's place?"

"To Bab-el-Louk?"

"Yes, Mr. Trent."

"Is he out of hospital? How is he?"

"He is in very good spirits."

"You mean he's drunk?"

CAIRO CABAL

"Oh no...he has recovered admirably. The doctor fixed him up very well, though he says the cleaning operation was very painful... He has even made an appointment for some...what shall I call it? For some fundamental surgery."

"Oh? Oh, I see."

"A very good man, the doctor."

"Well, I'll be round in about twenty minutes. I hope he hasn't finished that Scotch."

Trent put away his work, went and took a shower in the Colonel's private bathroom on the upper floor, locked up the office, and went out into the bright blue moonlight.

It was close to full moon now, and the sky was light with its gleam, no stars visible in the brightness except low down on the horizon across the river where Jupiter and Pollux glimmered faintly, trying to assert their distant temper over the cold brilliance of their closer rival. He walked down the driveway under the heavy-scented mango trees, watching the filigree of the jacaranda branches against the sky, feeling the crackle of a fresh layer of blossoms under his feet. He walked quietly in rubber-soled shoes, smelling the richness of the frangipani, reminding him as always of early mornings outside the night-clubs when little grubby children offered *leis* of their velvet petals, the thick white blossoms, tinged with bright yellow, strung together on khaki thread stolen from the Army depots. He remembered the cool sensual smell of them, watching them lying softly on full brown bosoms above low-cut dresses.

He thought of Jeannette and knew that she would be lying awake in bed with the gross Third Secretary and wondering if he would be sober, and then he went through the wrought-iron gates into the street; and the soft white cold of the Cairo night enveloped him in its rich blue shadows.

Bolec and Perugino were waiting for him when he arrived. He said at once:

"Well, what is it I'm going to disapprove of?"

Perugino glanced at Bolec. He said softly: "May I first offer you a glass of whisky?" Bolec nodded wisely. He said: "Maybe we all have little one. Is better. Is good Scotch. Very nice you bring it for me. I got good friends."

They spoke in subdued tones. Trent glanced at the kitchen door and saw that it was closed.

"All right," he said. "Who've you got in there?" There was an apprehensive nagging at the back of his mind.

Bolec said shortly: "Reizen."

"Oh, God..."

Trent sat down and took the glass which Perugino offered him. Glancing up in alarm, he said: "Is he...is he dead?"

"Oh no, Mr. Trent..." Perugino fell silent.

Trent drank and sat moodily for a moment, knowing that this was the answer, wondering what to do about it, knowing there would be hell to pay at the office. He gulped his drink down and sighed. "All right," he said, "let's have it. What's it all about? Are you trying to get me fired?"

"But no, Mr. Trent." Speaking quickly, volubly, using his delicate hands, Perugino said earnestly: "This matter does not concern you at all. It is only a matter of Bolec here, and as his friend, I do my best to help him. And as your friend—if you will allow me to call myself that—then as your friend, too, I insist that we must report it to you in case you can derive some good from it."

"I see. Got it all worked out nicely."

Bolec said stolidly: "This man try to kill me. What you think I do? You think I sit here and forget about this thing? Nobody stick knife in Bolec and me do nothing. Nobody. This Cairo. Not Prague any more. So I bring my friends here, say, 'You go out and get this man Reizen for me. Not my business how you get him. But you get him'. So they bring him to me."

"And then?"

Perugino said hastily: "We have not touched him, Mr. Trent. I insisted that you would not like such a thing. But he knows who Bolec is. He knows that Bolec's mother and father... He is a very frightened man. You said yourself, remember, that you would like to get hold of Reizen and beat the truth out of him..."

"I know, I know. There'll be the devil to pay about this..."

Perugino broke in eagerly. "But no, not at all. It is nothing whatsoever to do with you. If you wish, you can go now and forget that I ever telephoned to you. You have nothing to do with the local police...of course, we could hand him over to them, but we should never be able to prove a case against him. But since he tried to have Bolec killed..."

"You can't be sure of that..."

"He has admitted it." Perugino spoke softly.

"And so?"

"So surely we have a moral right to punish him for what he has done?"

"Moral right! You wouldn't know a moral right from a... The problem is not so simple, Perugino. Reizen knows me. I've met him a dozen times. And if saw you bring him here..."

Bolec said stolidly: "Nobody see him come. Ibrahim Shamar bring him in rickshaw. Abdul Ramia keep watch, Youssef hold little knife in his back. Reizen make no trouble. He come quick. No trouble and nobody see."

Trent looked at them both, knowing what he had to do, knowing he hated it and knowing that it would solve almost all his problems. He said: "You're a bunch of bloody scoundrels. If the office gets to hear of this..."

Pleased, Perugino said: "We'll keep this a good secret, Mr. Trent."

"Well...now that we've got him, what are we going to do with him?"

Bolec said impassively: "First, I teach this man little lesson. He not try to kill me no more." Trent shuddered at the sound of his voice. The big, fat, jolly man with the frying pan in his hand was no more. Bolec looked at him and said sharply, angrily: "This not a game!" He strode across the room and ripped the portrait off the wall, holding it out in his extended hand.

"Look!" he shouted. "Look this! You got family? Mother and father you got? One time I got, too. Now where are they? You tell me that, my friend, I not touch this man. You tell me!"

"I know...I know." He said at last. "Blindfold him. I'll talk to him myself."

Perugino glanced across at Bolec. His eyes gleaming strangely, he said:

"Perhaps it would be better, Mr. Trent, if you were to wait a little while. He will not talk so easily. Without a little persuasion, I am sure he will not tell you all you want to know. He will not even tell you the truth. In perhaps...in half an hour's time..."

Trent ran a tired hand over his face, feeling the stubble of his beard. For a long time he did not speak. He poured himself another drink and went to the window, opening the top of his bush-jacket and feeling the night air play on his chest. He would make no concessions to his conscience. At last he turned to them and said:

"Perhaps you're right."

He said bitterly: "I suppose you think I'm a bloody hypocrite."

"No." Perugino spoke gently. "But you have no interest in Reizen as the man who tried to kill Bolec. That is our affair only..."

"Our?"

"I will stay in case he needs my help. Two heads are better than one, don't you think? Don't you think so?"

Leaning against the wall, his face in his hands, pressing his fingers into his eyeballs, he said: "Then why the hell did you call me here now? You should have called me later...after..."

He felt sick suddenly. He said abruptly: "I'm going out for some fresh air. I'll be back in half-an-hour."

He stood up, averting his eyes, and went to the door, not looking at them, feeling them watching him. He stood for a moment at the doorway, pondering his Anglo-Saxon squeamishness, worrying over the essential differences between the fierce emotions of the Slavs and the soft restraints of those who had been cradled in the sacrosanct security of the English past.

"You English," Bolec had said, "you English always occupy; you have never been occupied..." And the fierce, cold calculation of hatred was beyond him.

He went quickly down the stairs, his feet making small padded sounds on the steps, and walked out into the night. He stepped off the curb and crossed the road, his hands in his pockets, his long chin sunk on his chest, unconscious of his open jacket, feeling the heaviness in his heart. He remembered a Czech he had known during the war, an officer whose legs had been coldly broken by some secret policeman or other, what was his name? "You English," he too had said, "you English will never make good soldiers because you do not hate enough. You want to live too much..." and he had gone out to fight and to bleed his life and his sophistry away in a burning, bombed-out building, and to leave his weeping women behind him.

"*You do not hate enough.*"

He kicked violently at the curb or the other side of the street and walked to the corner, buttoning up his jacket, and went into the bistro there.

At the door, he pulled up short.

Sitting in the corner, close by the window, a glass of wine and a saucer of sunflower seeds in front of him, sat Kamel Irani.

As Trent stared at him, he picked up a seed, split it delicately with his teeth, and blew the husk to the floor. He looked away.

Trent strode angrily over to the table and pulled out a chair. He was conscious of a rising temper and stood feeling the solid wood of the chair under his hands, his fingers twitching. Controlling himself with an effort, he said in Arabic: "Isn't it time we had a talk, Irani?"

Kamel Irani looked up, mildly surprised. There was mildness and inoffensiveness clear on his face. He spoke quietly. "If you insist." In English, he added. "Won't you sit down, please?" He gestured towards the chair, a mild and friendly gesture, his little eyes smiling.

Trent switched to English. "Would you mind telling me why you are watching that apartment? And just what the hell you're up to?"

Irani said gently: "Do you think this is a good place for us to talk?"

"No, I don't. Where do you suggest?"

"We could go to my hotel. It is not too far."

Trent laughed shortly. "No," he said. "I think not."

Kamel Irani raised his eyebrows. Trent saw with annoyance that he was faintly amused. He said: "I assure you, Mr. Trent, we have a great deal to talk about. And as for your wise precaution..." Still smiling, he pulled a Mauser automatic from his pocket, sliding it unobtrusively into his lap.

Trent gripped the edge of the table with his hands; he had a mental picture of the almost empty room behind him, the barman half asleep at the counter, a solitary woman perched on a stool at the bar.

Irani slipped the magazine out of the weapon, threw back the barrel, and laid the two pieces on the table.

"There," he said, "take it. Take it. I assure you I have no other. It is a good gun, a new one, as you see. I bought it only this morning." Nodding his head pleasantly, he insisted: "Go on, take it."

Trent said: "How did you know my name?"

Irani raised his hands, exhibiting the broad calloused palms.

"I must confess that until a few days ago, I did not know who you were. My officer suggested that I should get in touch with you when, and if, necessary. I did not think it expedient for me to be seen with you just yet; or even to come to you for help which I did not need. I'm afraid your own impetuosity has breached that little piece of security."

Trent said sourly: "This is all very interesting. Just who the hell do you mean by your office?"

Irani stood up and made a little bow, the friendliest of indications. He sat down and said:

"My name is Kamel Irani, and I am a major in the Turkish Army." He spoke softly, his voice soft and restrained, almost inaudible. Trent stared at him, disbelief clouding his features. Irani went on: "Naturally you will want me to prove this. I fear I do not carry my identification with me in a very accessible place...a precaution which has already proved a wise one. In any case...I will present my credentials to you at your office in the morning if I may."

Trent picked up the shell of the automatic. He scowled at it for a moment. "And you're here on official business, I take it? Have you reported to the Egyptian Government?"

Kamel Irani smiled gently, the creases at the corner of his eyes deepening humorously. "The nature of my business does not permit it... I am sure you will understand that. I came to take over the work that one of my agents had been doing alone...it became a little too much for one head to puzzle out. Shall we go for a stroll? There is much I would like to tell you. Or would you rather have a glass of wine here? We can talk quietly, I think." He looked around the room.

Trent put down the gun. He said briefly: "Let's go for a walk."

Irani dropped a ten-piastre piece on the table, slipped the automatic into his pocket with a gesture: "May I?" and stood up.

CAIRO CABAL

Trent noticed a long scar down the side of his neck as he pulled the chair away. They went out into the street.

The *midan* was deserted, and the babble of the market at Bab-el-Louk, where the trucks were beginning to arrive from the fertile countryside of the delta, bringing their goods for the morning's trade, off-loading their cabbages and melons and bananas and okra, the drivers and the porters distantly shouting and cursing each other, came to them muted and remote. They strolled along slowly, side-by-side, hands in pockets, taking in the cold fresh breeze.

Irani said: "Forgive me that I have not already been to see you. There was much I had to do first, and your own position here is a little...a little like mine, unofficial, is it not?"

Trent nodded. He said: "You won't mind if I say nothing until I've had a chance to check up on you?"

Irani chuckled. "Of course, of course. At this stage, I think we can help each other quite a lot." Walking quietly along the street, he said:

"As you know, my country is a partner with yours in the North Atlantic Treaty Organization. So...our defenses are against the same potential enemy. I should add that I am employed by the Turkish Government, not by NATO. Information has reached us from Moscow, where our penetration is tolerably good, that the Russians are organizing very considerable resistance to the NATO plans to bring the Middle East more closely into its defensive orbit...you are acquainted, of course, with all this political background—infiltration, sabotage, propaganda, the usual kind of thing which we are both quite accustomed to. But we learned from our agents there that a man named Racoski was coming out here to take over the Egyptian part of this business. Now, we know Racoski very well. He is a mechanically precise saboteur of very high caliber, Mr. Trent, and the party man of some consequence who does not waste his time on matters of any but the greatest importance. We learned that he was to bring the final plans—into this country, and to organize an uprising here which would make the 1952 riots seem a mere...a mere squabble by comparison. It is all aimed, I fear, at the British...as the handiest scapegoats, because of certain negotiations which your Government is at this moment conducting with the Minister of External Affairs. I cannot stress this too much..."

Irani stopped walking and turned to him. "I cannot stress too much the scope of this uprising and the damage that is being planned. Our agent here provided us with a great deal of alarming intelligence. And I was sent here to inquire into this matter and to report back to my Government. As soon as I arrived, I quickly found out that the position was far more serious than we had believed. I myself have been under almost constant surveillance, although I am sure that the Egyptians themselves do not suspect me. In fact, I was attacked and robbed in my hotel...not a common thief, I assure you. Meanwhile, my agent here, a young Turkish girl who posed as a cabaret dancer, was murdered."

"You mean Princess Higran?"

Irani looked at him sharply, standing silhouetted against the light of a street lamp, his hands raised in gesticulation, hesitating. He said slowly: "Then you know about Higran?"

"Go on."

Irani started walking slowly. He said: "Higran Hanem... Princess, of course, ...a *nom-de-guerre*...Higran was working for me, since I had to keep well under cover. I do not know how they discovered what she was doing. She was a good agent, a very good one, if sometimes a little careless on trifling, unexpected matters; you know how it is. An agent must be good all the time. In this business, there is no second try. But I found out who killed her."

"Yes?"

"Yes. She was killed by an Egyptian named Shakri bin Mohammed Youssef, on the explicit instructions of a man called Reizen, who is officially a Tass correspondent here, but actually an MVD man. I do not know how he penetrated her cover...what mistake she must have made. But I do know, Mr. Trent, that he found out and had her killed."

They came to the end of the street, and Irani took his arm and gently shepherded him back the way they had come.

Trent said: "I see. And why were you watching that apartment?"

Irani stopped again. He said: "Reizen is there now. I was going to see him, when I saw you arrive. Now, I am waiting for him to come out."

"I see."

Trent sighed deeply, filling his lungs with the clean air. "And what..." He broke off. "And when does this man Racoski arrive? It all seems to hinge on that. Do you know?"

"The last news I had was about six days ago. He left Moscow for Prague, and was about to travel to Athens. Our agents in Moscow are sure of that. They do not yet know when he moves on to Cairo. Unfortunately, in Prague, our people have not been able to find any trace of him at all." He said apologetically. "You understand, for a long time, the Russians have been our enemies, our traditional enemies. In Moscow, we are well organized. In Central Europe, it is a little more difficult for us and our information is not always so reliable. But this I do know. Racoski will shortly arrive to take over from Reizen, and when he does, then all the answers we have been seeking will become apparent. And then it will be too late to do anything at all but weep. I know this man Racoski. He is not a man to waste time. When he arrives, you may expect trouble. Bad trouble. Murder on an immense scale."

"Well..." Trent said abruptly. "This seems to have cleared the air a little bit. I wish I'd known who you were before. It would have saved me a great deal of trouble."

Irani was smiling apologetically. "You understand how it is? If you will forgive me...our sense security in my country has been sharpened by long necessity. We are not a great power. We cannot afford to make the mistakes that lead to wars. And so...we like to work alone. But," he added hastily, "very soon I would have come to see you, I think."

Trent said: "And now?"

"Perhaps in the morning I could present my credentials?"

"Please do. You know where my office is? Or is that a stupid question?"

"I know where it is. At about eleven o'clock?"

"At eleven then. Now, if you'll excuse me..." Trent offered his hand and Irani took it in a firm, heavy clasp. Still holding his hand, Irani said: "Mr. Trent..."

"Yes?"

"Are you going back to that apartment? To Reizen?"
"Yes. I am. Why?"
"Just curiosity...forgive me."

He dropped Trent's hand. He said "Goodnight, Mr. Trent," and turned and walked quickly back to the bistro. Watching his heavy form moving swiftly and silently away, plodding but quick, Trent had a feeling of relentlessness; at the back of his mind the fearful thoughts were worrying him again, nagging him, intruding upon his well-being. He thrust them roughly out of his way and walked quickly to the market at Bab-el-Louk. In one of the telephone booths by the lamp-lit, noisy stalls, he called the office. When the duty officer answered, he said:

"John Trent. Get an urgent cable to Istanbul, will you? I want to know all about a Major Kamel Irani of Military Intelligence. Get a detailed description, in a hurry. All right?"

The duty officer said: "Got it. John?" His voice was low and subdued at the other end.

"What is it? I'm in a hurry."

There was a pause. At last he heard: "There's a report just come in from Port Said...I'm afraid it's very bad news, John."

Trent felt a coldness creeping upon him. He said tightly: "Go on."

"It's Jeanette...and Saul..."

The fear was mounting up inside him. He felt a tingling at the back of his head.

"I'm afraid it's very bad news, John. Their car was ambushed...on the Port Said road...you'd better come and see the report..."

"Are they...are both...both dead?"

"Yes, John."

"Shot?"

There was a long pause at the other end. Trent said savagely: "Were they shot?"

"No. The car went off the road and then...you know how it is with the Arabs...I'm afraid they were...they were mutilated."

Trembling, he held the receiver away from his ear. Vaguely, he heard the muted voice of the duty officer. "John...John...are you there?" He put the phone down and leaned heavily against the glass. Then he pulled himself together and went coldly out into the market. He went straight to the rooftop apartment.

Bolec and Perugino were waiting for him. He glanced at the closed kitchen door, then at the two men. Bolec was sitting stolidly at the table, his big broad face set and lined. Perugino said smoothly:

"He is blindfolded, Mr. Trent. He will not recognize you. Perhaps it would be better if you spoke to him in Arabic so that he will think that you are...that you are not English. He understands it very well."

Trent nodded. The distaste of his work was hard on him. He said nothing and went into the kitchen.

Reizen was sitting on the wooden chair, his hands bound behind him, and his feet tied firmly to the legs. He was slumped forward, limp against a restraining cord around his shoulders, his thin, angular head fallen sideways on his chest. Trent looked at him carefully; he could see no sign of violence and he took a deep breath. Reizen's eyes were covered with a bandage fashioned out of a kitchen towel. His face was dead white, and he was breathing heavily.

Trent said curtly: "Reizen?" There was a peculiar sensation attached to the interrogation of a man who could not see his questioner. "I want to know the answers to a few questions." He spoke in Arabic, enunciating with precise clarity, talking the accurate, throaty Arabic of the educated Egyptian.

Reizen's breathing was labored. He nodded his head. Trent said: "What about the Englishman Pearman?"

"What...what do you want to know about him?"

"Tell me what you've been planning."

"He...they will kill him."

"How?"

"A machine-gun. They will fire on his car outside the Trade Delegation."

"Who do you mean by *they?*"

"His name...his name is Omar Said."

"A hired assassin?"

"Yes."

"And when is this to be?"

"I don't know...I swear I don't know..."

"Then who does?"

"Only...only...I don't know."

Trent said savagely: "Tell me who it is, Reizen, or by God..."

"Racoski." The word was no more than a whisper. He saw that Reizen was trembling.

"Racoski? Who is he?"

"He is...he is my boss. Vladimir Racoski. He will kill me..."

"And when is he coming to Egypt?"

"He is here already. In Alexandria."

Trent felt the blood draining from his face. He said: "Here? Already? And now?"

"Tomorrow he comes to Cairo, to my house. Could I have some water?"

"How did he get here?"

"By freighter. They put him ashore on the beach outside Alexandria just before...just before you picked me up. Tomorrow I am to meet him at my house in Maadi."

"At what time?"

"At ten o'clock."

"Does he know you? Have you met him?"

"Yes...we were...we were trained together."

"Any code words...any special plans for this meeting? Tell me about it, Reizen."

"Give me some water...please..."

Trent said relentlessly: "Tell me about the meeting."

"At ten o'clock tomorrow night...he will come to my house in Maadi and I will...I will hand over to him."

"Hand over what exactly?"

"There will be...demonstrations. Demonstrations against the Government. Some rioting."

"And the Englishman will be assassinated?"

"Yes. And others too...many others. They are going to blow up a ship in Port Said, and the cotton mills at Giza and burn the British banks again. And the hotels... Could I have some water?"

Trent remembered the Colonel's words. "Who's financing all this?"

"Racoski will bring the money. I don't know how much."

"And then...how long before they start?"

"He will pay the lieutenants their money...it will take a day or two. And then, he will give the signal."

"Which is?"

"Pearman...the Englishman. If they fail, then there is a bomb in his hotel. The Semiramis. Please...I have told you all this...can I have some water?"

"When I've finished with you. Tell me about this man Racoski."

"He comes from Moscow. He is...he is my chief in the MVD."

"Is he coming alone?"

Reizen hesitated. "I do not know. Perhaps he will bring one man from Alexandria...to drive the car."

"Do you know who that is?"

"No...an agent...an Egyptian. Nobody." Reizen's voice was weak.

"What about you? Have you any other contacts here? At the Embassy?"

"No...not at the Embassy. I send my reports to a *poste restante*. A tobacco shop...at the corner of Sharia el Assam. I swear I don't know who it is. There is a man here...I don't know him...I only send my reports to the tobacconist's."

"All this work will have been put down on paper, I suppose. Where do you keep it all?"

"At my house..."

"Or at your office? Be careful, Reizen."

"At my house. It is the truth. I swear it... There is a wall safe in...in the living-room."

"And the key?"

"Under the...under the turntable of the gramophone."

"And why do you keep this in your house instead of in your office?"

"It is for Racoski...I am to hand it all over to Racoski. He will bring the money and pay it out to the people I have recruited. Then he will give the signal..."

"Pearman?"

"Yes...Pearman. Pearman will be killed and the riot squads will start work. Pearman is working with your Ministry...Ministry of External Affairs...who is in the pay of the British. He is negotiating an arms deal...a very big one. When this news is made public...your Government will fall."

"And then?"

"I do not know." Reizen's voice was almost inaudible. "This is out of my hands...politics...perhaps my Government will offer to help. I do not know..."

"Please, please give me some water."

"What about the Turkish girl? Who killed her?"

"A man called Shakri."

"On whose instructions?"

Reizen's hand fell forward on his chest, rolling over to one side. Trent took a handful of hair and jerked his head back. "Whose instructions?" He said savagely: "Tell me who told him to do it."

Reizen whispered: "I did." His head fell forward again.

"And the others?"

"No others...I do not know..."

Now was the time. Forcing himself to keep control, Trent said: "On the road to Port Said they're shooting at cars. The British Third Secretary and...and his wife...were killed. That too?"

Reizen whispered. "I do not know...I told some of them to...to practice...to rehearse...Perhaps..."

Trent fought back the tears that came into his eyes and blinded him. He said, almost hysterically: "A rehearsal!" He lifted the flat of his hand and struck Reizen a savage blow across the face, then put his hand to his mouth and bit his knuckles. Reizen moaned softly, his head falling back.

Trent said over and over again: "Murderer...murderer... murderer..."

He took out his handkerchief, fumbling with it, and blew his nose. He wiped the tears out of his eyes and stared at Reizen. Slowly, a new horror came over him.

Under the broad grubby bandage, a thin trickle of blood was seeping down the sides of Reizen's thin, bony nose. It was coming from his eyes.

CAIRO CABAL

Trent stepped quickly to the sink and was violently sick.

He stood for a long time over the bowl, gripping the cold sides of it with his hands, then bent forward and splashed some water over his face. He dried himself on a roller towel that hung down behind the door and went into the other room. Perugino and Bolec were watching him silently. His eye fell for a moment on Bolec's family portrait on the wall. Then he went to the window and stared down for a moment at the lighted windows across the street.

Not looking at them, he said abruptly:

"I have to go to the office to make some urgent arrangements. Don't let him go. He must stay here." At the door he paused and turned to Bolec, their eyes meeting. He said bitterly: "All right, you've had your revenge. Now leave him alone. You understand? Leave him alone."

Bolec nodded solemnly, his face set.

"And don't let him leave this place. You understand. He must stay here at all costs, until I tell you to release him. I've got to decide how we can do this...I'm trusting you, Bolec."

Bolec nodded again. He said quietly: "I do what you say, my friend. He stay here."

"And for God's sake give him some water. Give him some whisky, a lot." Trent looked at his watch. It was nearly one o'clock. He said: "I'll be back here in about two hours. All right? Then we'll see what to do about this. Meanwhile... See that he stays here."

As he went out, they exchanged glances. For a moment, nobody spoke. Then Bolec said:

"You think maybe he is angry, our friend?"

Perugino shook his head. "You do not understand these Englishmen as I do," he said. "They live on the edge of hatred...they do not like the hot blood that you and I have. And yet they do not like cold blood, either. Strange, isn't it? Their blood, like their soups, must be tepid. It is not considered sporting to be otherwise. Let's go out and have a drink, what do you say?"

Bolec protested: "You want a drink, I give you my rakia. Or we got this good bottle of Scotch. We can't go out...we can't leave this man alone."

"You think he will escape? A blind man, bound to a chair?

Where would he go? No...he is well tied. Come, let us go and have a glass of wine. Tonight I feel like wine. You have no delicacy, Bolec; there are times when nothing will do except good Italian wine—even times for a particular Italian wine. Tonight, I feel like some Marsala from the hot slopes of the Sicilian mountains where the people are savages...but remarkably skilled vintners. Under other circumstances I would prefer one of the lighter wines from my own Fiorenze, but tonight...I think Marsala will take the smell of blood out of our nostrils. Come..."

Bolec hesitated. "I don't know...maybe we better stay here..."

Perugino went into the kitchen and looked at the cords that bound Reizen. He said softly: "*Communista!*" and spat in his face.

Then he went back into the room, and stood by the open doorway, waiting. Bolec said: "Ah, well...if you say so." Still protesting, he accompanied Perugino down the broad white stairway and out into the street. They crossed the road and passed the bistro on the corner.

Bolec said: "In here...is not too far..."

Perugino took his arm. "No, my friend. We go to the Italian restaurant across the *midan*. A few minutes only...we will come back in good time to meet our friend. And you know? To tell you the truth, I think he has gone out to get drunk."

They walked silently across the square to the bright yellow lights of Alfredo's and went into the bar. Perugino paused to pat the behind of a girl who was sitting there alone. "*Ciao cara*," he said, and the girl smiled at him. He leaned forward across the counter and said to the barman: "Two glasses of Marsala, *per piacere*." Turning to Bolec he said happily: "I pay...no, no, I insist. This time, it is on me."

They went to a table, opened the backgammon board, and began to play.

CHAPTER 18

The students were rioting again.

They raced through the streets, the coat-tails of their European clothes flying behind them, smashing everything that was European. For some of them, it was a sacred duty; for others, it was a way to let off steam; for others, merely a chance to beat up somebody in the street and thereby assert their manhood; and some thought: "Well, let's have some fun, let's burn something. Let's tip some cars over, let's tear something down, let's show them that we can govern ourselves."

This was the dangerous time. The minds of these young men were not all twisted. They were too young, and they had seldom known the rod. Individually, they would squirm, and argue, and giggle, and finally give way; but together, two thousand of them, it was: "Watch me, watch me beat up this old man, see what I did, I set fire to a car"; and then run off shouting: "Down with the foreigners", or "Down with the English", or "Down with the Americans", or the Greeks or the French; it didn't matter down with whom, as long as it was down with somebody, somebody to beat and revile and blame for a thousand years of poverty.

And there were stones and sticks lying in the square, and how did they get there?

And pavings were pulled up, and there was an iron bar, and somebody protested and a fight started, and when it was over there was blood on a crumpled white shirt on a silent, twisted figure, and the crowd raced on, a mob now. And there were knives and a few pistols. And the police, who had grinned and watched it at first, now started shooting teargas shells, and finally bullets, and when it was all over, the students stood silently watching the bodies that lay in that attitude that can mean only one thing, grouping furtively round corners, apprehensive and frightened, and then going back to their lessons.

The two men sat under the shadow of the grey stone statute of the great Khedive Ismail and watched.

Stubbing out his cigarette on the base of the smooth stone monument, one of them got to his feet; the other man rose quickly.

The first man said: "See how it works?"

"The police must be kept off the roads."

"Of course. That will be arranged. All you have to do is keep them at it. There will be no police."

The second man said suspiciously: "No police? It's not possible..."

"No police; just keep them at it. When it starts to flag, make a speech. Throw a bomb. Wave a flag. You know what to do..."

The second man nodded: "You mean the police will be on our side?"

"Of course. What else? But don't you worry about that. You're paid to do one thing only. If you don't like it..."

"No, no...I only thought..."

"Don't think. Do what you're paid to do. How much money have you in the bank?"

The second man stared. "In the bank?" He threw back his head and laughed, his face crinkling, his eyes shining. Now, he was a lovable character, happy with the incongruity.

"My friend," he said, "how would I get money in the bank? In the bank! Banks are not for the likes of us..."

The first man laid a long-fingered hand on his sleeve. He said earnestly: "I have money in the bank." The second man was suddenly respectful.

"In the bank?"

"By God. In the bank. Listen. How did I get money in the bank? I'll tell you. I got it by doing what I was paid to do. Not by worrying will the police be on our side. That's not my business. Somebody says: 'You do this, I pay you ten pounds'. I do it. I don't say 'What about the police?' You don't want to do this, *ma'desh*...I get somebody else..."

"No, no, I want to do it..."

"You see what I mean. Now I give the orders. Now I have money in the bank. Never mind how much. Money. In the bank."

Silently, awed, properly impressed, the second man looked at him and nodded.

CHAPTER 19

Trent let himself into his office with his own key, and went straight up to see the duty officer. It was Charlie Morgan. He was sitting back at his desk, his feet up, reading a pornographic novel by a man with the agreeable name of Walter Flogg. As Trent came in, he dropped his feet off the desk and sat forward with a crash. Getting up, slipping his novel out of sight, he stammered:

"Sorry, John...sorry I had to tell you about this. Do you...do you want to see the report?"

Nodding his head, Trent took the file from him and opened it.

Morgan said hesitantly: "If it's any consolation to you...Saul killed one of them with his bare hands... They left him there by the roadside when they made off...an Army lorry found them. If it had been a few minutes earlier..."

Trent said harshly: "I can read."

Morgan fell silent.

He put down the report and said: "Did you get my telegram off? To Istanbul?"

"Yes, of course." Morgan's handsome face was worried. Trying to get his mind off it, he said: "What's it all about...this Kamel Irani thing?"

"The Turks have sent one of their MI men here without letting us know about it."

"Well, we don't run things here anymore. No reason why they should let us know, is there?"

"True enough. It would have saved me a lot of bother if I'd

known before... But he's a good man. Seems to have done a lot in the time he's been here. Useful man to have around."

"This Pearman thing?"

Trent nodded. "It's falling nicely into place. Well, perhaps *nicely* is not exactly the right word, but... You know a man called Reizen? Sergei Reizen?"

"That bastard? Tass correspondent, among other things."

"Do you think anyone would miss him if he got killed?"

Morgan looked at him curiously. "Bit off your line, that sort of thing, isn't it?"

"Well, nothing to do with me really." He was talking quickly, forcing his grief to the back of his mind. "But I don't think he'll live very much longer. It's worrying me a bit. It's easy to think that you ought to step in and prevent...even with a man like Reizen..."

He paused and stared at the wall. He said bitterly: "They tell us not to blame the Egyptians...they're being misled...outside interference... Then who can we blame? Five thousand miles away a man sits at a desk in a cold office and stirs up trouble, and out here...five thousand miles away...they pass his orders on and somebody dies...like that...it's not even a clean way to die. She must have been wishing I'd been with her...I could have done something; something...or if not, it would have helped it I'd just been there with her..." He could feel the wetness on his cheeks. Morgan looked away from him.

He took out his handkerchief and rubbed it over his face. He said: "Have you got a drink on you?"

Morgan smiled quickly, nervously. He took a flask of brandy from the drawer in his desk and handed it to Trent. "Have to drink out of the bottle, I'm afraid. Won't do to leave the glasses lying around for the juniors on the day shift to smell..." His voice petered out.

Trent said: "You're a good fellow, Morgan. What about my cable? When do you expect a reply?"

"Any time now. I had them call on the screamer crystal rather than wait for the next schedule, so they know it's urgent. It doesn't take long provided they've got the information to hand. Where will you be for the next couple of hours or so?"

"Probably at the Colonel's. I'll keep in touch. Actually, it's just a precaution. I think the man's genuine enough. Let me use your phone, will you?"

He reached for the green enameled instrument and dialed the Colonel's house. As he heard the faint buzzing at the other end, he looked at his watch. It was nearly two o'clock. Presently, the Colonel's sleepy voice answered. He said:

"John here, Sir. Sorry to wake you up. Could you switch on your scrambler, please?" He waited till he heard the faint click of the switch and the Colonel said, wide awake now: "All right John, go ahead."

"It looks as though D-Day is almost on us, Sir. Any time now."

"Oh? Oh? What's happened?"

"First of all, there's a man arrived from Moscow to start the ball rolling and to take over from Reizen; he arrived this morning—or yesterday morning, that is—at Alexandria. At this moment he's somewhere between here and Alexandria, and the only place we can be sure of getting him is at Reizen's house in Maadi, which is his destination. The attempt on Pearman is set up, and they're waiting for him to give the word as soon as he's paid out all the group-leaders..."

"Where's Pearman now?"

"He's still at the hotel, Sir..."

"Get him out of it at once. Immediately. Get him round to the Malika Farida apartment and keep a man with him. Do it now; I'll hold the line."

Trent said to the duty officer: "Get Henson or Bradley on the other line. At the Semiramis. Tell them to take Pearman round to the apartment right away. Don't stop to pack his clothes or anything. He's to stay there till I get in touch with him." Morgan reached for the phone. Trent said into the receiver: "All right, Sir. Henson's getting him out..."

"I think you'd better come round and see me, John. Have you got time?"

"Yes, Sir. I'll be there in about ten minutes. There's one other thing, Sir, that'll interest you. I've been talking to Kamel Irani. He seems to be a Turkish Military Intelligence body. I'm checking on that now, but I believe he's genuine."

"Oh? Oh, that's very interesting indeed." There was a pause at the other end. Then: "In that case, what about Higran?"

"His agent here. She was killed by Reizen's men."

"I see...that's very interesting. It would account for a lot of things."

The Duty Officer was gesticulating at him, making signs with his hands as he replaced the other telephone.

Trent said: "Just a moment, Sir." He raised his eyebrows at Morgan.

"All right, Henson says he'll have him out in two minutes and round at the flat in five."

"Good." Into the phone, he said: "Pearman's on his way out, Sir."

"Good." The Colonel said: "Come and see me, John. I'll be waiting for you."

"In ten minutes, Sir." Trent rang off and flicked back the scrambler switch. He went out into the deserted garden, jumped into the Jaguar, and sped off to Gezira.

The Colonel was waiting for him in the big house on the island which stood just across the road from the smooth green turf that swept steeply down to the edge of the Nile, where the houseboats were moored and the long *dahabiyahs* lay close to the bank, their tall masts towering high above the bright-red frame-trees which now glowed faintly purple in the luminescence of the blue night sky, their sails furled tightly about their booms, and their long sweeping oars stowed darkly away out of sight.

He was in his dressing-gown. He said amiably: "Come on in, John, come in and sit down." Glancing at the clock, he said: "Have you had dinner, or breakfast, or whatever it is? I've got a very fine Stilton cheese if you're interested..."

"No, thank you, Sir," Trent said hastily. "As a matter of fact, I haven't got too much time."

"And Pearman's out of the hotel? Whisky and soda?"

"Yes, he'll be on his way to the flat already. Just a splash, please. Thank you."

The Colonel indicated a chair and sat on the grey leather sofa. Looking around the big room, finely furnished in taste and quality, he hardly knew how to begin. Walking up and down the deep blue carpet, feeling the beard on his chin, conscious of the pipes and the tobacco and cigarettes that bulged out of his pockets, feeling scruffy and uncouth in this comfortable elegance, he said slowly, staring into his drink:

"Well, there's a man here from Moscow, called Racoski, Vladimir Racoski, who's apparently a saboteur of some quality and a big man on the MVD; he was put ashore at a point on the beach just outside Alexandria. That's a good thing, because it means automatically that he can't go to the police if there's any trouble, which I suspect there might easily be..."

"No." The Colonel broke in. "Not at all. It's the safest way to arrive, and with eight hundred miles of almost unpatrolled beach on the coastline, it's the easiest. But he's certain to have friends in the police force...influential friends. He'll have no difficulty with the police, I can assure you."

"Mmm...yes, I suppose so. Anyway, he's going to Reizen's house in Maadi tomorrow night—tonight, that is, and I want to be there to get him when he arrives."

"You mean kidnap him? It's risky, John. Damned risky."

"Is there any other way, Sir?"

"And suppose you're successful. What then?"

Trent said carefully: "If all goes well, I think we should hand him over to the *junta* with an explanation of the case. After all, if Racoski were to pull this thing off, they are the people who would be put out of Government. Providing we take it up at a high enough level... I'm also hoping to get his papers, and Reizen's plans for the whole scheme; we'll have plenty to offer them..."

"Only a couple of days or so ago, you had never heard of this man Racoski. Where's your information coming from?"

Trent said uncomfortably: "I have a couple of new sources, Sir."

"New ones? Untried? Is Bolec one of them?"

"There's Bolec, and Perugino, and Kamel Irani...most of it comes from Kamei Irani..."

"Who may or may not be what he claims to be."

"I'm expecting a reply to my check on him now, Sir. Any minute now, from Istanbul."

"And if he's not?"

"Then we still have a few more hours to reconsider. But I believe he is what he claims to be...what he had to say was too...it rang very true, Sir."

"Have you cabled London about Racoski?"

"No, Sir."

"If he's an important figure, they just might have something on him. What about Reizen?"

"I have him under surveillance, Sir." He was dreading another question. He tossed his drink back, feeling the Colonel's shrewd eyes on him, knowing that nothing escaped them. The Colonel said mildly: "Help yourself to the Scotch, John. And your information about those papers of Reizen's that you hope to get...how good is that?"

"I believe it's good, Sir." Trent poured himself a glass of whisky and splashed some soda into it. The Colonel murmured: "I see..."

"You say that Racoski's bringing the necessary money for this picnic with him...if you get that, it'll hold things up considerably. Can't get very far in this sort of thing without a lot of money; a great deal of money." He was still watching him carefully. Trent said quickly:

"According to Kamel Irani, Racoski is bringing both the final plans and the money to pay off the leaders. Once that's been done they go to work. It gives us a little time, but not very much. May I use your phone, Sir?"

Colonel Brand nodded and sipped his drink, staring at him.

Trent lifted the phone and called the office.

"John. Switch your scrambler on." He waited. "Anything in from Istanbul yet?"

"Just come in. I'm in the middle of deciphering it. Be ready for you in fifteen minutes."

"Good, I'll be round by then. Meanwhile, ask London if they have anything on a man called Vladimir Racoski, of Moscow. MVD. Probably in their Oriental Affairs Branch, but could be anything else. Got it?"

"Have it off for you in five minutes." He rang off.

Colonel Brand said soberly: "You're sitting on a barrel of

dynamite, John. Be very careful how you go. Do you need more men?"

"I don't think they can be spared. I'll take Kamel Irani and Henson along to Maadi with me, and Bradley can stay with Pearman. He might need a relief, Sir. They've both been on day and night ever since this started. But I want Henson with me."

"I'll find somebody... Where is this meeting with Racoski to be?"

"At Reizen's house. In Maadi."

"What about Reizen? Will he be there?"

Trent said stolidly: "No, Sir. He won't be there."

The Colonel stood up, his hand thrust into the pocket of his red silk dressing-gown. "Be very careful, John. I'll take care of Pearman for you...keep him out of your hair. Have another drink before you go?"

Trent finished his drink and put it down. "No thank you, Sir. I've a great deal to do before tomorrow."

He went to the door. "There's one more thing, Sir." Feeling the pain inside him, he said: "Jeannette and Saul ran into an ambush on the way to Port Said last night. I'm afraid they're both dead. There's a report in the office." He blinked his eyes.

The Colonel stared at him for a moment, then dropped his eyes and turned away. For a long time he said nothing. Then he turned to him slowly. "I'm sorry, John," he said. "There's nothing much more one can say, is there?"

"No, Sir. Goodnight."

"Goodnight." The Colonel sighed and turned away again. Trent closed the door softly behind him.

He went out to his car and drove quickly back to the office, feeling the cold in his hair as he drove at speed through the deserted streets.

When he arrived, Morgan was just finishing the message, flipping the pages of the cypher books over rapidly with his left hand, writing with the other. He passed the top sheet across to Trent with a brief "First page..."

Trent read:

CAIRO CABAL

"Istanbul to Cairo. Subject is senior officer in local Military Intelligence, now working on 17-land infiltration of Arabic and Islamic countries stop he left Istanbul for Cairo about three weeks ago stop sorry about this but we would have informed you if we had known before stop he reports direct to Turkish C-in-C stop reported to be efficient and well organized in your home town stop his agent there is reported to be Turkish female dancer name unknown stop detailed description follows stop anything else you want to know about him query see my immediately following telegram ends"

Morgan looked up from the second sheet. "Bright boys. They sent the description separately. '*Five feet eight inches, weight two hundred pounds, complexion swarthy, eyes black, hair black...*' Well, what the hell did they expect in a Turk? Golden curls?" He went on: "'*Features heavy, scar on left side of neck, black moustache close-cropped...*'"

Trent said: "Skip it. That's the man. Did you get that cable off to London? About Racoski?"

"Of course. Enciphered and away before you'd put the phone down. Should have a reply by daylight. But they won't know anything; they never do, the poor dears."

"Well, I'll be at this number." He scribbled Bolec's number on the pad. "Give me a call if anything happens in the next couple of hours."

He went into the bathroom and had a quick shower, borrowed the Colonel's electric razor and cleaned the bristle off his chin, then went out and drove round to settle the Reizen problem.

He knew at once that something was wrong.

Bolec was sitting glumly on the edge of the table, his arms folded across his broad chest in the attitude of a man who knows there is going to be trouble and is prepared to face it. But Perugino... Perugino was plainly frightened. He looked away nervously as he opened the door and mumbled, "Come in, Mr. Trent, come in please..." His self-assurance was gone. His face was pale. His fingers were twitching.

Trent looked from one to the other. "Well?" he asked. Then he made for the kitchen door. "Reizen! He's gone!"

Perugino ran in ahead of him, scuttling under his feet like a rabbit.

"No!" he said. "No, Mr. Trent. Mr. Trent...please do not go in there!"

He stood with his back to the kitchen door, throwing out his arms like a wife whose love is hiding in the broom-closet.

Trent turned to Bolec. "Well?" he said grimly. "What is it?"

Bolec slipped off the table and stood scowling. He said:

"Shakri was here."

"Shakri? What the devil..."

"Shakri. Perugino and me, we go out to take little drink after you go away. I know this man Reizen not escape, we tie him good. When we come back, after maybe half-hour, I find front door open. I run in quick, because when we go out, I lock it. Don't know how he get inside, Shakri don't know how to open locks like this one, is very special kind, but never mind, he get in. I run in quick, go to kitchen, find Reizen dead. I not kill him, Mr. Trent, I promise you. I not kill him...somebody else do it. Must be Shakri."

"Why Shakri, for Heaven's sake? Did you see him?"

Perugino said: "No, Mr. Trent. We were too late, I'm afraid. But it could be nobody else. No one knows Reizen was here...indeed, I cannot suggest how even Shakri found out, but only Shakri could have the motive. In self-protection. He knows what would happen to him after his fiasco with Bolec...so he killed Reizen in self-protection. But I think we can deduce something else, Mr. Trent..."

"Oh, shut up! For God's sake shut up!" Trent sank into the chair and covered his tired eyes with a weary hand. He said: "I'm sorry, Perugino. Too much on my mind tonight. What were you going to say?"

Perugino said primly: "I was going to offer the deduction, Mr. Trent, that it was Shakri who killed the girl Higran."

"Oh? Why do you say that?"

Perugino said softly: "The method, Mr. Trent. It was the same way..."

"You mean...?"

"Yes, Mr. Trent. All over the floor."

There was that bestial look in his eyes again. Perugino was

trembling, his eyes bright, his fingers twitching nervously. He said:

"I think perhaps Shakri was watching this place, for some reason. He must have seen Reizen enter, and when we had all gone out, he must have realized that he was alone here. So he came up and killed him. The same way, Mr. Trent...it's horrible, isn't it?"

Bolec said sourly: "Make plenty mess in my kitchen. Now tell me how I get the body out of here, eh?"

"Just as I was on the verge..." Trent stood up. He said: "For God's sake give me some of that Scotch, Bolec."

Some of the load had slipped off his shoulders. He thought of Jeannette for a while, wondering if she had called to him while she died. He went to the window and watched the street for a while, staring moodily at the bistro across the way; the lights were still on and a woman was walking up and down the pavement outside. Kamel Irani, he knew, would have gone now; he would be sleeping peacefully under his mosquito net at the Lido, untroubled. Higran...Jeannette...they had something in common.

He said abruptly:

"Yes...how to get rid of the body. It's a problem. Can I leave it to you, Bolec? Perhaps one of your men...?"

Bolec nodded. "I fix. Is not too hard." He said to Perugino: "Maybe you go get Ibrahim Shamar for me? You know his place?"

"In the market?"

"In market. Tell him come quickly with two three men. Bring Army blankets. Only come quick, not too much time before daylight. I don't want no marks on the blankets, tell him. No numbers. You do this?"

Perugino nodded and scurried out. He shot a fascinated glance at the kitchen door before he went, and Trent felt again a sharp spasm of repugnance. He closed his eyes.

Watching him, Bolec said sympathetically: "Why you not take little sleep? You take my bedroom, I call you when you want. What you say, eh? Is good idea?"

Trent looked at his watch. It was nearly four o'clock. He thought for a moment.

"What about all this...? Reizen...?"

"Ibrahim and me, we fix this fine. You not worry."

"All right. It might be an idea...for a couple of hours."

He could hardly keep his eyes open. He said: "I'll lie on the bed for a couple of hours. Will you call me at six?"

Bolec nodded. He said hesitantly: "You think this is all my fault, Mr. Trent? Believe me please, such a thing should not happen..."

"No...it's just one of those things..."

"If I catch this man Shakri, I bring him to you." He said earnestly. "Is no-good, good-for-nothing Arab pimp. I catch him and bring him for you, yes?"

"Yes, you do that, Bolec. Will you call me at six?"

He went into the bedroom and laid down on the big brass bed that almost filled the room. He kicked off his shoes, opened his jacket, and before he could loosen his belt, he was asleep.

He woke a little while later and sat up sharply when he heard a bumping in the living room and subdued voices muttering in Arabic. Then he lay back and thought about Jeanette and about Higran, someone else's girl... He felt the tears coming to his eyes again.

Soon he was asleep.

CHAPTER 20

He was tall and thin and ragged, his aquiline features sharp in the bright blue light of the moon, the pale yellow glare of the lamp around the corner painting half his body with its aquatint, striking sharply on his hands as he gesticulated vehemently, using his fingers with short, expressive gestures, arguing angrily.

In the shadows about him, a dozen men hung on his words, watching him, agreeing with him, admiring the fine frenzy of his phrasing. One or two were smoking, cupping the lights from their cigarettes in their hands, watching carefully over their shoulders from time to time. Farther away, where the lane met the main road, a man stood in the darkness, watching for the police, his bright black eyes sharp and alert.

"*Islah...arms...baroud...gunpowder...rassas...bullets...*"

The words were whispered, but vehemently, angrily, with all the pent-up hatred of a man long oppressed. He threw his long coat open suddenly, a dramatic gesture. His cloth belt, a dozen yards of cotton wound tight around his thin stomach, was sagging with the weight of the pistols it carried. There were Brownings, and Lugers, and Walthers, and Berettas, some new, some old, some rusted, some bright and still gleamingly oiled. He pulled them out one by one and started handing them round, whispering their names as he did so:

"Ahmed...Suleiman...Musa...Said...Shafik..."

He took out a cigarette and somebody eagerly lit it for him.

He stood for a moment watching them as they tucked the weapons away in the deep dirty folds of their *gallabiyas*, sucking on the cigarette, drawing smoke of the pungent hashish deep into his wasted insides. He said:

"Hide them...do nothing...nothing...wait till the money comes. Is it understood? Nothing...nothing till the money comes..."

They nodded eagerly, tucking their guns away, making them comfortable about their waists, breaking into little chatting groups, whispering together, conspiring.

The man at the end of the passage whistled once, shrilly. The leader glanced over his shoulder towards him, moved quickly, spoke once. There was no more than the gentle pad of bare feet on the roadway, and when the policemen, fingering their slung rifles nervously, holding each other by the hand, their fingers intertwined in Muslim affection...when the two policemen walked into the alleyway, it was bare and empty and blue with the silent moon.

The pair stood there for a moment, staring about them in the empty silence, watching the long shadows of the lamppost, yellow-flanked with its own light on one side, blue-washed with the moonlight on the other. A cat walked solemnly across them, and paused as a garbage can suddenly clattered, tensing its body sharply, crouching in savage expectancy, its tail flickering.

The two policemen watched it for a moment, looked about them for a moment more, then shrugged and went on their way. The cat watched them go, then darted into the darkness and was gone.

Only silence was left.

CHAPTER 21

Bolec called him at six o'clock.

He stretched and yawned, in the strange brass bedstead, and scratched his stomach and ran a hand through his tousled hair, then slipped on his shoes, buttoned up his jacket, and went round to his own apartment. He took a hot bath with a bottle of rubbing alcohol tipped in it, shaved and dressed cleanly, wondering how long he would keep his khaki fresh and stiff, ate some breakfast, lit his pipe, and drove round to the office.

At eleven o'clock in the morning, he was sitting at his desk, two cups of Turkish coffee in front of him, talking with Kamel Irani.

The Turk was neatly dressed in a grey silk suit and white silk shirt, his thick fighter's wrists blackly hirsute in his French cuffs, his bull neck bulging over the top of his long-pointed collar. He sat hunched up on the chair, his broad forearm spread out on the desk, leaning forward, talking amiably. He said:

"You will agree, of course, that there was no need to announce myself to you when I first arrived here." Smiling, he said: "You know how we each distrust each other's idea of security in this sort of business? In my country, we are perhaps more zealous than most in guarding our secrets...but now that we are together, please count on me to cooperate in any way that I can." He spoke neat, precise English, accented faintly with the cosmopolite's French overtones.

Trent offered his cigarette case. "Of course...our methods may not be the same..."

"Methods? This is not a game, my friend. Any method is

permissible that has the desired results. In my country, we cannot take risks; a single mistake can mean...obliteration. For the great powers, the risk is just as great; but they can recoup with a war which they have the power to wage. We do not have that power."

Trent said mildly: "Nice to learn how we appear to the outside observer... Do your approved methods include murder?"

Irani shrugged his heavy shoulders. "If necessary. The life of one man...it is very little, is it not, to discount against the costs of war?"

"Reizen would have been far more useful to us alive."

"So? Then Reizen is dead? Well, I will not grieve for him."

Trent said nothing. Irani went on, speaking suavely, firmly: "As far as I am concerned, Reizen does not exist...either as a dead man or alive. The work he has done...that is what matters. And that...we know about. He has ceased to be of importance."

"We do not know all that he has done..."

"No? Then permit me to enlighten you briefly."

He smiled disarmingly. Watching him curiously, Trent ruminated, "You're a charming old bastard." He could feel the calm power of the man under his affable manner.

"First of all, your man Pearman is to be assassinated. This, I do not doubt, you already know about since it concerns you intimately. This is to be the signal for an uprising; the usual pattern of revolt and destruction which will turn into a major revolution. They tried it once before with near success, you remember. But in January 1952, they did not seize the opportunity when it was within their hands; they retired from the scene too early, thinking that the Wafd, which was then in power, would attain their ends for them."

He raised a didactic hand. "That was a mistake. Instead, the Wafd Government fell. The Army took control and shortly after succeeded in restoring some sort of order and in putting an end to the monarchy. *Tant pis*. This time, my friend, they will not retire from the battle quite so quickly. That is why Racoski is coming here. The Wafd will be put back into power, and then our Russian friends will start to move in. First of all, economic help; then technicians; then troops. It is as simple as that. There will be murder, and arson, and looting, and destruction, and utter chaos; but the real trouble for us, my friend, will come when the apparent dangers are over."

"Most of this...some of it, we already know, of course. What surprises me," Trent said with spirit, "is that having found out all this you did not think it necessary to advise us here."

"Why should I? Forgive me, Mr. Trent. The Western powers are, by our standards, a little...a little easy-going in their security. In England, some of your own Foreign Office officials are not above reproach...is it not so? Must I recall names for you? And in America...in America the patriots are those who shout the loudest. These are things which we cannot risk having shouted in election campaigns, nor bandied about in the dilettante drawing-rooms of your Mayfair. Forgive me...it is necessary that I tell you this. Unless you understand why, in Turkey, in my small country which lies at the foot of the Russian mountains...why we are so careful with our secrets, then I fear that you will not trust me as fully as you must. Do I make myself understood? Do you forgive my bluntness?"

"I understand you. What do you propose to do now?" Irani's great shoulders heaved eloquently. "Now...there is very little we can do until Racoski arrives. We have our men in Europe looking for him now...soon, they will tell us when he is to come here, and then...then, my friend, we must act quickly."

"And suppose they do not find him? Suppose he arrives here unknown to us? What then?"

Irani was troubled. Nodding his head, he said: "There...there, my friend, is the difficulty. If he should arrive unknown to us... Meanwhile, I am keeping my Government informed of events here. I do not doubt that they will inform your Government at the proper time. This, my friend, is not my responsibility. I report only to my own C-in-C. What happens after that is his responsibility. A proper chain of command, is it not so?"

Trent said again: "Suppose Racoski should arrive unknown to us? What then?"

"Yes...I know. That is the danger."

His heavy face was deeply creased, the lines about his mouth tightly set. "I have a good many informants here...since Higran died it has been very difficult for me, but you must understand, it was not too long ago that this country was part of our Ottoman Empire. A great deal of articulate Egyptian opinion would like to see us in control here once again; so my sources of information here are many and varied. In this respect also, that we too are Muslims, it is a great deal easier for us here than it is for you. None the less...I would be far happier if I knew of this man Racoski's precise movements."

"He is here. He arrived in Alexandria yesterday." Irani was lighting a cigarette. He stopped short, holding the lighted match in his beefy hands, the flame flickering under his heavy brows and casting weird inconstant shadows across his startled face.

"Here? In Egypt?"

Trent nodded, watching him, conscious of a sudden pallor on his swarthy features. He said slowly: "Eastern Europe is not an easy place for us to work in nowadays...but I cannot believe that he could have left there...are you sure, Mr. Trent? This is not a thing to make a mistake about..."

"A mistake like the murder of Reizen?"

He held up a placatory hand. "Please, Mr. Trent, please forget this man Reizen. Remember only that he killed the girl Higran. Very well...I will admit that perhaps it was necessary to kill her...but in such a way, Mr. Trent? In such a manner? And sometimes a man's personal inclinations...the personal equation, it always leads us to do things we sometimes regret. I regret nothing, and I admit nothing...the matter in hand is of forbidding importance. We must act quickly." Using his finger violently, poking it into the air, he said: "There is no time for recriminations. Do you know where this man is?"

"I know where he will be tonight."

"Then we, too, must be there."

"That's what I had already decided."

Kamel Irani smiled again. He said softly: "Forgive me. I will regard this as your own territory and put myself in your hands."

Trent stood up. "Good. Then let's go and see the Colonel; he wanted to meet you. Colonel Brand."

Irani lumbered to his feet. "Colonel Brand," he repented. "I know him by reputation, of course. A good man. You are lucky to have him here."

They walked down the long dark corridor to the Colonel's room. Joan came to greet them as they went into the outer office. She said:

"Major Kamel Irani? The Colonel asked me to have you come in as soon as you arrived."

She stood and held the door open for them. Irani smiled at her, inclining his head, smiling affably.

Colonel Brand rose from his desk and walked towards them, holding out his hand. "Come in, come in," he said cheerfully. "Major Kamel Irani? My name's Brand...do come in and sit down. John." He said easily: "I see John has checked up on you; we had to wire Istanbul during the night. We'd been a little worried about you."

Irani was pumping the Colonel's hand, beaming at him. He said:

"A thousand apologies...I would never have given you so much trouble... This is a very great pleasure, Sir. I believe you know my chief? General Aris Bey?"

"Yes, I do. I had the pleasure of meeting him during the First World War. I was a very green subaltern, then, and he was a captain. On the other side." His smile robbed the words of their import.

Kamel Irani said smoothly: "Yes, fighting your allies, the Russians."

"*Touché*. When he was captured, I was unfortunately chosen to interrogate him. He led me the devil of a dance. If anybody else had believed the fantastic things he told me, and which I swallowed wholesale, I should have been cashiered. As it was, when I made an urgent report to the General Staff, I was very nearly laughed out of the Army... How is he?"

"He is well, thank you. He told me to look you up if I found it necessary to announce my activities to you." Tongue in cheek, he said: "I do not think our friend altogether approves of my secrecy..."

"What, John? Why of course, I'm sure he does."

"I have offered him my unqualified assistance. My services are at your disposal entirely."

The Colonel said happily: "That's excellent. Are you getting your heads together?"

"Yes, Sir."

Trent said: "There's one thing you should know, Sir. Reizen...is dead."

"Dead? Oh...I see. What's the story?"

"He was killed last night by an unknown person." Irani said smoothly: "The assumption is, *mon Colonel*, that someone was avenging the murder of the girl Higran."

There was a moment of silence; the Colonel shuddered, it was as though the name *Higran* were a pebble dropped into a pool that could no longer remain placid.

Trent waited, and the Colonel said at last, very quietly: "I see. You think Reizen was responsible for her death?" He got up and walked to the window and stared out at the peacock strutting there, and said: "Yes, yes...I knew her too. I even suspected that she might perhaps be an agent for...for whom? We can never tell. But she was kind, and gentle, and...understanding. There was escape in the touch of her flesh. Escape from everything."

He turned to look at Irani, and said harshly: "If Reizen killed her, then perhaps she will rest a little quieter now."

Trent was fidgeting, remembering. Colonel Brand glanced at him and said: "Does Major Irani know about Racoski?"

"Yes, Sir. I've told him that he's already here."

Turning to Irani, the Colonel said: "Have you any ideas on the subject?"

"He must be stopped at once. At all costs. If he reaches Cairo..."

"Quite so. What do you think we should do to stop him?"

"What would you do?"

Colonel Brand smiled.

Irani said: "My methods are perhaps more drastic than those of which you would approve. But this is certain; it is quite useless to hand him over to the police. There are too many of them on his side, far too many. Perhaps the Army might be better, but that also is risky."

"Then what do you suggest?"

Irani said evasively: "I am in your hands..."

Trent got up and took the cigarettes from the table, offering them the box. Irani shook his head and took out his own case, holding it out to them. Trent said:

"Mrs. Beeton's recipe for jugged hare... *'First,'* she says, *'first catch your hare.'* Let's get hold of our man first and then see what to do with him. A lot will depend on the papers he's carrying..."

"Of this, you can be sure," Irani said. "We know that Racoski is the key man. Without him the whole scheme will collapse completely. As you say, let us first put our hands on him."

The Colonel nodded. "It's a tricky business. The department cannot be involved in anything...but you know that, of course. I'm afraid it means leaving the baby squarely in your lap, John."

Trent nodded.

Irani got to his feet. Holding out his hand to the Colonel, he said: "I shall be happy to tell my chief that I had the pleasure of meeting you."

"When this is all over," the Colonel said, "perhaps you'll come and have dinner with me? Will you?"

"You are most kind. And when you come to Istanbul...my house, my servants...everything I have is at your disposal."

"That's very good of you. How long are you staying in Cairo?"

"When this is over...for a few more days. I have to find someone to replace my Higran. It is not an easy task..."

"Yes, I know. But come and see me as soon as you can. I have an excellent cook at home."

"And I have an excellent appetite. Perhaps in a few days' time?"

"Early next week then. I'll keep in touch through John. And meanwhile, please come and see me if I can help in any way. In any way at all."

The Colonel watched them go. As they got to the door Kamel Irani put an affectionate hand on Trent's shoulder, and they made way for each other with elaborate courtesy.

They lunched together at an Italian restaurant on Sharia Suleiman Pasha, consuming enormous quantities of cold meats and salads washed down with a great deal of white wine. They talked about the war, and the Egyptians, and the Suez Canal, and Turkey, and women, and liquor, and food, and by the time they had finished their friendship was firm. Irani went back to his hotel for a siesta, and Trent drove to his office to work.

He went round to see Pearman and found him writing up his notes on the conference, happily at home in the little office apartment, with Bradley standing guard like a watchdog. He brought with him a couple of clean shirts and some socks and ties and offered to send his clothes out to be pressed. He was sitting by the desk that was once by the window, but now, at Bradley's insistence, had been dragged into the center of the room. One of the Colonel's servants was there too, fussing about in the kitchen and making coffee.

Trent said, grinning: "How is the prisoner? Bed comfortable?"

Pearman nodded eagerly. "Very. I do think I'm putting you to an awful lot of trouble...Bradley's been awfully helpful."

"Good. How's the conference going?"

"Excellently. If nothing happens to upset it all... It's going very well, really. I didn't dare hope for such results. It's really a very delicate business." He hesitated. "How long...how long do you expect this to last...I mean, I'm escorted to the office and back, I'm not allowed to move out of Bradley's sight...I feel it must be an awful nuisance..."

"You mean you'd like a visit to the Pigalle again? I can send one of the girls over if you like..."

"Really, Trent, really...it isn't that at all." He said resignedly: "I'm not used to the scent of danger. I live a very prosaic sort of life, you know. I find it a little exciting...is that childish? But it's a little bit dull, too, you know, being cooped up like this. How's everything in the world outside?"

Trent protested: "Come now, you've only been here a few hours...it might go on for weeks..."

"Oh no...not really?"

"No, not really. Tonight's liable to see the end of it all."

"Good, that's splendid. What about those people we met the night before last...Jeannette and, what was his name? Saul something? How was the wedding? You know, in the excitement, I quite forgot to send flowers. I hope they won't think it remiss of me."

Bradley got up from his chair and went out on the verandah, turning his face away. Trent said: "No...I don't suppose it matters very much." He was silent for a moment. He said abruptly: "Is there anything I can get you? I'd better be on my way. Lots to do before tonight."

"No...there's nothing, really. Bradley's taking great care of me. And Colonel Brand told me to call him if there was any difficulty at all. And thank you for coming over. It was very good of you."

Trent nodded and went out.

At his office, he sat down and made plans for the evening's assault on the house at Maadi.

They set out at eight o'clock, soon after the moon had risen. The heat of the day had gone, and a thin wisp of cloud had drifted lightly in from the east, so thinly spread over the vast pale sky that it was no more than a faint and wispy gauze, a ghostly white transparency of the early night, as though this were all that had been left over from the harsher skies in other countries to the north where all the cloud that God could lay his hands on was needed to make men miserable. Here there was just a glimpse, a fragment, a suspicion of cloudiness left over that would have to do for the enormous open stretches of the desert where not very much was needed, really; and finally it had spread so fine and thin that it was almost gone and only the past suggestion of its presence was left behind, lightly floating over the vast infinities beyond the fertile strip of the river's banks. The *feluccas* were sliding silently by on the glass of the river that ran beside the road, their tall white cuneiform sails cutting like sharks' fins against the sky, sliding softly by in incredible silence.

Kamel Irani sat beside Trent in the front of the big black Humber from the office. In the back was Benson; sitting beside him, remotely pressing himself into a corner, was Kamel Irani's Arab.

That was how he had introduced trim. *"This is my Arab,"* he had said, and Trent had been content to leave it, at that.

He was tall, and thin, and his light blue Berber eyes were almost hidden in the thousand wrinkles of his brown and ageless face. He sat hunched up in his corner, muttering to himself at frequent intervals: *"Allah hu akbar, Allah hu akbar,"* as though to reassure himself that God in his greatness knew what he was doing and would protect him from the infidel who was driving the car...

"Allah hu akbar," he muttered, over and again, *"Allah hu akbar."*

The black tarmac road was smooth and seven miles straight as they followed the course of the wide river, the filigree trees tall and delicate beside them, and soon they came to the turn-off which led to the pretty little village, the garden village of Maadi. Trent pulled over on to the grass verge under the flame-trees and wild walnuts, and they got out and stood in a conspiratorial group around the car, standing quietly in the shadows of the trees and the tall thick hedges, listening to the sharp insistent croaking of the frogs, a monstrous cacophony of strident discord piercing the beautiful night.

Trent said:

"All right. It's fairly simple. The house lies down there..." pointing to the west, "at the edge of the village. It's the last house on the road, and the only one with two stories. Henson was out here to reconnoiter this afternoon, and there are what? Two servants in the house?"

"That's right, Sir. Just the two of them. Far as I could see, nobody else. Unless, of course, somebody turned up after I got back."

"Good. It's Friday, so the gardens will be flooded and the boards will be out..."

"Boards?" Kamel Irani asked. "What boards?"

"Twice a week, on Tuesdays and Fridays, they flood the whole of the village with water from the river. It brings in the fertilizer, the silt...they put duckboards down from the roadways to the doors of the houses. It's of no consequence, really... In any case, I'll try to get into the house quite openly by the front door. Henson, you go straight round to the back and come in as soon as I call you. Kamel Irani, will you take the garden with your Arab? There's plenty of time, so after I've got in I suggest we all have a look round, leaving the Arab outside to stand guard, and then about half-past-nine, if you'd go back to the garden and watch... Two of us in the house and two outside. I think it's fairly simple. Then we simply wait for him to turn up, hold him under guard until the morning, and then the Colonel will talk to the Army and see what to do with him. All right?"

Henson nodded. Irani said shrewdly: "We expect to take this man very easily. I hope we are not being too simple. I know him by reputation. He is a clever man. And quite ruthless. Let us make up our minds about one thing; we must be ready to shoot him down at once if necessary. If I had my way, that is what I would do. It would be safer."

Trent shrugged his shoulders. "There are four of us. He's bringing one man from Alexandria, a driver. We need expect no trouble from him. According to Reizen, he'll be coming straight to the house at ten o'clock."

"Suppose he should telephone first. What then?"

Trent kicked at the tires of the car. "Yes," he said slowly. "It's a point, isn't it? I thought perhaps we might leave the telephone off the hook. If he gets the busy signal, he'll wait and try again. Finally, he should decide that it's out of order and come in anyway. Don't you think so?" He turned an anxious face to Kamel Irani.

"Yes...yes. I imagine so. I don't think he will be expecting any difficulty. But please, we ourselves must expect it...we must be prepared for anything. For anything at all."

"Of course. Then shall we go? It's about two hundred yards to the house. I think we'd better leave the car here."

They walked quietly on the grass past the Maadi Club where the faint chatter of late diners came to them softly across the green lawns and the hedge, alongside the narrow irrigation canal under the red poinsettias and up under the hedge to the wooden gate of the big two-storied house on the corner. The tiny irrigation gates were open and the faint gurgle of water mixed with the throaty barking of the frogs. The crickets suddenly faded in their shrill and rhythmic shrieking in the mango tree that stood beside the gate. A six-inch layer of water covered the garden, a black layer of liquid mud that shone brightly in the moonlight. By morning, the tiny gates would be closed and the water would have seeped away, leaving behind it richer, riper, blacker soil, steaming gently in the morning sun.

Trent waited at the gate while Henson went quickly along the duckboard to the back of the house, and Kamel Irani, lifting up his trousers, stepped on tiptoe through the water and splashed gently off into the shadows of the hedgerow. Watching his great bulk move delicately through the mud, Trent laughed to himself.

He watched the Arab fade suddenly into blackness beside him, an unobtrusive, silent disappearance into the shadows of the foliage, and marveling at the eeriness of it, he went slowly towards the front door.

In the house itself, the lights were on. Through a lighted window at the side he could see a white-robed cook moving about, talking to someone who was out of sight, brightly moving about behind the mosquito netting. He raised the knocker and let it fall heavily.

He heard the soft pad of the servant's feet and his voice through the door:

"*Min?*"

Speaking careful Arabic, he said: "I want to see Mr. Reizen."

"He is not here, *essidi*."

"Well, open the door, then. Open."

The servant hesitated. "The master is not in, *essidi*."

"Then I will come in and wait for him. Open the door."

"I do not know when he will come, *essidi*."

Trent said roughly: "Open the door. This is the police."

After a moment, he heard the bolt drawn back and the door slowly opened. The old servant peered out, squinting up at him. He pushed his way past him and closed the door behind him. He said: "Is there anyone at home? Anybody?"

"Nobody, *essidi*." The servant's tired old eyes were puzzled. He said hesitantly: "But...but you are not the police, *essidi*."

"All right, go to the kitchen. Henson!"

He heard the back door open and Henson came in. The servant looked round in alarm. The cook came out of the kitchen, a worried, inquiring look on his face. Henson waved them back to the kitchen and shepherded them into the pantry.

Trent went with them and closed the shutters of the window. He took out his pistol and showed it to them. While they watched him, frightened, he said gently: "There is nothing to be afraid of. Only do not leave this room, or open the window. If you do, I shall have to shoot you. There are others outside. Sit here, and stay here. Nothing will happen to you. Is that understood?"

The old man nodded violently: "*Na'am, essidi, na'am...*" he said. The cook, staring wide-eyed at the gun, chimed in, nodding his head. He said eagerly: "We will stay here, *essidi*...your servants...we will do as you say...only...but..."

"Well, what is it?"

The cook, embarrassed, indicated his bare head. Trent picked up his tarboush from the table and handed it to him. The cook put it on and sat down. Trent took out a packet of cigarettes and handed it to them. "You can smoke. But don't try to leave this room. Where's the telephone?"

"There, *essidi*, there...in the study." Nodding towards the hallway.

Sitting silent, the cook stared at Trent, a wrinkled old man from Nubia, his hands gnarled and creased, his thin body clothed in long starched white, his splayed feet bare. He sat patiently, minding his own affairs.

Henson came in from the hall. "Nobody seems to be in the house, Sir. I'd better search it thoroughly, shall I?"

"Yes, do that. But get Kamel Irani first, will you?"

While he waited, he studied the house. It was big, and old, and comfortably furnished. The rooms were high and spacious, their walls distempered after the local fashion, the floors covered with skins and camel-hair rugs. A safe was let into the wall by the doorway. There was a big American radiogram standing in the corner, an expensive hi-fi set in polished walnut. He went over to it, prised up the turntable, and found the key to the safe. When Kamel Irani came in, wiping the mud off his shoes on the thick coconut fiber doormat, he had opened the safe and was pulling out its contents. He threw them down on the table. A bundle of money, three or four notebooks, an account book, some letters, a diary, a tightly-folded sheaf of papers tied with a piece of thick twine. He opened them up and spread them out. He looked up as Kamel Irani came over to him.

"Do you understand Russian?"

Irani nodded. "Yes, fairly well. But I think the material we need will be in code. There seems to be quite a lot here."

He was thumbing through one of the notebooks. "Payments to agents and informers. This will be very useful, my friend. The names are all in code, but I do not doubt that in your office there will be someone who can decipher it."

Trent was grateful for the implied acceptance of authority.

Irani said: "He has friends in the police force. Otherwise he could not possibly afford to leave these papers so carelessly about. A safe like this...almost anybody could open it."

"He's to hand it over to Racoski. Normally, he'd keep all this in his office, in a better hiding place."

"Or at the Embassy, perhaps."

"Perhaps. I believe there is another man here to whom Reizen reports. He sent his reports to a tobacconist on Sharia el Assam. Do you know about that?"

Kamel Irani was turning over the papers. "No, I did not know that. A *poste restante*. There might be twenty Reizens in Cairo, all handing their reports in to a tobacconist, and hence to...where, I wonder? A note of his monthly expenses." He tossed one of the notebooks back on the table.

"And this..." He held up a sheet of foolscap full of neatly typed figures. "A simple code, I think. It will not take long to break. Really, sometimes the simplicity of these people amazes me."

He took out a pocket knife and slit along the edge of an envelope. It was full of English five-pound notes.

Trent picked them up and counted them. There were twelve of them. He turned the envelope over in his hand; it was unmarked.

Henson came in and said: "All clear, Sir. Nobody in the house. I found a couple of pistols though." He laid them on the table.

"Good. The telephone?"

"I took it off the hook, Sir."

"The servants? Are we going to have any trouble there?"

"No, Sir. They're too scared to move, and I've locked them in the pantry. No trouble there, Sir."

"All right. See if you can find a bag or something and get these papers gathered up, will you? We'll take it With us to the office when we leave here."

Henson went out to the kitchen. Kamel Irani was walking about the room, opening cupboards.

Smiling happily, he came over to the table with a chess set and a bottle of vodka.

"What do you say?" he asked. "We have more than an hour to wait. Shall we have a game?"

The mud from his shoes was leaving marks all over the carpets.

CHAPTER 22

In the little silent group that gathered round the body, the policemen pulling at the bloody Army blanket and dragging the mess clear of the noisome garbage cans at the back of the market, two men were whispering quietly:

"That's the man with the money."

"Is it true? Are you sure?"

"Yes. The Russian. He was the man who paid us."

"Is it true? Now who will pay the rest of it?"

"I don't know, by God! Better we go to our homes. They will get in touch with us."

"That's Shulam *effendi* there. You know him?"

"The policeman? A clever man."

"They say he's with us?"

"Is it true? What will happen now?"

The blue-bottles were still buzzing round the bloody mess. The stench around the garbage cans was intolerable, though the sun had long since gone down.

A cat darted in and crouched by the body, snarling and looking up at the uniformed police constable. The policeman kicked at it with his heavy boot and it darted away into the darkness, then turned and sat watching, licking its mouth, the lamplight shining from its eyes, watching and waiting.

The policeman bent and picked up a piece of watermelon rind and hurled it and the cat watched it sail through the air close by, not moving, crouched in feline expectancy.

Up on the third floor of the building beside them, a man leaned over the iron balcony, wearing pajama trousers and a singlet and smoking a cigarette, watching them. Another light went on and a woman came to a window and leaned out to watch.

Standing slim and aloof and angry and watchful, Shulam said to the man beside him:

"Reizen. Sergei Reizen. You know where he lives?"

"No, Sir."

"At Maadi. In the old Water Company's house. The one at the end of Helouan Road. You know it?"

"Yes, Sir."

"Get a squad ready. I want the place searched thoroughly."

"Yes, Sir." The man saluted and made to move off.

"Wait. I'll come with you."

Shulam spoke to his sergeant briefly, dabbed at his nose with a clean white handkerchief, and stepped fastidiously over the body.

CHAPTER 23

The ormulu clock on the marble mantelshelf was striking eight forty-five. The tall beige curtains of thick velour were tightly drawn across the windows, and the amber shades of the standard lamps cast an inviting glow over the room; they might have been in a comfortable London flat.

They faced each other across Reizen's chess-table. The middle game was on and Trent was cautiously bringing out his queen.

Irani said: "There may be a pre-arranged signal between them; if the radio is playing, he will not come to the door. Or if the upstairs light is out, he will go away. A drawn curtain...a light in the porch...an open gate...there are a hundred tricks they may have arranged between them."

"That is why I want you to stay outside; the Arab alone is not enough. To get any sort of message like that, he has to come at least as far as the gate. If you wait there, that is where we will catch him."

"He might leave his car farther away and walk in; I noticed that there are several places where he could easily get through the hedge on the other side of the house."

"That is where the Arab must be. Can we rely on him? Check."

Kamel Irani interposed a bishop. "Absolutely. To tell the truth, I think he is a better man in many respects than either of us. He is a desert man. He can move as quickly and as silently as a snake."

"A Berber, isn't he?"

"A Senussi, from Libya. By profession a bandit, and a good one. He had some trouble during the war, and could not go back home. Higran found him here and recruited him."

"I noticed his blue eyes."

"Yes...Berber stock. In Libya, in Tripolitania, as far as the coastal towns of Tunisia, they would give a great deal to know where he is. They want him for murder, for robbery, for banditry, for cattle theft. Even for rape, I believe. His father was a bandit before him, and his father's father before that. He has fought the French, and the Italians, and the British, and the Turks, and the Germans. His family were long supporters of Abdel Krim. He speaks very little; he thinks a great deal. And I believe him to be immensely loyal."

"To whom? To you?"

"No, not to me only." He moved out a knight and took a pawn. "Check. There was some bond between him and Higran; she never told me what it was, but I saw at once that he worshipped her. That is strange, for, as you know, the desert Arabs do not think of women except as workers and mating companions. Yet he had the highest respect for her. Now...he knows that she is dead. He is like a savage animal."

Trent studied the board carefully and moved his king out of danger. Irani moved his knight again and said: "Queen." He drained his glass and held up the bottle. "This is very good vodka. Far too good for a simple newspaper correspondent. May I fill your glass?"

"Please. You know, I have a nasty feeling about the two servants. I wish we could have got them out of the house."

"I do not think we need worry. They are Nubians, both of them. The Nubians are simple, honest people. They do not take easily to deception. If the servants here had any other role to play, they would be Arabs or Egyptians, who are better suited by nature to fraud and deceit. The Nubians are harmless. Good people."

"Perhaps you're right. All the same, I could wish we had the house to ourselves."

Henson came in from a tour of inspection in the garden.

"Quiet outside, Sir. Not a sign of anything."

"Is the Arab out there?"

Henson grinned. "Yes, Sir. Still as a statue. Didn't see him till I was right on top of him. Nearly scared me out of my wits. Never saw a man stand so still...I watched him for quite a while; I don't believe he's even breathing, and he can't be seen more than a yard away. Smart boy, Sir."

"And the servants?"

"I had another look at them. Quite happy, Sir. The cook's fast asleep."

"So much the better. Do you play chess?"

Henson came over and stood watching them for a moment. "No, Sir. Never had much time for that sort of thing."

Kamel Irani said amiably: "In this profession, one wastes a lot of time. If one can find a chess-board, it makes the waiting less tedious."

"Yes, I suppose so. Never had much time for it, myself. A good game of darts, now...I'll be upstairs, Sir, if you want me. There's a good view of the road from the bedroom windows."

"All right, Henson." Trent moved his queen back. Studying the board he said:

"You play a good game. I'm in trouble."

Irani nodded comfortably. He said: "Colonel Brand said he had met Higran. I'm surprised he let her get to him."

Trent sighed. "We all have our weaknesses. The Colonel needs...relief. Escape, he called it. He's a lonely, savagely-battered man. Before the war, he was a concert violinist, one of the best in the world. Of course, he'd been doing this sort of thing in the first war, as you know, and in 1939 he joined up in Cairo, where he was giving a recital when the war broke out. He has a special talent for this sort of work. But his music... He lost his arm in the first, almost the only enemy raid on Alexandria. You know...two or three aircraft several miles up that dropped their bombs hopefully and disappeared again? One of them landed on the balcony of the hotel where he was staying...he was almost the only casualty that Alexandria ever saw. Can you appreciate that? A damn-fool little bomb that hardly damaged the room it fell in. But it took his arm clean off. After that...his wife was killed in London by a V-bomb, and his son was killed at Alamein. Since the war started, his history has been written in destruction. Can you wonder he goes overboard once in a while? So...he looks for kindness, wherever he can find it. He was with Higran, the night before she was killed. His description was on the list of her visitors that Perugino got for me from a friend of his in the police force. So was yours, of course."

"I see. How did you connect her with all this? Did you know of her...of her clandestine activities?"

"No. And I don't think the police did, either. But she had and lost, a list of names...including yours and Pearman's."

Irani said sharply: "A list? On paper? That was very careless of her. It's quite extraordinary..."

"There was yourself—your name was added in afterwards—and Pearman; a fellow called Shulam who is a political officer; an Army officer named Saleh; Bolec; and Reizen."

Irani muttered: "These are the people I told her to make inquiries about when I first arrived. She already knew a great deal of the background, of course. I wanted detailed notes of those very people. She came to my room at the Lido Hotel, and I briefed her there." He said sadly, "I am disturbed about this, John. I know that sometimes she was...how shall I put it? Extravagantly indiscreet. But to write out a list of names...and to lose it...it is against all the principles of her training. She was a good agent. And a fine woman."

Watching him, Trent said: "The list was typed. On your typewriter. Your move."

"On my typewriter? She should have known better." He said suddenly, suspicion clouding his face; "How did you know it was my machine?"

Trent said gently: "You were my first lead. At one time, everything seemed to point to the fact that you had killed her. Then your interest in Bolec, which we knew about, made it appear that you were on the other side. If we'd known about you earlier, it would have been a lot easier. As it was..."

He shrugged his shoulders, and taking out a bundle of hundred-dollar bills from his hip pocket, He tossed it on the table beside the chess-board. He said:

"I'm sorry I had to hit you so hard, but you're too damn big to play about with...I couldn't risk it. In the morning we'll go and get your passport and your pistol from the office. There are some papers, too. I might add that it was your report that put me on the right track."

Kamel Irani stared at the notes. Then he touched the top of his head a little angrily. "You might have killed me like that."

"Better like that than the way Reizen was killed."

"H'm..."

He recovered his good humor quickly and picked up the money. "Perhaps it is one of the hazards of my profession that our friends sometimes mistake us for enemies." Then he said: "But why are you carrying all my cash with you? Should it not have been in the office with the rest of my things?"

Trent said, smiling: "What was that you said about the personal equation?"

Irani wrinkled up his face, the humor deep in his eyes. "I thought it was one of Reizen's men. I must confess that I was worried when I thought they had found my report."

"What about Saleh? The Army officer who was killed?"

"Ahmed Saleh was very unfortunate. He found out quite a lot of what was going on and reported it to his superiors. Unhappily, one of those superiors in with the other side...a great many of the Army officers are strongly opposed to the present regime, you know. This is Egypt; here, there will always be scheming and counter-scheming. It has always been this way. That is what makes our task here relatively easy. In this country, the custom of selling men's secrets is an ancient one." He moved out his queen's castle, sliding the carved ivory piece with a slow, patient movement along the board. Trent saw that he had fallen into a trap. He said, smiling: "Two moves to mate. I'm afraid you're too good for me." He laid his king gently down.

Kamel Irani stood up and stretched himself. Looking up at the clock, he said: "Nine-thirty. I will take up my post in the garden." At the door, he turned. "And when we have him? What do you propose to do then?"

"Well...we can hold him in the office. Not a very good policy, really... We have a flat in town, but Pearman is holed up there. Henson lives on a *dahabiya* on the river; that might be a good place for him. Then I'll get a quick report out, and I think the Colonel had better take it from there. The *junta* will be very sure of seeing that he does no damage, one way or the other."

"Yes. I think that is the second best way."

"And the best?"

Smiling gently, Kamel Irani drew an expressive finger across his throat. Then he turned, and went out into the garden.

Trent went upstairs to speak to Henson.

It was exactly ten o'clock when he heard the car pull up at the gate, and at the same moment Henson came running down the stairs, gesturing.

Calmly, he went into the hall and waited. He knew exactly what he had to do. He slipped the pistol out of his pocket, checked it, and put it back in again. Henson was holding a massive .45, standing close to the door, his body pressed tight against the wall.

Trent said quietly: "As soon as I open the door, slip out and get behind him." Henson nodded.

Standing silently waiting, Trent could hear the soft ticking of the clock in the other room, and thought he felt the beating of his heart getting stronger. He strained his ears to catch the sound of footsteps on the duckboards outside. For a long time, nothing happened.

Then, so close beside him that he jumped, the door knocker was banged, a rat-tat-tat repeated. Remembering the old servant, he said:

"*Min?*"

"*Iftah.*" The order telling him to open was in Arabic. He wondered if Racoski would speak Arabic.

He said again: "*Min hada?*"

"*Iftah, ya ibn sharmuta!*"

The curse was straight out of the gutter, an Arab-to-Arab oath. He hesitated and glanced at Henson, seeing the repressed spring in him, watching his light stance on the balls of his feet, his gun held commando-fashion close into his side. Inclining his head he reached out and turned the lock of the door, then quickly flung it open.

Henson was out in a flash. Trent reached out and grabbed the visitor by the lapels of his coat, hurting his hand on the yellow enameled taxi-driver's badge that he wore, then yanked him savagely into the house. Henson half pushed him and stumbled in after him.

The visitor was an Arab.

Trent flung him against the wall, shouted to Henson, "Watch him!" then sprinted out of the house and into the garden, running fast, slipping once off the boards and splashing into ankle-deep water, running as fast as his lungs would allow him down the long stretch to the garden gate.

He saw the dim outline of the car under the trees, a long American car with a taxi-plate from Alexandria, and he ran out into the roadway and ducked behind it, suddenly afraid, suddenly fearing for his life, waiting for the danger and expectant of it. He ducked quickly behind the car, crouching down, his pistol ready, the safety-catch off, staring into the darkness.

The car was empty.

He heard Kamel Irani come running, splashing through the water, the silt flying up around his feet with a sharp splashing sound, and then he heard a commotion in the hedge beside him, close by the gate, a quiet scuffle, a heavy breathing, a muttered oath in Arabic with a desert accent, and he turned quickly and moved towards it.

The tall Arab was there. His back was arched, tall and slim in the shadows, his dark face almost invisible. His left arm was round the neck of his captive, from behind, his left wrist tight in the man's throat, his right hand grasping a handful of hair and forcing the head drawn tight over the compressing wrist.

The man was gasping, struggling convulsively, struggling desperately tor air, his hands pulling wildly at the Arab's arms, his legs kicking uselessly, his feet twitching. Trent knew that in another minute he would be dead.

Kamel Irani reached them and touched the Arab on the arm. "*Bas*," he said, "*Basta...*" The Arab released the man and stood back into the hedge. His captive fell groaning into the mud, splashing limply into the water, collapsing and twitching on the ground.

Standing over him, his pistol ready, his feet wide spread, Trent said curtly: "Get up, Racoski."

Rascoski was gulping in air. Still breathing heavily, cowered with wet mud, rubbing his throat with an uliginose hand, the black water dripping from him, clutching his throat and coughing, he climbed unsteadily to his feet. He stumbled and fell again, and for a moment remained on all fours in the black water, like an animal, leaning on his hands and knees. Then slowly his white face came up, a long, angular, cruel face, the white moon shining on its pallor, the vicious eyes peering at them, the pallid face turning slowly from side to side. He began to grope in the water, patting the surface with his hands, feeling for something. Silently the tall Arab stepped forward; he was holding out a pair of thick spectacles.

Racoski looked at him and staggered slowly to his feet. He took his glasses silently with a muddy hand and slipped them on, curving them round his ears with a slow, precise, mechanical movement. His breath was still labored. He rubbed his throat again, streaking mud all over his features, and looked at the Arab. Trent shuddered at the venom in his weak eyes. Fingering his automatic, he said roughly:

"Do you speak English?"

Racoski turned his malevolent eyes on him. Then he looked at Kamel Irani and back to the Arab. At last he answered coldly:

"Of course."

His voice was thin and slow and malignant.

"Then get into the house." Trent waved his pistol.

Irani bent and retrieved a briefcase that was lying at his feet. Racoski looked at him and said nothing, then turned slowly towards the house. He walked slowly with a light, precise step. Trent was surprised to see how small and insignificant he seemed from the back; and then the memory of his virulent eyes made him shudder.

When they reached the house, Henson was standing in the hall, running his hands over the taxi-driver who was leaning forward into the wall, his hands raised high. Henson said briefly: "Nothing, Sir," then turned his attention to Racoski, gesturing with his .45.

Racoski silently put his muddy hands on the wall above his head. Henson slipped his gun back into his pocket and ran his hands up and down Racoski's arms and legs. He pulled a Mauser automatic from his belt and handed it to Trent, then shook his head. "Nothing else, Sir. But I'd better strip him..."

"That can wait. Get the taxi-driver into the pantry with the others."

They trudged into the living-room, a viscid trail under their feet, tramping mud over the camel-hair carpets, the water dripping on to the polished floor. Irani dropped the briefcase on to the table and tried the lock, then ripped it open with a sudden wrench of his powerful hands. He said, cheerfully:

"This, my friend, will solve all our problems."

CAIRO CABAL

The case was packed tight with money.

As Irani tipped it out on to the table, Henson came back into the room. Trent said to him: "Watch Racoski," and waited while Henson pushed him down into a chair and took up his post behind him. Then he put his automatic into his pocket and went to the table.

There were bundles of American notes, mostly hundred-dollar bills; there were four thick packets of English five-pound notes; there was a great thick wad of Egyptian money; there were eight tight rolls of gold sovereigns; and wrapped incongruously in a white handkerchief, there was a little pile of diamonds, twenty-eight of them, glittering brightly on the polished red teak of the table-top, scintillating in the light of the lamps, sparkling radiantly, a marvelous coruscation of brilliant color. Trent stared at them, fascinated.

He looked up at Kamel Irani and scratched the back of his head. "Well..." he said. "Well..."

He ran his fingers lightly over them, watching the brilliance shoot off them. "I wonder what the hell those are worth..."

He gathered them up and slipped them back into the white handkerchief, then turned his attention to the briefcase again. In the second compartment, there was a notebook and a sheaf of papers. He thumbed through them, staring at the Russian characters, then tapped them lightly with the back of his hand.

"This," he said, "this is the thing we want."

He began stuffing them back into the briefcase, picking up Reizen's papers and putting them in too, bulging the briefcase out tightly, pulling on the straps that slipped over the broken locks. He said: "A nice present for the Colonel...I wonder how much there is there?"

"The money? A fortune. A great fortune, my friend, for you or me. For them...nothing. Money is like manure, John; spread it about and you may see great changes. If this had been spread about..."

"A spadesful of manure for Pearman's life... It's a harsh thought."

Henson said diffidently: "He ought to be stripped, Sir. I don't like the thought of him hanging around like this with all that stuff lying about."

Trent turned to them. Racoski, his muddy face set and cold and emotionless, sat rigidly in the chair, not moving. His venomous eyes were watching him. He had the impression that he was waiting...waiting for something to happen, watching them warily like an animal in a trap waiting for the door to be sprung.

He said: "Yes. Strip him and search him. Wait...I'll help you..." He said to Racoski: "Stand up and get your clothes off, all of them."

Kamel Irani said sharply: "Listen!"

There were the dying notes of a long shrill whistle on the air, coming clearly to them out of the garden, the shrill staccato peepeeping of a night bird.

Irani said quickly: "It's the Arab..." Then, as they heard the soft rumble, "It's a car...quickly...!"

Trent stepped rapidly into the hallway and opened the door a little. Peering out into the moonlight he saw a jeep draw up at the gates; another pulled in behind it and braked heavily to a stop. He went quickly back into the living room and said urgently: "It's the police. Let's get the hell out of here. The back way...make for the car."

He went to Racoski and took out his pistol. He said: "One sound out of you...just one sound, that's all..."

Kamel Irani said something to him in Russian. Trent saw a sudden fear come into his eyes, a cowardly, vicious fear. He went meekly to the door, the others following. Irani picked up the muddy briefcase and handed it to Henson.

Trent said: "What about the Arab?"

"By now he will be on the roadway waiting for us. If not...*ma'alesh*, he knows where to find me."

They talked quietly, moving silently out of the back door. Trent took Racoski's thin arm in his hand, clenching his fingers tightly over the stringy biceps. He closed the door behind them quietly, and they made their way in the shadow of the house across the vegetable garden to the hedgerow.

Trent whispered: "This way...the car's over there..."

In the distance beyond the house they heard the police calling to each other, not hiding themselves, shouting out orders, an authoritative voice among them. Trent stood still and listened. He said excitedly: "That's Shulam! Do you know him? Ibrahim Shulam?

CAIRO CABAL

What's he doing out here?"

Irani did not answer. He was watching Racoski, walking quickly and silently beside him, his feet squelching lightly in the mud. They came to the end of the long shadow cast by the house, and hesitated, then ran quickly across the open space to the hedge. Trent glanced over his shoulder as he ran, then pushed Racoski unprotestingly ahead of him, running fast, bent almost double.

As Irani reached the hedge, Trent saw the gleam of a steel blade in his hand; he was gesturing with it to Racoski. They dived into the shrubbery and forced their way through it, feeling the pliant twigs on their laces, choking on the pungent scents of the wild and fragrant weeds in the ditch.

Henson was through first and sprinted for the car, Trent and Racoski hard on his heels, Kamel Irani bringing up the rear. They heard a shout in the distance behind them, and then another, and then a rifle was fired, and Trent shouted: "Quick! The car..." and they tumbled in as Henson started the engine. They heard the splashing sound of running feet on the other side of the hedge and the car shot forward with Kamel Irani hanging on to the open door and running beside it, then leaping in the back to fall, a jumble of legs and arms and solid flesh on top of them. And then another rifle shot sounded sharply and with a screech of tires the big car gathered speed and was away, tearing and lurching across the road with Henson hugging the wheel. They picked themselves up and heard Henson say jubilantly: "All in, Sir? I hope?"

Racoski was on the floor of the car, Trent on top of him, and Kamel Irani sorting himself out on top of both of them. Trent said happily:

"We're away...that was Ibrahim Shulam, the political policeman...you know him?"

Irani said softly: "I know him. I think our friend does, too."

"Oh? Oh indeed... Are you sure?"

"No, my friend, I am not sure. But I was watching his face...I think perhaps I am right." He added gently: "It will be a simple matter to find out."

Panting, Trent said: "I thought Racoski would make a break. He could almost have got away then if he'd tried hard enough."

"No...he could not have got away. He is a coward. It is as simple as that. Like many of his kind, he is a coward. His job is to sit at a desk and organize murder...for men like him, danger is best controlled from a distance. He is mortally afraid, John. A coward."

Henson, slowing down a little, said: "Where to, Sir?"

"Anybody on your *dahabiya*? We've got to hold him till the morning."

"Nobody there, Sir, but..." he hesitated.

"You don't like the idea?"

"It's not that, Sir, but...well, if anything should go wrong, it's not an easy place to get away from in a hurry. Just a precaution, Sir. Of course, if you think it's all right..."

"No...perhaps you're right. Pearman's at the flat. I don't think we should go to the office...I think we might take him to Bolec's place. Yes...we'll go to Bab-el-Louk. And drive fast; it'll take them a good fifteen minutes to phone ahead of us and get any sort of a check organized...step on it."

The car shot up to eighty and the black tarmac slipped by silently under the wheels, and in less than ten minutes they slowed down to turn into the *midan*.

Trent said: "Drop us off at Bab-el-Louk, then get round to the office. Hand that briefcase over to Mr. Morgan and tell him to get an interpreter to work on the notes in it. Right away. I want it all done by morning, right? And then go round to the Colonel and tell him what's happened. Tell him I'll phone him as soon as I can."

"Right, Sir."

They pulled up outside the apartment house. Across the road, on the other corner, two policemen were standing under the lamp-post.

They sat in the car and watched them. They were holding each other's hands, Arab fashion, and arguing with quick, urgent gestures, saying over and over again, "*Ismah, ismah,* listen..." and "Listen to me...listen, my friend...my friend, listen..." each insisting with the other and both talking together and neither paying any attention to the other's arguments, and laying their hands on arms and hearts, insisting urgently. They were arguing about some woman and nobody was listening.

Trent grinned to himself and turned to Kamel Irani. He said:

"Keep an eye on this bastard. I'll go and see if the coast is clear."

Kamel Irani nodded and spoke to Racoski in Russian again. Racoski turned his cold eyes on him and said nothing. Trent saw him turn and look at the two policemen. He said softly:

"Don't do it, Racoski, don't do it."

And Irani said: "Go ahead, my friend. I will look after him." The level of his voice was glacial; Trent remembered Reizen and shuddered.

He went quickly up the stairway two at a time and knocked on the door.

Bolec said: "*Min hada?*"

"It's me, Bolec. Open up." Bolec opened the door and stood there, a heavy cast-iron frying-pan in his hand, his belly bulging out over the top of his belt. He said happily, noisily: "Come in, Mr. Trent. You just in time. I make some *kebab*. Non like *kebab?*" He was swaying slightly.

"One of these days you'll poison yourself with that wood alcohol you drink," Trent said affably. "I've got some company for you. Are you alone?"

"Only the girl. Company?"

"A couple of friends."

"Then bring them in. I got plenty food. Plenty drink too. We have party, eh?"

"Kamel Irani and Reizen's boss."

"Oh. Reizen's boss?" He sobered quickly. "You want to hide them here? Is that what you want? I make them very comfortable..."

"Well, until the morning. Are you expecting anyone?"

"Nobody come here, Mr. Trent. Nobody. Who is this man, Reizen's boss?"

"A visitor. Just arrived from abroad."

"A Russian?"

"A Russian."

"I look after him for you. I look after him good. I take good care of him..."

"I'll bring them up. You're a good fellow, Bolec. How's the wound?"

"The wound? Oh, that. Is finish. Little scratch, no more."

"Where did you put Reizen's body?"

"Well..." Bolec looked uncomfortable. He said unhappily: "I tell Ibrahim Shamar to put him in river, take him out in boat and drop him in deep water, fix him with chains to keep him down, nobody find him. But you know...when we get him out, is too late, getting too near daytime. So Ibrahim come back and tell me he put him in garbage can in market. Is a good place, but I think they find him pretty soon..."

"So that's it. Yes, I think they found him. Anything on him to bring the police to you?"

"Mr. Trent..." Bolec was hurt. "Nobody find anything of mine on him."

He said hastily: "This the first time I do such a thing, but..." He laughed quickly. "Nobody find anything of mine on him. Me and Ibrahim make good job. If they find him, I'm sorry, but you know...too near daylight..."

"Never mind. I'll go and get the others."

He went quickly back down the stairs. The two policemen were still across the street, still arguing, still saying *Ismah ya habibi, ya habibi ismah, ismah minni, ismah ya abui, ismah, ismah, ismah...* In the back of the car, Racoski was watching them, contriving to watch Kamel Irani at the same time, wondering. The Turk was smiling quietly; it seemed to Trent that he was waiting for the Russian to make a break.

He said quietly: "All clear. Can we get him inside without any trouble? Shall we wait for the police to move off?"

Irani shook his head. He said softly: "No trouble, my friend. He will not make trouble."

He spoke a few words of Russian again. Not speaking, his eyes cast down, Racoski got out of the car. He moved stolidly, unprotesting, like one of his own political prisoners, Trent ruminated, a sullen but unprotesting robot, moving on order, quite passionless, unmoved, almost inhumanly obedient. Trent watched him carefully. He said to himself, "I know this type; the smallest chance is all he wants..."

Irani climbed out of the back seat. Trent said to Henson: "All right, off you go. You know the phone number here?"

"Yes, Sir."

"I'll be here for a while. When you've seen the Colonel, go to the office and stand by." He was very tired suddenly.

They went up the stairs together, a procession. Bolec was waiting by the open door. As soon as they were inside, Trent introduced them. Irani said:

"Ah, yes. Stefan Bolec. My information was that you were working with our mutual enemies."

"He changed his mind when he found out who was behind it all," Trent said. "He's done some good work for us."

Bolec beamed. He had wet his hair and plastered it down over his forehead. He said: "Maybe you like little bit arak, Major? I got the best arak in Cairo."

Kamel Irani nodded pleasantly. "And if you have some rope?"

"Sure, I got rope. I tie him up so he not get away. But first, I pour you little drink of arak. You too, Mr. Trent?"

Trent was at the window, watching the two policemen across the street. He said: "How do we get out of this place in a hurry? If we have to? Is there a back way?"

Kamel Irani looked at him sharply. Bolec put down the bottle he was holding. He said briefly:

"Any trouble, we get out over roof. Get down into market at Bab-el-Louk. Why, we got trouble?"

"No, I don't think so. But I wish those two police would go away." He went to the phone and dialed the Colonel's number.

When Colonel Brand answered he said carefully: "John here, Sir. I'm at a place in town."

"All right, John, go ahead."

"I have our friend from overseas with me. Henson is on his way round to see you and tell you all about it."

"Good. Good. Anything you want done?"

"Well, I think we may have a local headache on our hands, Sir. The sooner we can get rid of him, the better. I think it might be best if you were to speak to...to the authorities."

"Yes, yes, of course. How soon can you let me have a report?"

"Well, there's some translating to be done first..."

"That means it will have to wait till the morning. Unless...who's the duty officer?"

"Morgan, Sir."

"Well..." He waited a long time before the Colonel went on. "No. It will have to wait till morning. Let me have a full report just as soon as you can. What's your number there?"

Trent gave it to him. He said: "I think we might perhaps have visitors. If so, it's going to be very difficult."

"What about the apartment?"

"Not with Pearman there, Sir."

"No, you're right, better not go there. Any other ideas?"

"If there's trouble, I'll get to one of our Czech friend's hideouts. Our Turkish friend can handle things this end, and I'll come round and see you."

"Good, do that. Be careful, John. Be careful. Call me back if there's anything. As soon as I have your report, I'll see that he's handed over to the right people."

Trent put down the phone. He said to Kamel Irani: "A fine state of affairs when we can't even trust the police."

"In a matter like this? Half of them are on the other side. It would save us a lot of trouble if we simply disposed of him."

"Yes, I know."

Bolec was cutting up a piece of stout cord. Irani had pulled a wooden chair over to the door and was sitting down, leaning back against it, watching Racoski. Racoski stood in the center of the room; he said nothing. His small frame was still and relaxed, his eyes were averted but restless under their heavy lids. Trent was aware of the tension in him. He suddenly wished he had told Henson to come back here.

He went to the window and looked down on the street. The two policemen were still there, still arguing.

As he watched, a jeep drew up and slowly stopped beside them. They stopped arguing and watched it, then went over to it, and saluted.

Trent said quickly: "Trouble. They're on to us."

Kamel Irani leaped to his feet and joined him. He stared at the police car for a moment. Bolec said: "Over the roof, Mr. Trent?" He picked up his butcher's knife and stood beside Racoski. Racoski's eyes were narrowed. Trent said briefly:

"Let's go. You lead the way. Can we get to one of your friends' places?"

"Ibrahim Shamar lives not far. We go there. Better we hurry."

He went quickly to the bedroom and spoke to the Arab girl, then went to the door and opened it for their. "Quickly! We get on the roof quickly, then they not catch us."

There was the beginning of a smite on Racoski's cruel face. Trent said to himself bitterly: Much more of this and he won't even have to try to get away. He went to the door. Bolec said urgently:

"One minute please."

He ran to the kitchen and turned out the gas under his *kebab*.

They ran quickly up the half-flight to the roof, pushing Racoski ahead of them, uncomplaining. Out on the top, in the open, the fresh air was cool and moist. Trent ran a hand over his eyes and felt the stubble on his chin. He took out his gun as they ran across the wide flat space to the edge of the roof.

There was some laundry hanging here, a long white line of underwear and towels and pajamas and sheets, motionless in the still air. At the low stone wall at the edge, they stopped and looked down. Below them was the roof of the adjoining building, a story lower. Bolec said:

"We got to jump. Is not far."

"You go first."

Bolec climbed over the wall, hung by his hand for a moment, then dropped from sight. He called up: "Is not far, just little bit."

Kamel Lani followed him. As he hesitated he said: "I'll watch Racoski. Send him after me." He dropped down quietly.

Trent prodded the Russian. He said:

"All right, down you get." Carefully, almost fastidiously, Racoski climbed over on to the outer ledge. There was a smile on his cold white face. Trent restrained an impulse to jab the pistol savagely into it. Then he was gone, and he jumped quickly over and joined the others. Bolec said:

"This way..."

They ran quickly over the thick hard clay of the white-washed rooftop and followed him along the edge of a wide balcony that was somebody's private verandah. Through an open window beside them, Trent could see into a lighted room; a woman was washing her hair over a tin basin. As they ran past he saw her look up, and he stumbled.

The woman squinted at the bare electric light bulb, then crossed to the window and looked out at him. She called out:

"*Qu'est-ce que tu fais là, cochon que tu es? Voyeur! Va-t'en! Crétin!*"

She was wearing a skirt only, and her long black hair hung down over her white breasts. Trent ran on, the woman shouting at him as he ran. He reached the others at the edge of the building. They stopped and looked over. Bolec said:

"We jump down again. Same like last time."

Trent peered over the edge and looked up at Racoski. He was still smiling cruelly. Kamel Irani saw the expression on his face and said smoothly:

"I told him, my friend, that you would not shoot him if he tried to run away. I told him that I would."

Trent saw the smile disappear from Racoski's face. Irani said:

"If I were doing this alone, my friend, we would not have all this trouble. One more dead Russian...a very small thing."

"Let's keep going. Where is this place, Bolec?"

"Not far. We get to the street behind the market. Ibrahim live close by. All dark there. Nobody see us."

Trent looked up behind them and saw a figure on the wall above, framed against the sky, fifty yards behind and above them; it was one of the policemen. His rifle was slung across his shoulder.

He pressed deeper into the shadows, holding out his arm to draw the others with him. He whispered savagely in Racoski's ear:

"All right, you bastard. Just make one sound..."

He held his pistol tight into his side, watching the other man carefully. Bolec whispered: "This way. He not see us."

He climbed over the iron railing and dropped quietly down on to the roof below them. Irani followed and Trent jabbed his gun again into Racoski's side. The Russian swung himself over, took hold of the railing with his white hands, and again Trent saw the malevolent smile on his face as he dropped from view. He looked back and saw that the policeman was still there. He was shining a flashlight now, searching the roof above them. He heard the woman calling out and saw the policeman in the dark distance slip his arm out of his rifle sling and stand there with the stars behind him, the rifle across his body. Saw him turn away and call out something to the others behind him, and he swore softly, a long and violent string of blasphemy, then he slipped his pistol back into his pocket, swung himself over the railing, and dropped on to the roof below.

Across on the other side of the lower roof, beyond the wide expanse, there were open windows again, and the sounds of a rowdy party came across to them. The yellow light spilled out on to the broad flat roof where they stood, but fell far short of them as they crept quietly past in the shadow. And then below them suddenly lay the market, its bright bare lights busily crowded with the insects flying about them, the stench of meat and vegetables and flour and coffee coming powerfully up to them as they stood and looked down on it all; and the cries of the ubiquitous coffee-seller and somewhere a raucous gramophone, and the noise of fluttering, squawking chickens, struggling to get their tied legs free from the pole slung over the vendor's shoulder, and the sound of cats in garbage cans and the stench of rotten tomatoes and melon-rind.

Bolec whispered: "This way."

They eased their way slowly along the edge of the roof to the other side where it was dark, and Trent looked down gratefully into the blackness below, seeing the greasy cobblestones of the lane shining bleakly in the dim lamplight. He turned to Irani and whispered:

"Same again. Last leap."

The Turk looked down and nodded, then turned to Racoski and said in English: "Remember, my friend, I will be very happy to kill you."

Racoski looked at him and said nothing. Trent suddenly realized that all evening he had spoken two words. "Do you speak English?" *Of course*. A cold, disdainful reply, no more, then silence.

Bolec said softly: "Better be careful, Mr. Trent. Is long drop this time. Not too long. But more long like last time. Better be careful." He sat down on the cold clay, dangling his legs over the edge for a moment, then twisted his great body, slithered his belly over the edge, and dropped. They heard the dull thump as he hit the ground, and at the same moment a police whistle sounded above and behind them.

Trent said urgently: "Quickly!" and Kamel Irani dropped to the edge and slid down, then lowered himself to the extent of his long arms, disappeared from sight. Trent nodded his head to Racoski. He thought, if he looks at me again like that, I'll kick his teeth in...

The Russian sat down on the edge, twisted round, and looked down into the lane below. He pushed himself clear of the wall and jumped. Trent peered over the edge.

He saw Racoski fall heavily, twist over, and fall to the ground. He heard a soft, moaning murmur and swore again. Then, as he lowered himself quickly over the edge, looking down into the yellow-lit darkness below him, he saw Kamel Irani bend down over the recumbent Russian and drag him to his feet.

And then it happened.

Twisting himself freely with an incredibly animal movement, Racoski broke loose and bolted toward the light. He ran fast, unbelievably fast, sprinting with sudden energy towards the corner where the market lay bathed in brilliance.

Hanging by his hands, Trent looked down and swore, and by the time he had picked himself up, the Russian was already round the angle and out of sight. Irani was running fast close behind him, Bolec standing by gaping at them stupidly. He shouted:

"Come on! Don't stand there!" and took off after them.

When he reached the corner, panting, Kamel Irani was standing still, breathing heavily, his face flushed, staring into the late crowds milling about the stalls. He was cursing quietly and violently, swearing to himself with long and carefully modulated vehemence. He was trembling, and the look in his eyes was frightening.

Racoski was nowhere to be seen.

CHAPTER 24

They met by chance in a coffee shop down in the *mousky*, in the dusty depths of the market behind the Opera House which opened up like a strange and brightly-colored city far removed from the sophisticated bustle of Cairo itself, yet only a few sandstone walls away from it.

Here it was Oriental, a mass of chattering color, with carpets and bronzes and carvings and beaten brasses, with hot bright daubs of color lying in the sun in front of windowless shops that opened like caverns leading long and dark into unknown depths where more bright colors lay; and everywhere there was the noise of tiny hammers tapping on silver trays, and the sing-song of the coffee-seller, and the soft plunk-plunk-plunk of the squatting weaver's bow as he strummed the long taut wire that trembled and plucked out the cloudy mass of raw white wool that lay about his haunches, and the rich ripe smells of *shish-kebabs* scorching in front of upright charcoal fires, the mutton-fat sizzling over them, and sesame-oil dripping over honeyed cakes, and paper-thin pancakes of bread cooking in brown clay ovens, and coffee spiced with cardamom, and the tric-trac noises of backgammon boards on the tables of the cafés, and the quiet gurgle of *nargilehs*, and everywhere the shade and the escape from the heat.

As the other man passed him, he put out a hand to stay him, and said "*T'fadal*", nodding at a chair close beside him.

The other man stopped and held out his hand, smacking the outstretched palm lightly with the flat of his fingers, then dragging up the cane-bottomed chair with the other hand, sliding it under him as he bent his knees, and somehow contriving to push his tarboush away from his brow all at one and the same time, his movements quick and fluid, a precise exercise in smooth coordination; at one minute he was walking carelessly by, and at the next he was seated, his tarboush pushed back, his chair pulled up, his hand shaken, his movements all lithe and fluid and incredibly Egyptian.

He took a mouthpiece from his pocket and called to the waiter to bring another *nargileh*. As soon as it was brought and the small boy had come running with the red-hot charcoal between the tines of his long black tongs, blowing on it as he ran so that the sparks flew off it cheerfully; and when he had placed it carefully on top of the wet tobacco in the clay bowl, and the smoke was billowing down and bubbling up through the scented water into the amber mouthpiece and down again to his wasted lungs, then they began the elaborate rigmarole:

"How are you?"
"Thank God. And how are you?"
"I am well if you are."
"And how is your health?"
"Thank God."
"How is your father?"
"Good, by God."
"How is your house?"
"By God, good."

And then a long pause, both looking away and watching the *shesh-besh* game at the next table, and the other man beginning:

"How is the world with you?"
"Thank God."
"And your father?"
"Good, by God."
"And your family?"
"Thank God."
"And how is your house?"
"By God, good."
"And how are you?"
"Good, by my life."
"And how is your health?"

"Thank God."
"And how are you?"
"If you are well, then I am well."
"Thank God."

And at last, looking over shoulders, eyeing the next table suspiciously, speaking softly:

"Have you been paid?"
"No. I do not like this. I am frightened."
"The money is good."
"The money? What money? They tell me fifty pounds. Where? Where is fifty pounds? I have not seen it."
"By God. Neither have I."
"I tell you, no money, no work. I tell him too. I tell him the same thing."
"Yes? Is it true? What did he say?"
"He said 'Wait. You get your money.' All right, I wait. But I do not like it. It is dangerous. Too dangerous."
"The money is good."
"Yes."

Then the long silent pause, broken only by the soft bubbling of the blue smoke and the faint crackle of the lively charcoal. And then again:

"How are you?"
"Thank God."
"How is your father?"
"Thank God."
"How is your family?"
"Thank God."
"How is your house?"
"Thank God."
"How is the world with you?"
"Thank God."

They were worried, both of them.

CHAPTER 25

The stalls were tightly packed under the insect-worried yellow glare of the bright arc lights above them.

The trucks were moving in from the villages, crowding their way through the narrow entrances, weaving dangerously among the stalls, piling up their watermelons and sacks of rice, and flour with weevils working their way through it, and rancid butter in greasy tins stamped: *Petrol; poisonous. Not to be used for food storage.* There were trucks piled unbelievably high with wicker baskets of live poultry, tied on with string and leaning drunkenly outward, and crates of softly cooing pigeons seeming oblivious of the pastry-crusts awaiting them; and sticky sacks of golden dates from the tall palms of the desert to the west, and figs and bananas, and tomatoes and cabbages, and plantains and sweet potatoes, and papayas and custard apples. And everywhere noise and bustle and smell and curses, and the intent animation of the shopkeepers preparing their stalls for the early-morning opening when the first housewives would appear in bedraggled housecoats, their hair in curlers, their feet in sloppy sandals, and followed by their barefoot servants silently carrying their baskets.

Trent and Bolec and Kamel Irani stood staring into the seething mass, an angry, frustrated trio. Irani was muttering, half to himself, saying over and over again, "My fault, Mr. Trent, my fault...it was my fault," and cursing in a mixture of Arabic and Turkish, swearing horribly, fuming, white with anger. Trent said quickly.

"Get round to the other side...watch the other exit...quickly...

Bolec, you come with me."

They separated and worked round to cover the ways out of the market, hopelessly frustrated, knowing that by now he would be gone, just hoping desperately for a glimpse, no more than one glimpse of him. The truck drivers and the porters and the merchants glanced at them as they thrust their way roughly through them. They all recognized Bolec and greeted him:

"*Ahlan wa sahlan, ya Bolec effendi...*"

"*Hawagga Stefan, zeiak?*"

"*Zeiak Stefan effendi?*"

"*Keef halek, ya Stefan Pasha...keef halek...?*"

And looking up from their work to clap him on the back:

"*Ya Stefan effendi...zeiak?*"

One of them stopped his work and seized Bolec's hand, pumping it vigorously, saying, "*Keef el dunya andak*...how is the world with you?" And Bolec answered growling, "How's the world? It's like a couple of cucumbers, friend. One in your hand for supper, and the other stuck up your ass..." The other man threw back his head and roared with laughter.

Trent pushed him, then stopped and grabbed Bolec urgently by his lapels. He said feverishly:

"You know all these people here...?"

"Sure, these people all my friends, Mr. Trent." The pride showing on his face, he said: "This is my home. I got plenty friends down here...all know me..."

"Then for God's sake ask them if they've seen him..."

Bolec said calmly, patiently: "I do better. All these people help you find him. Maybe I offer little bit money...?"

"Whatever you like...but hurry, be quick about it..."

Bolec was perfectly composed. He looked around him for a moment, ignoring the friends who greeted him, peering into the jostling crowd. He called out suddenly:

"*Ali...Ali Mohammed! Ta'al...ta'al ya ibn hmar!*"

A small boy who was darting between the legs of the porters stopped in his tracks, swung round, and came running up to them, a boy of ten or twelve years old, dressed in a ragged shirt that came down to his ankles, barefoot and tousled, his brown precocious old-man's face beaming happily; a homeless, ragged, unpossessed night-urchin chewing on a piece of sugar-cane, all the self-sufficient wisdom of the gutter gleaming in his bright black eyes. He came to a sudden stop in front of Bolec, looking up at him expectantly.

Bolec laid a friendly hand on his shoulder. He said proudly:

"One of my sergeants..."

He took the boy to one side and stood talking to him, low-voiced, using his hands descriptively, looking up from time to time and squinting at the people near him. Another child came running up and joined them, and Bolec brought him into the circle with a gesture.

He said: "Go and get Ibrahim...tell him, come now...*yallah, bil'agil*..." and the child went running off, darting between strong bare thighs and long white gowns and baggy white *sharawallis* as he twisted and turned among the porters and the drivers and the lorry-boys, running lightly, effortlessly, out of sight in a moment. Bolec went on explaining to the other child, tapping him on the shoulder, gesticulating. The boy nodded and was gone.

Bolec said placidly: "I think they find him, Mr. Trent. If he is in Cairo, they find him. This boy tell all other boys. In ten minutes, you got twenty boys looking for him."

"In ten minutes," Trent said angrily, "in ten minutes he'll be ten miles away."

"*Ma'alesh*... In half-an-hour, you got fifty boys. By morning all my boys working for you, maybe more than a hundred." He said anxiously: "I promise ten pounds to boy what find him, Mr. Trent. Is too much? But for ten pounds you got every boy in Cairo..."

"That's the least of my worries."

Trent glared around the brightly-lit square. "A hundred places he could hide here...if we don't find him at once... Wait for me here."

He went into the telephone box at the entrance and called the office.

"John here. Listen, Morgan...is Henson there yet?"

"Just came in, John. Want to speak?"

"No...but get his briefcase off him...who's on call for Russian?"

"Russian? That's Connie again. John, I dare not get her out of bed again..."

"Get her. I want every damn thing in that case translated. Some of it will be in code; I don't care if you have to get the whole bloody cipher office out of their beds, but I want that stuff on my desk by the morning..."

"By the morning? But John, Russian cipher? It's going to take a week..."

"I don't care if it takes a month...I want it on my desk by daylight and that's all there is to it. If you have any trouble with the cipherenes, ring the old man..."

"At this time of night? He'll have my guts for a necktie..."

"He'll be waiting for a call from you. Tell Connie to look first for anything that resembles a list of names...tell her to pull her finger out and hurry up with it. I'll call you from time to time for a progress report."

He heard the beginnings of a sigh at the other end and slammed the instrument back on the hook and went out.

Bolec was talking to a tall slim Egyptian, whispering urgently. There was a huge gold ring on one of the man's fingers and he carried a gold-mounted cane. He had a neat brown jacket over his *foustan* and wore sandals of yellow camel-hide. As Trent came up to them he flashed a quick toothy smile, showing his gold inlays proudly, and held out his hand. Bolec said quietly:

"This is my friend Ibrahim. Together we catch this man. Now, you got nothing to worry about, we catch him quick."

Pointing a finger at Ibrahim, he said: "You see him easy. Mud all over clothes, on trousers, on jacket...black mud, from Maadi, you understand? Very thick glasses...and his clothes, not Egyptian, not French, not English, but different, very foreign, you see him easy, very *frangi*...when you catch him, you bring him to your house, O.K.? We wait for you there?"

Ibrahim nodded wisely. He said softly: "If God wills..."

"You believe me," Bolec said. "You get this man, you go straight to Paradise when you die. I fix it for you."

The Egyptian tucked the cane under his arm and stood for a moment looking around him. It seemed to Trent that he was wasting a lot of time to study the lie of the land in a place he seemed to know so well. Then he nodded briefly and walked off towards the shadows that lay beyond the market.

Trent and Bolec walked across to the other side and joined Irani.

Taking command, Bolec said placidly: "We go wait in Ibrahim's house."

"No...we'd better stay here... We might see him..."

"No," Bolec said firmly. "This is my job now. We stay here, this man see us, we never catch him. We got plenty people looking for him already. He don't know none of them. Better we get out the way. Go and have coffee at Ibrahim's place. He make pretty good coffee..."

"Well, I suppose that makes sense. If we don't find him soon..."

They pushed through the crowd and worked their way to the mud hovel that was Ibrahim's hiding-place.

When Racoski picked himself up and fled, speeding to the security of the crowds in the marketplace, he knew that he was safe.

He waited for the shots he thought might follow him, flinching fearfully in anticipation of them. As he reached the corner and ducked round it, his heart pounding, he knew that once away from the lights they would never find him. The elation he felt was badly tempered by the loss of his briefcase, and the damage it held was gnawing at him, tugging the vicious anger in his heart; the rage was deep in him, clamoring for relief in terms of empty violence, of taking, suppressing, killing... He slipped into the deep shadow behind a pile of potato-sacks and waited...

He saw Kamel Irani walking quickly to the exit at the other side of the square, and then Trent came and stood beside him for a moment, his back turned, his hands on his hips, his thin head twisting quickly at every move around him. He held his breath and waited, crouching deeper into the shadows.

For a long time Trent stood there.

Racoski wormed his way backward and turned in behind a truck crossing a bright path of light and darting into the friendly darkness of an abandoned stall. He watched again and saw Trent standing in the near distance, looking the other way, then saw him move into the telephone booth. Bolec was nowhere to be seen.

He edged away again, looking for the exit, and when he found it, he saw that Kamel Irani was placed strategically in view, and he moved away quickly, looking desperately for a way out. He saw a truck starting up and wondered if he could get aboard it while it went through the big iron gates, and he half-moved towards it and stopped when he saw some porters standing up in its back. He watched it rumble out on to the main road and thought of running for it, and instead moved away again. He looked at the telephone booth on the other side of the square and saw with alarm that Trent had left it; now there were both Trent and Bolec to be accounted for...

He found a dark alleyway and ran down it, then found himself in a murky courtyard, deep in shadow. The mud wall at the end was no more than five feet high. Looking quickly over his shoulders, he hoisted himself up on it, then dropped lightly down on the other side.

He was in a dimly-lit side street. He hurried on, worrying about finding a police station. An Arab passed him, carrying a load on his shoulders. "Once in a police station," he said to himself, "all I need say is *Get Ibrahim Shulam for me...Ibrahim Shulam, get Ibrahim Shulam...*"

He tapped the Arab on the arm and said in English:

"Where can I find a police station?"

The Arab twisted his weight to look at him, spat, and hurried on. The savageness welled up inside him, and he began to raise his hand, then turned away quickly instead and hurried on, hoping to find a main street and a taxi, walking fast.

The moon was bright and once out of the narrow side street he was conscious of his disheveled appearance. He walked quickly along, close to the tall buildings, crossing the road frequently to avoid the brightness of the street lamps, looking fearfully over his shoulders. Once he thought someone was following him and he looked back in alarm and saw only a small child.

He walked on, his heart beating fast.

Next time he looked back the child had been joined by another, and he thought he saw them dart into the shadows as he turned; when he stopped, they were suddenly gone, and then as he started to walk again he turned and saw them once more. They were whispering together, looking at him.

One of them came up and ran abreast of him for a while,

dancing along beside him, running, half-hopping, half-in-front of him, studying him. He raised his hand to strike him and said angrily: "Go away, go away..." and the boy darted back, moving quickly on the balls of his bare feet, darting away like an animal, moving lithely with night-quickness, an animal from the remote holes in the slums taking over the tarmac pavements for the night, sleeplessly at home on the dark streets.

He stopped and looked back again.

Now, he thought, there was only one of them, hanging back out of range of his anger, ready to move to further safety. He strode on quickly.

A car turned in ahead of him, and drove past him, then stopped abruptly in the middle of the street and backed up a few yards. He waited, ready to run.

The driver leaned out and called: "Taxi, *effendi?*" Jubilantly, he stepped forward. Opening the door, he said: "Take me to the nearest police station," and stepped into the back. He heard the child behind him run forward shouting, and the taxi driver looked at the boy, called out something in Arabic, and when the boy shouted back at him, running lithely up, the taxi driver leaned over the partition and grabbed him by the lapels of his suit, pulling him towards him, grinning into his face, reaching for him.

Racoski struck out viciously at the man's neck and tore himself free, hearing the man grunt as his bony knuckles struck him in the throat, then pushed himself out of the car and ran, ran down the street, hearing the door of the taxi slam behind him, and knowing that the man was after him, too. At the first corner he came to, he sprinted round, and a passerby reached out a foot and tried to trip him, laughing as he jumped clear and raced on.

He ran fast in the darkness, the sweat pouring into his eyes, feeling the cold wetness under his arms, knowing that he was desperately afraid. Then he rounded a corner again and slipped into a doorway.

He found himself in a long dark hall, a flight of ancient wooden stairs leading to the flight above. He slipped underneath them and crouched on the ground, close down in the darkness, forcing himself like an animal into the deep recess, then lay crouched and panting and watching the doorway.

He saw the taxi-driver stop and stand framed in the light of the street, then saw him move away and heard the gentle padding of his slippered feet on the roadway, and then the boy came and stared into the doorway and came into the hall and looked up the stairs, and he lay there silent, not breathing, the floor cold under his hands, his armpits wet and clammy, silent and still. Then the boy went away and he took a deep breath and waited a long while, listening carefully. When at last he heard the friendly sound of a bus passing on a nearby street, he stood up, dusted himself down, grimacing at the hard-caked mud on his clothes, went to the doorway and cautiously looked out, then stepped briskly out into the street.

A moment later, the boys were behind him again. Now there were three of them. He took to his heels and ran.

In Ibrahim's house, Trent sat sipping his strong black Turkish coffee, the strain of the sleepless night plain in his eyes. Kamel Irani was silent and scowling, Bolec volubly taking charge of the operation.

From time to time a boy came running in with a message from Ibrahim, reporting the various phases of the search with all the communications efficiency of a military operation. Perugino had appeared from nowhere and sat with them. He said eagerly:

"They will find him, Mr. Trent. A man in foreign clothes, lost at night in Cairo... There is something about his clothes, as Bolec says... These people know these things. They will look at a tourist on the streets and know at once that he is an American with a lot of money, or an Englishman with five pounds in his pocket, or a Frenchman who will spend only pennies, or a German who wants to see only the night-clubs... This is their living, believe me." He raised his hands delicately, stressing the point.

"And then...mud on his clothes...a European in Cairo with soiled linen? Such a thing is unheard of..."

Trent said briefly: "He'll brush it off."

"Even so, Mr. Trent. You do not know these boys. They have eyes like eagles. Not a hotel, not a street, not a single dark passageway will escape their attention. I know. I tell you, if I myself were in this man's shoes, I could not hope to elude them."

An Egyptian came in and introduced himself as Ibrahim's cousin. Perugino said deprecatingly:

"Ibrahim...everyone in the demi-monde of Cairo is Ibrahim's cousin. A man of many intricate relationships, Mr. Trent."

The Egyptian sat down and took the coffee-cup that one of the household women brought him from the dark recesses of the kitchen. He was calm, unhurried, poised. He sipped his coffee noisily through his teeth, put down the cup, and began his routine. He said to Bolec:

"How are you?"

Trent said: "For God's sake, we haven't time for all that."

The cousin spat carefully into his handkerchief with exaggerated politeness. He announced, raising a pedantic hand:

"There is always time for the courtesies. How is your father?"

Trent sighed. "He is well, thank God. And yours?"

"Thank God. And your family?"

"If your family is well, then mine is too."

"And how is it with your house?"

"For Christ's sake..." A pause. "My house is well, if yours is."

"Thank God."

"Yes. Thank God. God is good."

"Ah, yes, God is greatest. Everything comes from God."

"So? For God's sake? So?"

"He is not in the market. He went from it."

"We know that... Go on, go on..."

"I leave two boys there. The taxi-drivers have been warned to look for him. This will cost a lot of money. By God."

"Never mind the money..."

The cousin nodded. "Good...good. The beggars have been called out of their beds. The boot-boys are looking for him, and most of the pick-pockets. If God wills, we shall find him. It will cost a lot of money." He said his piece, turned his coffee-cup upside down, and left.

Trent said wrathfully: "I don't think we're getting anywhere at all." He stubbed out his cigarette and fumbled in his pockets for a pipe, then went out to the telephone box in the market and called the office.

When the duty officer answered, he said:

"John Trent. How's the translation coming on?"

He heard Morgan sigh at the other end. "Connie's here, hopping mad, and one of the girls from ciphers. They're working at it now. There's an awful lot, you know..."

"Anything concrete yet? Any names or addresses?"

"Nothing like that at all unless it's in code. Connie's working on it, John. It'll be some time before you have anything. She says there's a couple of days' work there at least..."

Trent said sulkily: "I'll call you again in an hour-or-two."

He put back the phone and stood looking at the market for a while. The sight depressed him and he went angrily back to the house. Kamel Irani was still sitting disconsolately on the edge of the bed. Bolec had found himself a bottle of something. Perugino was standing by the kitchen door, talking to the maid-servant.

He sat on a wooden stool, put his head in his hands, and waited. He looked up once and said wrathfully: "Is that man Ibrahim any damn good at all?"

Bolec answered placidly: "A good man," and Perugino came into the room and reiterated: "A good man. If only the police knew the things that man has accomplished..."

Trent looked at Bolec's placid face curiously. He said: "You're not worried about this at all, are you?"

"No, Mr. Trent."

"Why?"

Bolec said simply: "We find him. Maybe take two three hours, but we find him. I got nothing to worry about."

"And if we don't get him by daylight? You realize then we'll never see him again?"

Kamel Irani spoke heavily. "The police. That is my fear. If he goes to the police...he will have a good many friends here, John, highly-placed friends. That is what I fear."

Trent nodded. "Thank God we've got the briefcase. But it's not enough... We want him, too." He said stubbornly: "We've got to have the man as well."

"You get him," Bolec said. "You take my word. You get him. Maybe you have little drink now?" He held out the bottle.

He shook his head. "God knows, I need it..."

The *jezveh* of coffee was being brought in again when Ibrahim arrived. His black eyes were gleaming, his gold teeth showing. He sat down and took out a silver cigarette case, then extracted four cigarettes and offered them round, holding them extended at the tips of his fingers, offering them individually. He waited for someone to question him, taking his time, looking from one to the other. He said at last:

"Please God you are all well?"

"Thank God, and for God's sake, Ibrahim, tell us what's happening..."

Ibrahim raised a pained hand. He was unhappy with the uncouth briskness of the affair. "A little coffee, first," he said. "A little coffee first, then we talk."

"There's no time," Trent shouted. He threw up his hands in disgust.

Ibrahim said gently, a courteous reproof: "There is time. Time is from God, like all things."

Kamel Irani said quietly: "Everything is from God, Ibrahim."

Ibrahim nodded wisely. Having established himself among fellow-Muslims, he said carefully:

"I have found him. By God."

"What!" Trent jumped up from his chair. "Where? Where is he?"

Ibrahim drew slowly on his cigarette. He said: "First I put two boys in the market. But, by God, I know he will not stay there for long; there is too much light. There is a proverb: 'In the sun, all men have eyes—at night, only the camel and God'. So I ask myself, where will this man go? To the darkness, I say. All right. I go to the lane where it is darkest. By God, he is not there."

He raised his hands elegantly.

"Then more boys begin to arrive, and I say to them, watch the streets leading from the market. But do not search them from the market end, that would not be right. Run as fast as you can, like the Saluki dogs that chase the gazelles on the desert, run to the other ends of the streets and work your way back towards the market, in all the alleys... Then one of my boys comes running to tell me, I have seen him; he was hiding under the stairways of a house on Sharia el Antikhana, and young Mohamed the son of Youssef the son of Ahmed the son of Saleh, is following him now. He tells me that this man tried to take a taxi to the police station, and I say to myself, 'By God, Ibrahim, that is a mistake.' My friend, I do not often make mistakes, is it not so, Stefan *effendi*? So I quickly send a boy to warn the taxi-drivers, and soon they are looking for him, too. Also, I send four of the older boys to wait outside the Kasr-el-Nil police station, just in case..." He clapped his hands, and when one of his wives came in, he said angrily: "Bring more coffee. Why do you not pour coffee for my friends?"

Trent sat down patiently. He looked at Kamel Irani and raised his hands. Ibrahim went on:

"And then word comes to me that he is running away from my boys on Sharia Sufula, and I go quickly in my cousin's taxi to that area. I send my other cousin to bring more boys to that place, and I know, my friend, that we have him; he cannot escape. We are too many. Everywhere you look, there are my boys. On the corners, in the passageways, hiding in the shadows... Even the police become suspicious, and a patrol moves in to see what is happening. Fortunately, the corporal in charge of the patrol is also my cousin, so I give him a little money and tell him to go away and drink the health of his commanding officer. I know that my good friend will reimburse me for this?"

Trent nodded solemnly, forcing himself to be patient.

"So, he goes away." Ibrahim shrugged his shoulders. "Even the police must live; they are very poor people. Then one of my boys reports to me. The man has entered a building near the *midan*, he says, running hard. Three of my boys are following him, and he climbs on up and up and up, trying to find somewhere to hide. He finds an open doorway and he goes into the apartment." He sipped his coffee again and said: "Now this, my friend, my father, my brother, my good and generous benefactor, is very amusing. Because this place is a brothel, and the *karakhanji* there is also my cousin." He said apologetically: "It is hard that he should have to do this work, but he is not very clever, and he makes a very good living this way. By God. As soon as I arrive there, your man is asking the Madame for a telephone, but my boys are there too, and my cousin...I have a few words with Madame, she is my friend, understand me? 'And I leave my cousin with him and come here to tell you the news. Have I well?"

"Better than you," Bolec said emphatically, "is nobody."

Trent said: "Let's go get him."

When they climbed the five flights of stairs to the bordello and burst in like a boatload of eager tourists, Trent and Kamel Irani and Perugino and Bolec, with Ibrahim leading the way like a dragoman from one of the big hotels, they found the cousin mounting guard over the prisoner.

Two of the girls were gathered in the doorway, whispering to each other, and the Madame was fussing about saying, "No trouble, please, *Messieurs*, no trouble, a respectable house..." and Racoski was sitting dejectedly on the edge of the bed, quite naked, his thin legs incongruously white and bony, almost all the menace gone from him, only the vice in his eyes still gleaming cruelly. He seemed to know that his scheming had come to its end and that so had he.

The Arab was sitting on the floor by the doorway, paring his nails with a dagger, and there was a thin red streak across Racoski's face.

The Arab said, grinning: "I make him take off his clothes. Now, if he wants to run away...not so much trouble to find him." He slipped the dagger into the folds of a cloth at his waist and stood up. He was the biggest man Trent had ever seen; he had the flabby cheeks and high-pitched voice of a eunuch.

Racoski looked at him coldly and said: "My clothes."

Trent picked them off the chair and threw them to him. He said: "Get dressed."

Irani's black eyes were watching him. Racoski slowly put on his clothes. He was a pathetic figure. Irani said softly, half mocking:

"You must not feel sorry for a man like that, my friend, simply because he has lost his trousers... He is still a very dangerous animal..."

Trent said sharply: "No...no." Watching Racoski closely, he said: "Under other circumstances...but not now. The personal equation..."

Racoski put on his shirt and fastened the old-fashioned collar on with studs, and put on his tie and slipped on his waistcoat and jacket, then went to the dressing-table and poured some eau-de-Cologne on a handkerchief and dabbed at the cut on his face, and then brushed half-heartedly and ineffectually at the caked dirt on his clothes.

One of the girls whispered, in Arabic, "No, not English. French perhaps..."

Racoski was standing by the window, staring at his rejection in the long mirror, fiddling with his tie, straightening it. He said:

"What now?"

"Now? The Army will want a word with you. Tonight, you'll stay with us. In the morning, you'll be handed over to the right people, together with the decoded contents of your suitcase and Reizen's safe..."

"What happened to Reizen?"

"Reizen's dead."

Racoski picked up a comb from the dressing-table, smelled it curiously, then began to run it slowly through his lank hair. He patted his hair into place, staring at himself in the mirror. His thin-lipped face was hateful. Trent said harshly:

"All right, let's get going."

Racoski put down the comb and turned to look at them. They stood in a semi-circle round him, Trent in the center, his fists on his hips; Irani by the door, a thin smile on his face; Bolec beside him, staring stolidly at him: Perugino standing close to the two girls in the two doorway; and his cousin discreetly to one side, waiting, wondering what was going to happen.

Racoski looked at them, and seemed to sway momentarily; then he put his shoulder to the window close beside him and pushed; as the glass shattered, and he swung inclining out of sight, Trent leaped across the room, his arm outstretched.

There was a little moan from one of the girls as the horrible sound came up to them distantly from the pavement below. Hearing her little faint cry whimpering behind him, Trent thrust his head and shoulders out of the window, feeling the blood running down his wrist where a jagged piece of glass had scored it. He heard a car squeal to a frightened stop beside the broken body, and he looked away.

Kamel Irani had not moved. He was still smiling faintly.

Trent pulled himself back from the window and went to the door, pushing himself past the scared, half-naked girls who stood there wide-eyed, clutching their flimsy veils about their breasts and staring at him. He turned at the door and motioned to Kamel Irani.

"Let's get the hell out of here before the police arrive."

He stared at Ibrahim a moment. "I'll see you at your house tomorrow. Bolec too." The Arab put his hand over his heart. "By God, you are my friend. By God." As he went out, he heard Ibrahim patiently, urgently instructing his cousin. "When the police come... This is what you must say..."

He went slowly down the stairs and out into the cold night air of the street, binding a handkerchief round the cut on his wrist. A small group of people, five or six of them, had gathered round the body. Somebody said, in Arabic, "Shouldn't we send for the police?" And a shoulder-shrugging voice answered: "Why should we...no affair of ours. They'll come in time..."

He said: "This way."

He put his hand on Kamel Irani's heavy shoulder and fell in step beside him. A solitary horse-drawn cab was clop-clopping along, its driver fast asleep on his box, his tall thin whip rising like a plume above his head, the big wheels turning slowly; the horses were lazily walking, half asleep. Far away somewhere a train sounded off, distantly, the noise coming to them hushed and almost melodious across the wide soft sands that lay beyond the sprawling mass of the city.

Only in Egypt, he thought, could the whistle of a train sound beautiful.

The sharp staccato of the horses drifted to a stop and all was silence. The night was cold and moist and pleasant.

The city was softly asleep.

THE END

ABOUT THE AUTHOR

Alan Lyle-Smythe was born in Surrey, England. Prior to World War II, he served with the Palestine Police from 1936 to 1939 and learned the Arabic language. He was awarded an MBE in June 1938. He married Aliza Sverdova in 1939, then studied acting from 1939 to 1941.

In January 1940, Lyle-Smythe was commissioned in the Royal Army Service Corps. Due to his linguistic skills, he transferred to the Intelligence Corps and served in the Western Desert, in which he used the surname "Caillou" (the French word for 'pebble') as an alias.

He was captured in North Africa, imprisoned and threatened with execution in Italy, then escaped to join the British forces at Salerno. He was then posted to serve with the partisans in Yugoslavia. He wrote about his experiences in the book The World is Six Feet Square (1954). He was promoted to captain and awarded the Military Cross in 1944.

Following the war, he returned to the Palestine Police from 1946 to 1947, then served as a Police Commissioner in British-occupied Italian Somaliland from 1947 to 1952, where he was recommissioned a captain.

After work as a District Officer in Somalia and professional hunter, Lyle-Smythe travelled to Canada, where he worked as a hunter and then became an actor on Canadian television.

He wrote his first novel, Rogue's Gambit, in 1955, first using the name Caillou, one of his aliases from the war. Moving from Vancouver to Hollywood, he made an appearance as a contestant on the January 23 1958 edition of You Bet Your Life.

He appeared as an actor and/or worked as a screenwriter in such shows as Daktari, The Man From U.N.C.L.E. (including the screenwriting for "The Bow-Wow Affair" from 1965), Thriller, Daniel Boone, Quark, Centennial, and How the West Was Won. In 1966-67, he had a recurring role (as Jason Flood) in NBC's "Tarzan" TV series starring Ron Ely. Caillou appeared in such television movies as Sole Survivor (1970), The Hound of the Baskervilles (1972, as Inspector Lestrade), and Goliath Awaits (1981). His cinema film credits included roles in Five Weeks in a Balloon (1962), Clarence, the Cross-Eyed Lion (1965), The Rare Breed (1966), The Devil's Brigade (1968), Hellfighters (1968), Everything You Always Wanted to Know About Sex* (*But Were Afraid to Ask) (1972), Herbie Goes to Monte Carlo (1977), Beyond Evil (1980), The Sword and the Sorcerer (1982) and The Ice Pirates (1984).

Caillou wrote 52 paperback thrillers under his own name and the nom de plume of Alex Webb, with such heroes as Cabot Cain, Colonel Matthew Tobin, Mike Benasque, Ian Quayle and Josh Dekker, as well as writing many magazine stories.

Several of Caillou's novels were made into films, such as Rampage with Robert Mitchum in 1963, based on his big game hunting knowledge; Assault on Agathon, for which Caillou did the screenplay as well; and The Cheetahs, filmed in 1989.

He was married to Aliza Sverdova from 1939 until his death. Their daughter Nadia Caillou was the screenwriter for the film Skeleton Coast.

Alan Caillou died in Sedona, Arizona in 2006.

LOOKING FOR ACTION & ADVENTURE
AUTHOR ALAN CAILLOU
DELIVERS!

AVAILABLE IN PAPERBACK AND EBOOK

ADDITIONAL ACTION & ADVENTURE FROM ALAN CAILLOU

AVAILABLE IN PAPERBACK AND EBOOK

CALIBERCOMICS.COM

DON'T MISS ANY OF MICHAEL KASNER'S HARD HITTING MILITARY NOVEL SERIES

BLACK OPS

Formed by an elite cadre of government officials, the Black OPS team goes where the law can't - to seek retribution for acts of terror directed against Americans anywhere in the world.

3 BOOK SERIES

Armed with all the tactical advantages of modern technology, battle hard and ready when the free world is threatened - the Peacekeepers are the baddest grunts on the planet.

4 BOOK SERIES

CHOPPER COPS

America is being torn apart as criminal cartels terrorize our cities, dealing drugs and death wholesale. Local police are outgunned, so the President unleashes the U.S. TACTICAL POLICE FORCE. An elite army of super cops with ammo to burn, they swoop down on the hot spots in sleek high-tech attack choppers to win the dirty war and take back America!

4 BOOK SERIES

FROM CALIBER BOOKS
www.calibercomics.com

FROM FANTASY AND SCIENCE FICTION
AUTHOR ROLAND J. GREEN
THREE EPIC SERIES

FROM CALIBER BOOKS IN PAPERBACK AND EBOOK

DON'T MISS ANY OF NEIL HUNTER'S NOVELS FROM CALIBER BOOKS

Reporter Les Mason is completing an expose on the Long Point Nuclear Plant. But before he can finish he dies an agonizing death. The doctors are baffled—and there are similar cases to follow...Chris Lane, his girlfriend, and organizer of the Long Point Protestors, discovers Mason's notes, and decides to find out for herself what the plant has to hide.

2 BOOK SERIES

In middle of the 21st century America – over-populated decaying cities are ruled by hi-tech gangs pushing every vice and wastelands are controlled by bands of mutants. Ordinary citizens are oppressed and face a hopeless future. But Marshal T.J. Cade is a new breed of law enforcer. Teamed with his cyborg partner, Janek, Cade takes on these criminals and works in the gray areas of the law to get the job done.

3 BOOK SERIES

The village of Shepthorne England wasn't being gripped, but strangled by a winter's blanket of heavy snow and Arctic temperatures. The trouble began innocently enough with a massive pile-up of autos on frozen roads leading to and from the village. Then, from the sky, a military transport plane with its top secret cargo of devastation crashed down towards the center of the village. Hell was just beginning to touch Shepthorne and its unsuspecting citizens...

FROM CALIBER BOOKS
www.calibercomics.com

www.ingramcontent.com/pod-product-compliance
Lightning Source LLC
Chambersburg PA
CBHW072153070526
44585CB00015B/1122